Dedicated to my mother

Ada Viola Elias
who has adventured in more exotic
places than I ever will.

Rocky Mountain Books

From Grassland to Rockland

An Explorer's guide to
the Ecosystems
of Southernmost Alberta

Peter Douglas Elias

Front cover photograph: *Mount Blakiston from Mount Galwey.*
Title page photograph: *Near Whaleback Ridge.*

Copyright © Peter Douglas Elias, 1999

All rights reserved. No part of this work may be reproduced or transmitted in any form or by any means, electronic or mechanical, including photocopying and recording, or by any information storage or retrieval system, except as may be expressly permitted in writing from the publisher.

We acknowledge the financial support of the Government of Canada through the Book Publishing Industry Development Program (BPIDP) for our publishing activities.

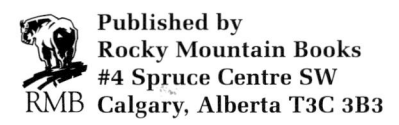

**Published by
Rocky Mountain Books
#4 Spruce Centre SW
Calgary, Alberta T3C 3B3**

Printed and bound in Canada
by Houghton Boston, Saskatoon.

ISBN 0-921102-62-3

Canadian Cataloguing in Publication Data

Elias, Peter Douglas
  From grassland to rockland

  Includes bibliographical references and index.
  ISBN 0-921102-62-3

  1. Natural history--Alberta--Guidebooks. 2. Biotic communities--Alberta--Guidebooks.
3. Hiking--Alberta--Guidebooks. 4. Alberta--Guidebooks. I. Title
QH106.2.A4E44 1999   508.7123'4   C99-910266-4

Contents

Preface — 6
Acknowledgements — 6
Introduction — 7
1 Space and Place — 13
2 Parts of Space and Place — 19
3 Dry Mixed Grass Ecoregion — 41
    1 Pinhorn Grazing Reserve — 45
    2 Writing-On-Stone — 53
    3 Davis Coulee — 62
    4 Red Rock Coulee — 63
    5 South Saskatchewan River — 71
4 Mixed Grass Ecoregion — 83
    6 Lethbridge Coulee Trails — 87
    7 Twin River Grazing Reserve — 97
5 Fescue Grass Ecoregion — 109
    8 Exploring Kimball Park — 113
6 Aspen Parkland Ecoregion — 123
    9 Wishbone Trail — 126
    10 Trout Creek Ridge North — 132
    11 Trout Creek Ridge South — 138
7 Montane Ecoregion — 144
    12 Carbondale Hill — 148
    13 Whaleback Ridge — 156
    14 Beaver Creek — 167
    15 Cypress Hills — 177
8 Subalpine Ecoregion — 194
    16 Goat Lake—Avion Ridge — 197
    17 Upper Oldman River Cabin Ridge — 205
    18 The Oldman's headwaters — 211
    19 South Twin Creek — 216
9 Alpine Ecoregion — 226
    20 Mount Galwey — 230
    21 Table Mountain — 239
    22 Thunder Mountain North Ridge — 247
    23 Southfork Lakes — 254
Recommended readings — 265
Index — 269

Preface

Southernmost Alberta lies between the Oldman River and the Crowsnest Trail on the north, and the United States border on the south. This is a very small part of the Earth, a mere fragment, perhaps, but a place of great landscape diversity and beauty. In only a few hundred road kilometres, the Crowsnest Trail rushes east across the Continental Divide from sheer mountain walls through towering forests, along mighty rivers, across swelling foothills and sweeping grasslands and into deep valley badlands.

There are plenty of places to enjoy the splendours of this fascinating part of Canada and for many walkers, sheer immersion in splendour is enough. But, others want to know why things are the way they are and why a particular place possesses an unmatched ability to fascinate.

The natural history of southernmost Alberta is well documented, thanks to the efforts of several generations of scientific researchers. However, few of their texts put scientific details into the perspective of walkers, riders, skiers, snowshoers, climbers, canoeists or cyclists. I hope people in southernmost Alberta will find enough information in this book to tell them about the main features of the landscape they are experiencing, without drowning in rich scientific details.

The robust landscape of southernmost Alberta is the product of many powerful forces. The first part of this book discusses the prime elements of landscape—space, climate, geology, soils, water, plants, animals and humans—in just enough detail to account for the main distinguishing features of the entire region.

The rest of the book is a guide to Special Places where important features of southernmost Alberta's natural history can be seen and experienced firsthand.

Of course, my Special Places are not the only fascinating places in southernmost Alberta. My places are selected for four reasons. First, each Special Place illustrates an important part of the natural history of southernmost Alberta. Second, they are off the beaten path, not the kind of place visited by just anybody. Third, they require effort to see and experience. Finally, they are each knockout places where people can satisfy a lust for thrills and a natural curiosity about the landscape around them.

Acknowledgements

The maps at the beginning of each ecoregion chapter were adapted from Wayne Strong's report Ecoregions and Ecodistricts of Alberta and also from Natural Regions and Subregions of Alberta: Summary, produced by Alberta Environmental Protection. The maps in this book merge the main features of the maps contained in these volumes. Both are listed in the Recommended Readings section of this book.

My thanks to the people of Alberta for the maps and for the opportunity to travel freely over our splendid public lands. I have three best companions in my backcountry adventures—Claudia Notzke, Joe Zink and Greg Hardy. They are trusted backcountry friends, experienced, knowledgeable and durable wilderness adventurers, ready to go anywhere at any time.

Introduction

In this book, southernmost Alberta has a particular meaning. Southernmost Alberta lies south of a line following the lengths of the Oldman River and South Saskatchewan River. The Oldman River flows from just beneath the rockland summits on the Continental Divide and heads southeast through the foothills before turning east across the grasslands. The South Saskatchewan River begins where the Oldman ends and completes the journey across Alberta's grassland. These two great western rivers tie together near-desert grassland and barren alpine rockland. Southernmost Alberta is bounded on the east, south and west by the borders with Saskatchewan, Montana and British Columbia.

The Crowsnest Trail is the straightest east-west road in the province, and cuts right through the heartland of southernmost Alberta. The highway runs 330 km from the Saskatchewan border on the east to the British Columbia border on the west. From a speeding car, the way many people see southernmost Alberta, the landscape unfolds all too quickly.

On the road

The first 90 minutes of highway travel from the western border of Saskatchewan crosses flat and gently rolling dry plains. Imperceptibly, the highway gains elevation, and somewhere between Taber and Lethbridge the landscape becomes noticeably more rolling. The low swells are cloaked in taller grasses than along the highway behind, and a few shrubs appear along larger waterways.

Two hours from the border and the highway reaches Lethbridge, poised above the splendid valley of the Oldman River. The city's luxuriant green is a fresh contrast to the endless domesticated grasslands spreading away from each side of the highway.

Less than an hour west of Lethbridge the highway crosses a landscape of even taller grasses and more streams lined with shrubs and trees. The rounded southern end of the Porcupine Hills rises on the horizon to the west and north. In a little more than an hour, the highway passes Pincher Creek on the boundary of a landscape of windblown grasses, swelling hills and pockets of trees scattered amongst broad, rolling meadows.

Introduction

West of Pincher Creek, Highway 3 crosses a last narrow band of tall grass prairie and parkland, and in half an hour enters a landscape of hills ridged with rocky spines and cloaked with pine, fir and spruce. The foothills landscape follows the highway deep into the Crowsnest Pass. On all sides, just a short distance away from the floor of the pass, subalpine forests and then towering rocky peaks of mountains take over. This trip traverses grassland to rockland in four hours.

Science and sense

However, a fast highway trip is not the way to really see southernmost Alberta. The real splendours of the changing landscape are only seen close-up and at a pace where every little place is special, a unique collection of merging and melding landforms, plants, animals and other elements of landscape. The splendours are enhanced with a little help from the wealth of scientific information describing the region.

In a scientific sense, landscapes are defined by their measurable features—especially geology, climate, plants and animals, soils and human history—and interactions between the features. Scientists have described many of the features of landscape, and our libraries are well endowed with their reports.

For walkers, important features of landscape are qualities that are sensed and experienced as well as learned and understood. Landscapes are memorable in part for their natural features and in part because of the sense of meaning and harmony a place conjures.

The scale of adventure

Landscapes can be very large. All of southernmost Alberta is a single landscape about which a unified story may be told. Walkers, however, experience things at a more intimate scale, and there is no place in southern Alberta from which all the big landscape can be seen. Still, there are plenty of very big landscapes, measured from the perspective of a walker.

This book is in part a guide to interesting places in southernmost Alberta, where the defining features of the region can be explored at a walker's natural pace. More than a trail guide, the book also contains enough deeper information to help enquiring walkers understand why the landscape they are enjoying is so interesting.

The deeper information is organized around the key concepts of "ecoregion," "ecodistrict" and "ecosite." These are tools used to organize information and knowledge describing and defining the features of a landscape. While senses are important for understanding a landscape, many features of ecoregion and ecodistrict cannot be directly observed—chemical constituents of soils and rock, minute life forms, extremely slow geological processes or the origins of a region's climate. Fortunately, scientists have spent several lifetimes making close-up observations for us, and we can learn from the scientists.

Landscape organization

Ecoregions are typically large areas where many features of the landscape are essentially and measurably the same—generally the same climate, landforms, soils, geology, plants and animals prevail throughout an ecoregion. For the enquiring walker, ecoregions are too big to fully appreciate unless you are hurtling along in a car or, better yet, overhead in an airplane.

On direct flights from Winnipeg to Vancouver, aircraft cross the Saskatchewan boundary at over 10,000 m. On a really good day—mid-winter, cold, high barometric pressure, no wind, clear skies—the Cypress Hills will lay off the port wing and the summits of the Continental Divide will be on the horizon ahead. The landscape from that altitude in the right conditions is all of southernmost Alberta. It is a splendid sight from high above.

However, huge ecoregions are not as uniform as a speeding, distant glimpse would suggest. More likely, the veneer of sameness hides places where the common elements of the ecoregion are well displayed, along with measurable variety that makes each place different. Ecodistricts are the many parts making up the whole.

Ecosites are identifiable places where specific combinations of key characteristics occur. They are destinations where hikers may see and experience how the landscape is expressed. The Special Places described in this book are ecosites.

Book organization

Chapter 1 begins with a detailed discussion of landscape, ecoregion, ecodistrict and ecosite and the features that help define them in southernmost Alberta. This part of the book is keyed to a model of landscape classification that has gradually emerged in Alberta to meet the needs of land and resource planners and managers. Scientific, academic and even a few adventure writers have adopted the model in their research and writing strategies. Using the model, many of the best trail and species guides listed in the Recommended Readings section of this book can be easily keyed to the Special Places.

The model landscape

A good example of the model was prepared by Wayne Strong of W. L. Strong Ecological Land Surveys Ltd. for the government of Alberta in 1992. Strong organized his landscapes primarily on the basis of climate similarities and differences—places with generally the same climate are classed as ecoregions. Strong related his climate-based maps to other features in the landscape, including local geology, soils, weather patterns, plants, animals and human history. Places with the same climate and a constellation of other shared features are ecodistricts.

Of course, there is more to a place than climate, but climate seems like a good principle on which to organize the landscape from a walker's pace and perspective. Climate shapes the immediate and sensible features of the landscape—the surface landforms, soils, plants, animals and human impacts are all easily understood and experienced as a consequence of climate. And climate, expressed through the medium of weather, helps decide how comfortable most walkers will be while travelling in a particular place.

Alternatives

Strong used climate as his primary organizing principle, but with just as much logic landscapes could be organized on the basis of any other feature. In fact, there are several maps that organize Alberta's landscape from the perspective of earth sciences, biological sciences or human sciences. Each map offers an alternative view of how a key feature of natural history relates to other features. Chapter 1 sets out these relationships.

Chapter 2 describes the natural history of southernmost Alberta in terms of the broad elements shaping the landscape walkers will see and experience—the mighty forces of land and life. Chapter 2 is indebted to the many scientists who have provided the depth of details. This book only distills their knowledge into a condensed description of what is known so far about the diverse landscapes of southernmost Alberta.

Introduction

Special Places

The next seven chapters each deal with one of the large ecoregions in southernmost Alberta, beginning in the far eastern grasslands and ending high in the western mountains. Each chapter starts with a description of an ecoregion, pointing out and illustrating its unique characteristics and natural history. Then, there are descriptions of Special Places where walkers can see and experience key features of each ecoregion.

The Special Places were selected for several reasons: They contain a good lesson in the natural history of southernmost Alberta; they offer a variety of challenges for walkers; they are well documented in the scientific literature, and they are accessible.

There are many other places of equal beauty and splendour in southernmost Alberta, but there are only so many pages in a book. I have included Special Places that are off the beaten path. Some of these places are almost unknown even to the people who live in southernmost Alberta. And perhaps most important, they are all great fun to visit.

Trail information

The descriptions of each Special Place are accompanied by a sketch map and a table in which the essential challenges of a particular trail are laid out. The table suggests the best mode of travel for each route. Some routes can only be done on foot, but others can also be done on horseback, skis, snowshoes, canoe or bicycle, each offering a different experience.

The trails are rated according to how much work walkers must do to complete the route. Easy routes are straightforward, with little elevation gain or loss, and can be completed wearing running shoes. Moderate routes are longer, involve more elevation gain and loss, may require a little routefinding, and usually hikers will need heavier footwear. Difficult routes are strenuous, with more elevation change, and require familiarity with maps and compasses. Scrambles are the most difficult, requiring the use of hands to climb past more-or-less dangerous obstacles.

Distances are given for a return excursion from the trailhead back to the trailhead. Time is counted as the number of hours needed to travel the route on foot, calculated at a rate of one hour for each 300 m of gain and one hour for each 3 km of cross-country travel. Of course, the time for appreciation or dealing with the unexpected must be added to the times given in the route descriptions.

The maps named in the route descriptions are all National Topographical Series 1:50,000 sheets published by the government of Canada. The small sketch maps in this book are for orientation only: they are not a substitute for real maps.

As for the unexpected, I always travel in the backcountry with more gear than I need. I always have my basic first aid kit, water purification tablets, flashlight and mechanics kit and backup clothing, even on short day trips. The whole package fits into a small backpack along with my camera, guidebooks, water and snacks. For hard-work routes leading several hours away from the trailhead, I carry an advanced first aid kit, a water filter, a GeoPositioning System, an emergency shelter, a fire-making kit, a complete change of clothing and two days of food.

Thankfully, I have only needed to use a few patches and fixes and never the whole kit, but by now I know enough not to take southernmost Alberta for granted. Almost anything could happen at any time: Be prepared.

Introduction

Choices

Any one book can only describe a few of the splendours awaiting in southernmost Alberta, and the ones in this book were selected because they immerse walkers in an important lesson in natural history. Each chapter includes places where the essence can be seen and experienced, without a great deal of effort. If you only have a few hours, or you don't have the necessary technology, or if you are not as limber as you once were, these sections describe accessible ecosites that help tell Alberta's history.

Appendices

There are two final parts in the book—a list of recommended readings, and a concordance index.

Recommended readings

The list of recommended readings includes three kinds of publications. The references in the first part—Landscape Perspective—offer a broad overview of the prime character of ecoregions, ecodistricts, ecosites and Special Places. The books and reports under this heading will help walkers get oriented in Alberta's big and complex landscape. Mostly, they are written by scientists and scholars with extensive backcountry experience, and include some of the best descriptions of Alberta available in print. When I travel by truck, these books go with me and are now frayed from use.

Next in the recommended readings are the Natural History guidebooks. These are guides to identifying plants, animals, landforms, soils and geology encountered in southernmost Alberta. Some of these books travel with me in my truck and in my backpack, pannier or saddlebag.

Finally, the recommended readings include Trail Guides. Alberta's experienced and talented adventure writers have produced trail guides to many of the Special Places described in this book. There are trail guides for hikers, climbers, canoeists, cyclists, strollers and horse riders. The trail guides are valuable sources of additional information about the challenges on a route.

Index

The common names used in this book are the ones most familiar in southern Alberta, but common names change from place to place. In the index, each common name used in the book is matched with its scientific name. This should help readers who want to look up a plant or animal in a detailed natural history guidebook.

The rest of the index concentrates on connecting the concepts discussed in the first two chapters with the Special Places described in each later chapter. Readers can browse with purpose.

Introduction

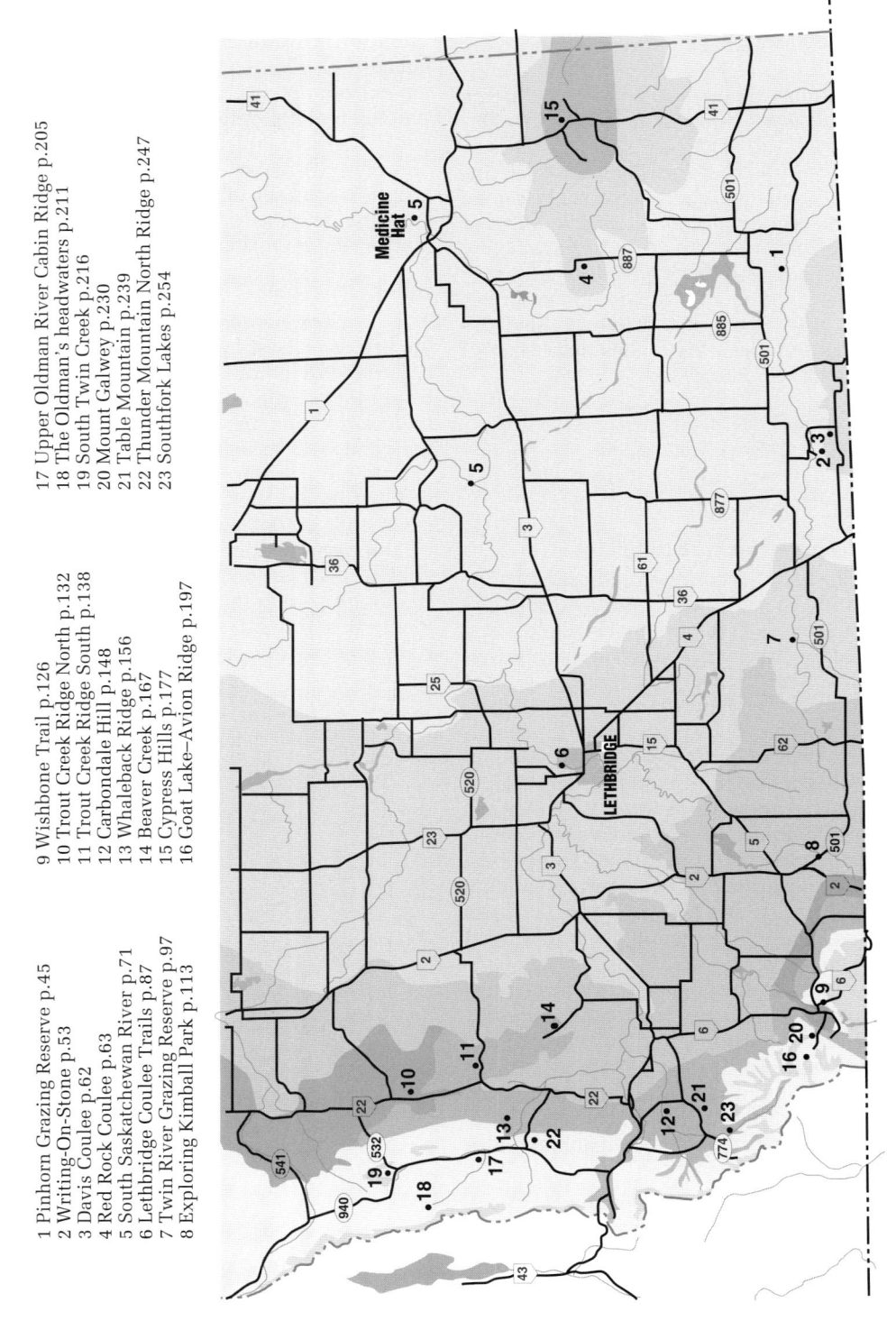

1 Pinhorn Grazing Reserve p.45
2 Writing-On-Stone p.53
3 Davis Coulee p.62
4 Red Rock Coulee p.63
5 South Saskatchewan River p.71
6 Lethbridge Coulee Trails p.87
7 Twin River Grazing Reserve p.97
8 Exploring Kimball Park p.113

9 Wishbone Trail p.126
10 Trout Creek Ridge North p.132
11 Trout Creek Ridge South p.138
12 Carbondale Hill p.148
13 Whaleback Ridge p.156
14 Beaver Creek p.167
15 Cypress Hills p.177
16 Goat Lake–Avion Ridge p.197

17 Upper Oldman River Cabin Ridge p.205
18 The Oldman's headwaters p.211
19 South Twin Creek p.216
20 Mount Galwey p.230
21 Table Mountain p.239
22 Thunder Mountain North Ridge p.247
23 Southfork Lakes p.254

1

Space and Place

Landscape, ecoregion, ecodistrict and ecosite are connected to ideas of space and place. They can only exist with reference to particular places even if those places are very large, extending over thousands of square kilometres. Walking, of course, involves moving within space or across a place. Space and place are central concepts in this book.

Landscape

In 1857, the British government sent Captain John Palliser west to describe and assess southern Alberta's resources and suitability for settlement. In his three years of exploration, he was impressed and dismayed by the near-deserts he crossed, the unwooded rivers he forded and the other elements of nature he battled.

Palliser saw only dormant prairie overgrazed by bison, dry sloughs and ponds, sluggish rivers, very few animals and not many other people. He concluded in his report to government that the region had little agricultural potential, few important natural resources and an intolerable climate.

Perhaps Palliser missed the west's wetter and more abundant years. He would never know, because Captain Palliser could only work with information he and his team produced using their own senses and the tools of 19th century science. There were no libraries or archives of comparative descriptions he could use to confirm what he saw and experienced. Neither could he extend his limited information toward a thorough understanding of the landscapes through which he travelled.

Space and Place

A revised perspective

Palliser's description of the Interior Plains as a barren and desolate landscape unsuited for agricultural settlement lasted until the 1890s when a spate of much more complimentary descriptions appeared. Some of these were written by scientists of the day, who visited the Interior Plains in exceptionally verdant years—and described the opposite of what Palliser saw. Many were purely promotional pieces written to attract European settlers away from the United States and into Canada. These "reports," published in most of the languages of northern Europe, were as excessively optimistic as Palliser's report was pessimistic.

The promotional effort was successful, though, and settlers came to western Canada in the thousands, expecting a land of sweet temperament. As usual, the hard truth lay somewhere between, but the pull of good publicity and the push of conditions in Europe resulted in a flood of immigrant settlers that did not abate until the start of the First World War. Reality swiftly sorted the naive from the knowledgeable.

Science

Since the days of Palliser and the publicists, researchers have built on their work, using more information and better science. We now have maps and detailed descriptions showing regions of common soil types, climate, animal and plant populations, surface landforms, bedrock geology, cultural forms, economic activities and so on.

No one map of a particular feature can define a landscape; it takes several overlapping common features to show that a certain bounded space is all of a single kind.

One result of science and a history of observation is the model of organization adopted for this book. The model defines and describes 13 "ecoregions" and 92 "ecodistricts" in the entire province. Of the 13 ecoregions in Alberta, seven are found in southern Alberta and one ecoregion, the Dry Mixed Grass Ecoregion, is found only in southern Alberta.

Ecoregions

An ecoregion is an area characterized by a distinctive combination of regional climate and vegetation. The regional climate is the primary environmental influence, associated with characteristic plants, geology, soils, animals, birds, fish, insects and human history.

Naturalists use the concept of ecoregion to describe very large landscapes and to specify the look and feel of an "average" place within a landscape. Ecoregions cover extensive territories, measured in tens of thousands of square kilometres.

The largest ecoregion in the province, the Mid Boreal Mixed Wood Ecoregion in the far north, covers almost 32 per cent of Alberta's 661,000 km of territory. The smallest is the Montane Ecoregion in southwestern Alberta at about one per cent of the province. Even the smallest ecoregion is still a very large place.

Space and Place

Dry Mixed Grass Ecoregion

The Dry Mixed Grass Ecoregion is found in the southeastern angle of the province. It is a landscape of flat, dry short grass prairie, cut with deep and heavily-eroded river valleys, including much of the Milk River, Alberta's share of the South Saskatchewan River and the lower part of the Oldman River.

Medicine Hat, Bow Island and Taber are the landmark communities in the central part of this ecoregion. Manyberries, Foremost, Coutts and Warner are in the southern and driest parts of the Dry Mixed Grass Ecoregion.

Mixed Grass Ecoregion

The Mixed Grass Ecoregion forms an arc around the north and west margins of the Dry Mixed Grass Ecoregion. Here, the land is more rolling, the grasses somewhat taller and thicker, and the rivers more gently eroded. The middle part of the Oldman River, the lower St. Mary and Waterton rivers and the upper Milk River are located in this ecoregion.

Lethbridge, Fort Macleod and Brocket are spread across the midsection of the Mixed Grass Ecoregion. Farther south are Raymond, Magrath and Milk River. Agriculture in the Mixed Dry Grass Ecoregion relies on irrigation, and most of the central part of the ecoregion is penetrated by elaborate water delivery systems.

Fescue Grass Ecoregion

The Fescue Grass Ecoregion lies in a narrow band to the west of the Mixed Grass Ecoregion. It is much hillier and clothed in taller and richer grasses, with more trees and shrubs along the waterways. The St. Mary, Waterton and Oldman rivers all cross this ecoregion.

Cowley and Pincher Creek are in the central part of the fescue grassland, and Cardston, Mountain View and Del Bonita are in the south of the Fescue Grass Ecoregion.

Aspen Parkland Ecoregion

The aspen parkland is hilly country, cloaked with large meadows of fescue grassland and dotted with aspen groves. In places, there are forests of aspen and few other trees. Compared to the dry grasslands to the east, there are plenty of wetlands and small lakes.

The aspen parklands in southernmost Alberta are squeezed into select places between mountains and plains. The small landscapes of aspen parkland are remnants and outliers of the much larger parkland closer to Calgary and Edmonton.

Little of the aspen parkland has survived the chainsaw and plough and there are no communities in the southern aspen parkland.

Space and Place

Montane Ecoregion

The Montane Ecoregion merges fescue grassland meadows with pine, fir and spruce on a series of parallel, north-south ridges. The ridges are foothills formed when the Rocky Mountains were built. Southernmost Alberta is the main place in Canada where the montane landscape can be enjoyed.

Almost all the important rivers in southwestern Alberta flow through some part of the Montane Ecoregion before joining with the Oldman River. The Crowsnest Trail is lined on both sides with a fringe of montane forests and hills almost to the Crowsnest Pass.

All the communities in the Montane Ecoregion are spread along Highway 3 from Lundbreck in the east to Crowsnest in the west.

Subalpine Ecoregion

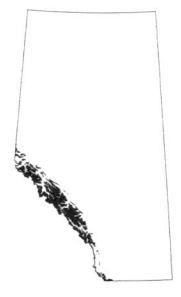

The Subalpine Ecoregion cloaks the lower elevations of the Rocky Mountains and the high mountain valleys. The subalpine landscape is seen from afar as a dark green or black band of towering conifer forests broken by thundering mountain streams. The band of forest ends abruptly at the tree line, beyond which trees do not grow.

There are no communities in either the Subalpine or Alpine ecoregions.

Alpine Ecoregion

Seen from a distance, the Alpine Ecoregion is a gray band of exposed rock looming above the highest tree line on the mountains. The entire western boundary of southernmost Alberta lies within the Alpine Ecoregion along the Continental Divide.

Learning from ecoregions

Because of the generally uniform conditions found throughout an ecoregion, people familiar with one place in an ecoregion are comfortable elsewhere in the same ecoregion. For walkers, all places in an ecoregion have a familiar feel, because knowledge and experience are highly portable.

Perhaps the best example of learning and living on the move is found in the history of the North-West Mounted Police. The Mounties, as they were later known, were sent by the government of Canada in 1873 to enforce Canadian law and sovereignty in the far west. Most of the recruits to the force had no experience whatever in western travel. They were recruited in eastern Canada and England. They arrived at the railhead in Manitoba and from there marched west across the arid grasslands.

In two months of gruelling travel, they reached the site of Fort Macleod in southern Alberta. The force learned its environmental lessons about grasslands as it marched, and in a short while it was transformed from a pack of novices into a company of hard and tough adventurers. By the end of the century, the force had built and staffed a string of outposts along the border from eastern Saskatchewan to Police Outpost Lake in the shadow of the Rocky Mountains.

Ecodistricts

All places in each of Alberta's ecoregions share key characteristics, but particular places are just as obviously different. Even the most uniform ecoregion contains plenty of smaller, distinctive areas. The concept of "ecodistrict" accommodates these distinctive areas.

An ecodistrict is a subdivision of an ecoregion based on distinctive patterns of topographic relief, landforms, geology, geological origin of soils, vegetation, animals and water. Ecodistricts are distinguished at a basic level, but they each share the general characteristics of the parent ecoregion.

A map of ecodistricts is quite fine-grained, showing distinctive places as small as a few square kilometres in size, any one of which promises a new view of the landscape.

Differences and similarities

The seven ecoregions represented in southern Alberta are divided into 34 ecodistricts. Some ecoregions are divided into only a few ecodistricts, indicating that the ecoregion is either relatively small or very uniform throughout its extent, or both.

The small Alpine Ecoregion, for example, is divided into only two ecodistricts—the high mountain peaks ecodistrict, and the high foothills ecodistrict of northerly Alberta. These two ecodistricts share and express the characteristics of the Alpine Ecoregion, and they differ mostly in the details of elevation, aspect and exposure.

Other ecoregions are divided into many ecodistricts, suggesting greater extent, greater variability or perhaps both. The Dry Mixed Grass Ecoregion and the Mixed Grass Ecoregion together cover 77,223 sq. km, and each is divided into seven ecodistricts. These 14 grassland ecodistricts suggest the grasslands are far more variable than rocklands. This is reflected in the amazing variety of plants and animals found in the eastern part of southernmost Alberta.

In between, the Montane Ecoregion is divided into four ecodistricts, suggesting great complexity in a landscape a fraction the size of the grasslands.

Size of ecodistricts

Some ecodistricts are small and confined to an outstanding feature in the landscape. The valley of the Oldman River, for example, forms its own ecodistrict within the Mixed Grass Ecoregion near Lethbridge because grassland river valleys are so strikingly different than the level plain above.

Ecoregion	Area (km)	Ecodistricts
Dry Mixed Grass	47,299	7
Mixed Grass	29,924	7
Fescue Grass	12,291	4
Aspen Parkland	52,148	7
Montane	5,714	4
Subalpine	26,060	3
Alpine	14,656	2

Space and Place

Other ecodistricts are quite large. The largest ecodistrict includes the famous, infamous and endless plains in the grasslands of southeastern Alberta. The entire ecodistrict, covering almost a quarter of all southernmost Alberta, is remarkably uniform.

The ecodistrict is closer to the walker's sense of landscape—small enough to sense and experience in a good day or so of travel. But, ecodistricts are still too large to show the places where a walker may sample the distinctive delights of an ecodistrict, and where the uniqueness of an ecodistrict may be seen up close. The smallest unit, the ecosite, leads directly to these Special Places.

Ecosites

Ecosites are places that exemplify key characteristics of an ecodistrict. Because ecosites are fairly small, no one site may fully express the reality of an ecodistrict or ecoregion.

An example of ecosites

The entire length of the lower Oldman River valley where it flows through the grassland is considered a single distinctive ecodistrict, apart from but still a part of the surrounding sea of grass in the Mixed Grass Ecoregion.

Some shores along the river valley are quite treeless. Other parts support a narrow and sparse fringe of cottonwoods, rarely more than one or two trees in depth away from the water's edge. Nearby is another place where there is a large forest of cottonwood. Slightly farther upstream or downstream is still another much larger site that is mostly lush meadow on a low floodplain with a thick fringe of willow and a modest forest of cottonwood.

Each place has a familiar feel and look—the broad river, a low floodplain, cottonwood trees, grassy meadows, tall valley walls—but each includes a special thing, such as rattlesnakes along the hottest and most exposed shore and raccoons in the lush and cool floodplain forests. Rattlesnakes won't be found wallowing in mud under a tree, and raccoons won't be found basking on a parched shoreline shingle. If you want to see it all, you must go to several ecosites.

No one of these ecosites tells the whole story of the river. Together such places along the Oldman River are a good expression of the entire valley through the grassland part of the river's run.

Learning from ecosites

Ecosites are connected to particular places that can be named and pointed out on a map. Such a particular place embodies an inventory of characteristic plant and animal species, soils, slope and aspect, climatic and weather conditions and signs of human presence.

The Special Places described in the later chapters of this book are ecosites. Each records an important chapter in the natural history of southernmost Alberta. The descriptions of the Special Places will help walkers connect their sense of place with the science.

2

Parts of Space and Place

Landscape, ecoregion, ecodistrict and ecosite are made of many parts, including climate, weather, geology, soils, water, landforms, elevation, topography, plants, animals and human modifications. These are all measurable variables, and the precise combination of variables results in the distinctive character of a place.

Natural history
Naturalists have been hard at work defining each of these variables, and as a result there are entire fields of science dedicated solely to understanding how each variable is represented in the whole of a region. Some results of the scientists' work are exceedingly complex.

The standard text on the plants of Waterton Lakes National Park is almost 700 pages in length and discusses the characteristics of over 900 species in an area of only 512 sq. km. The volume on wild prairie plants is over 500 pages and discusses 1,200 species. Even the book describing the plants of a single ecosite—the tightly constrained coulees in Lethbridge's city parks—is 130 pages in length and describes 124 plants. Similarly, there are professionally complex descriptions of climate, geology, soils, animals and human impacts.

Fortunately, each field of knowledge has its systems of indicators—key, essential characteristics that tell what a place is like in respect of a range of possible variations. Scientists have distilled the smallest details of the entire range of possibilities into descriptions that say what is usual and easily recognized in a region. In other words, the kinds of things walkers want to see and likely will see in their travels through a landscape.

This chapter brings together and co-ordinates knowledge created by scholars and researchers in several fields of natural history. These summaries supply information for people wanting to satisfy their curiosity about the places and spaces of southernmost Alberta.

Parts of Space and Place

Geology

Usually, walkers only see and contact the very surface of the landscape—sky and horizon, plants, animals, humans, exposed soils, rocks and waters. Underlying the surface elements of the landscape is the heritage of two billion years of geological history.

It is impossible to escape the effects of many millions of years of dramatic geological events. These events gave us the surface shapes we experience today—flat lands, undulating lands and hilly lands, coulees, canyons, river valleys, foothills and mountains.

Visitors in southernmost Alberta will see and walk, ride, ski, paddle or drive over the consequences of three major geological events. First are the events that resulted in the formation of the Interior Plains, then the events that resulted in the western mountains, and lastly the events of continent-wide glaciation.

Continents

Over the past two billion years the crust of the earth has been in constant motion as continents formed, broke up and then reformed. Crustal heaving repeatedly allowed shallow seas to invade dry lands and take over a large part of the globe.

In very ancient times, during the Proterozoic period about 1.5 billion years ago, the atmosphere was rich in carbon dioxide, and when this gas dissolved in rain and seawater the resulting corrosive solution combined with abundant calcium and magnesium dissolved in the seas. The resulting calcium and magnesium carbonates settled out in thick beds and eventually formed the limestone and dolomite typical of mountains in southern Alberta.

Life

A few million years later, life appeared in the oceans in the shape of bacteria feeding on hydrogen sulphide and excreting sulphur. Still later, blue and green algae-like microbes learned to use the energy of the sun to split plentiful carbon dioxide into carbon and oxygen. The oxygen was excreted as a gas into the seawater, and as oxygen is toxic to sulphide-eating bacteria, the early algae quickly took over the well-lit upper layers of the seas.

The oxygen excreted into the sea by algae was bonded onto iron dissolved in the seawater. The result was thick beds of iron-rich mud, awaiting compression into flat rock and then crumpling into the red and green mountains of southwestern Alberta. Visitors can only walk over fragments of southern Alberta's most ancient rock, in places like Waterton Lakes National Park, where the eastern front mountains are composed of red rock 1.7 billion years old. Everywhere else, the underlying ancient rock is deeply buried under much younger material.

When the dissolved iron and other metals had combined with the oxygen and settled to the sea floor, the surplus oxygen escaped into the atmosphere, providing the means for life as we know it today.

Lands standing above the seas were lashed with torrents of rain laced first with acidic carbon dioxide and later with oxygen, the metal eater. The surface of the exposed land was pried apart, stripped off the mountains, and carried far out to sea in tremendous rivers. This debris formed beds of ancient freshwater sandstones alternated with beds of equally ancient marine limestone, dolomite and shale.

Mountain building

At various times the business of building flat and level ocean bedrock was interrupted by cataclysms of sinking, rising and splitting land masses and fluctuating sea levels. Continental drift and collision drove the flat water deposits into each other, tipping, folding and bending them. Once above the seawater, the new mountains began to erode immediately, filling the shallow seas with fresh deposits of sediment.

The seas receded from time to time, leaving a flat dry land surface fringed with mountains and bordered by seas. Then, the cycle started over using fresh rock materials, highlighted by episodes of volcanic rock-making. The process of continent building, mountain building and erosion went through several long cycles before creating the landscape of today.

Building the Rocky Mountains

The latest episode of mountain building gave us the mighty Rocky Mountains and the eastern foothills. About 200 million years ago, in the late Triassic and early Jurassic, the continental landmass that would eventually become North America was drifting slowly toward the northwest on a collision course with two chains of offshore islands that were then drifting to the northeast. In a protracted collision lasting 55 to 75 million years, the islands were scraped off the floor of the ocean and welded onto the western edge of what is now Alberta.

The new mass of rock ground slowly eastward, riding over the older sedimentary rock of the continental shelf and pushing the uppermost layers of ancient seabed into a towering heap—the Rocky Mountains.

Erosion immediately began to wear the mountains down, but in the meantime drifting pieces of the earth's crust continued to collide, adding new mass to the western edge of North America.

By the end of the Cretaceous, 65 million years ago, 42 separate masses of land had been gathered into the shape of British Columbia. The crushing forces of mountain building rippled eastward to form the foothills.

Glaciation

In the past billion years there have been at least three great glacial ages, each lasting 100,000 years or so. The exact number is not known. Glacial ages were interrupted by long periods of mountain building, marine inundation and erosion, and any signs of a glacial age that survived this onslaught were eventually ground beneath the ice of succeeding glacial ages.

With such sparse evidence, it is still only possible to offer expert guesses on the causes of the great glacial ages. Most likely, the cause is related to the ever-changing position of continents adrift on the fluid core of the earth. For most of time, continents were arranged so there was an easy exchange between warm equatorial waters and cold polar waters. Ice could not build up in the polar regions because they were constantly bathed with warm water. Today, as it happens, the Antarctic landmass blocks the flow of water toward the south, and the Arctic Ocean is hemmed in on all sides by Canada, Alaska, Siberia and northern Europe. Warm and cold waters are almost cut off from each other. Conditions today are almost ideal for the birth of glacial age.

Glacial ages are not one, long and unbroken winter. Rather they are made up of a string of relatively colder and warmer periods. Ice and glaciers build up during the cold periods and recede during the warm periods. The period of advance within a glacial age is called a glaciation, and the warmer periods are called interglacials.

The most recent, third glacial age is still underway and has been for the past two million years. During that time, there were at least 19 distinct glacial advances and recessions. Since glacial ages last about 10 million years, we are living in a single warm interglacial that will sooner or later revert back to a time of cold when glaciers will again cover the polar regions of the earth. With our usual lack of modesty, humans tend to call the latest episode of glaciation as *The* Ice Age, but there is nothing to distinguish this glaciation from all the rest except, of course, this last one was experienced by humans.

A mere two million years ago just before the beginning of the last glacial age, southern Alberta had weathered into a mellow and rounded landscape, with high gentle mountains, winding rivers and streams and dense forests in all the valleys and high up on the mountains. The land looked somewhat like the moist interior mountains of British Columbia today. The glaciers changed all that, turning the landscape of southern Alberta into one of rugged and almost barren mountains, wild broad rivers, sparse forests, deeply carved plains and utterly flat grassland.

The look of the land

All of southern Alberta bears the dramatic marks of ancient rock making, mountain building and glaciation, but billions of years of geological history resulted in great complexity. The details of certain geological landscapes are contained in the descriptions of the Special Places, including discussions of the bedrock under the Interior Plains, glacial effects on the plains and in the mountains, drainage patterns and other major features in the landscapes of southernmost Alberta.

Soils

Soil is a key component of any landscape, and one of the factors influencing the chief characteristics of a region, along with geology, climate, plants and animals and human history. Soils lie on the very surface of the earth and help directly shape the subjective part of landscape—what walkers can see, feel and smell as they move through the countryside.

Because of extensive agricultural domestication, visitors will see endless kilometres of exposed cultivated soil in the spring and autumn. Elsewhere soils are exposed by roads, rivers and natural land movement. In much of the grassland, especially in the Dry Mixed Grass Ecoregion, plants cover the ground sparsely and surface soils lie naked to the eye. But soil is not just dirt; there are many different kinds of soils, each with its own special history of formation. The peculiarities of soil help account for the differences walkers can experience in the various ecoregions and ecodistricts of southernmost Alberta.

Making soil

Geologists describe soil as the loose material forming the uppermost layer of the earth's crust. In a geological sense, most of the earth's land surface is covered with soil.

Biologists define soil more narrowly as loose material that has been modified by physical, chemical and biological agents so it will support rooted plants. In this sense, much less of the earth's land surface is covered with soil because there is plenty of loose material that will not support rooted plants.

The biologist's soil begins with the raw material of the geologist's soil. Rock fragments are broken down by physical force and weathering, especially freezing, thawing and wind.

Water carries chemicals that alter, dissolve, oxidize and hydrolyse the rock material. Physical and chemical forces may reduce rock to very small grains, but this material is not yet biological soil.

Biological soil begins when organic materials are incorporated in the mineral material and when plants begin to grow and decompose. Once plants have taken root, physical and chemical forces continue to act on the soil, along with the actions of soil organisms.

Describing soil

Scientists have created complex systems for uniform descriptions of soils throughout Canada and indeed the world. Since the 1920s, Canada adopted a system of soils classification published in Russia simply because at the time there were no better ways of accounting for all the varieties of soils. Over the years, scientists throughout the world modified the Russian original, and now the classification system includes technical terms in Russian, English, French, German, Arabic, Greek, Latin and local terms in many of the world's languages.

As a result, myriad soil types bear such user-unfriendly names as "Orthic Dystric Brunisol," "Rego Humic Gleysol," "Sphagno-Fibrisol" and scores more just like these. Alternative systems are no better. For example, the most common class of soil in southern Alberta is named "Chernozem," using the original Russian name, but identical soils in the United States are named "Borolls," and the official United Nations name is "Kastanozems" in Russified Anglo-Persian. There is nothing common sensical about systems of soils classification.

Canada is a leader in soil science and the Canadian classification system is a model of scientific order. Two thick volumes and three large maps, published by Agriculture Canada, contain the standard definitions and descriptions of soil types throughout Canada. As well, there are hundreds and perhaps thousands of reports describing the soils contained in the coverage of single 1:250,000 map sheets, or a surface area of about 960 sq. km.

At the fine grain, there are descriptions for much smaller areas of special interest. For example, the soils of Waterton Lakes National Park are described in two hefty volumes and nine large maps at 1:25,000 scale. The park is only 512 sq. km in size.

Whatever the scale, systems of soil classification take into account a bewildering variety of factors, including dominant slope, texture, depth, landforms, nature of parent materials, presence of permafrost, nature of vegetative cover, climatic phases of soil temperature and moisture and chemical composition. Each of these many variables is combined with others to produce definitive classes and subclasses of soils. There are 13 classes and subclasses of soil temperature, and 10 classes of moisture, and these are only two of over 60 environmental variables taken into account by the classification system. Altogether, there are 170 defined and described soil types in Canada and each of these includes numerous sub-types.

Fortunately, there are only seven orders of soils in southern Alberta, the highest class of soils in the Canadian system, and their names are no more unwieldy than the names for geological eras, or the Latin names for plants and animals. Each order is divided into numerous suborders, but soils included in an order all share more or less the same characteristics.

Soil orders in Alberta

Chernozemic order

Chernozemic soils are associated with grasslands, the Montane foothills and the Aspen Parkland ecoregions. Chernozems are the soils of the Interior Plains, from southwestern Manitoba to high in the subalpine of the eastern Rockies and north to Edmonton and Prince Albert, Saskatchewan. Wherever dryland grasses are found there is likely a patch of this kind of soil.

The top layer of Chernozemic soil is usually richly organic from generations of supporting dryland plants. Chernozems are crumbly, well drained and have a rich, earthy smell. Climate and especially sparse moisture limit the profusion of plants and animals, including humans. Humans have tried retaliating with irrigation, fertilizers, herbicides and insecticides to thwart nature and increase the soils' ability to produce commercially valuable crops.

Thanks to agricultural technology, almost all the Chernozemic soils of Canada are under the plow, but few humans actually live on these soils. In southernmost Alberta, it is said the ungulate to human ratio is about 20:1, 20 ungulates for every person. This does not include thousands of horses or hogs, which are not ungulates, but it does include all the other large mammals visitors will see somewhere in southern Alberta, including wild goat, sheep, elk, moose, deer, antelope and domestic bison, llama, goat, sheep, perhaps a few yak and of course cattle, cattle, cattle.

Science, like soil, accumulates. Soil scientists have long known of a particular heavy clay soil that when it dries forms deep vertical cracks. This soil, named Vertisol, was assumed to be a variety of Chernozem. In 1996, scientists urged a revision of the Canadian classification of soils to recognize Vertisols as an order of soils in its own right. Science never sleeps.

Solonetzic order

Solonetzic soils are salty Chernozems. Solonetzic soils are mostly found in the southeastern part of the province near the border with Saskatchewan and the United States. The presence of Solonetzic soils defines an ecodistrict within the Dry Mixed Grass Ecoregion, set apart by its saline soils and the kinds of life sustained in salty soil.

There are only small patches of Solonetzic soils elsewhere in southern Alberta, but salty soils are fairly easy to spot. Low-lying places may collect sparse rain and then dry up, leaving a rime of white crystal visible on the surface of the land.

To live with Solonetzic soils, plants, animals and humans must be salt tolerant as well as drought tolerant. Compared to unsalted Chernozems, Solonetzic soils underpin a hard-scrabble way of life for humans, since the agricultural productivity of salty soil is limited. As well, water in contact with salty soil is often corrosive and unpalatable.

Luvisolic order

Luvisols are usually found under better nourished woodlands where tree litter has decomposed and leached the soil with acids. Acidic water has carried the organic content and clay component of the upper layer deep below the surface.

Luvisols are often imperfectly drained with a shallow organic layer thinly spread on a base of clay, glacial till or windblown silt. When they dry, Luvisols tend to form hard clods, limiting penetration of seedling roots and increasing the amount of surface runoff.

Brunisolic order

Brunisols are soils on the frontier of soildom, amongst the youngest soils found throughout Canada's mountains, and in tundra, arctic and glacial landscapes and windblown places. In southern Alberta, Brunisols are especially associated with post-glacial forested subalpine and alpine landscapes.

Brunisols are rich soils, capable of sustaining trees, but are often little more than a skim of rich organics overlying a bed of mineral parent material—usually gravel or bedrock. Brunisols are easy to identify by the presence of a strongly coloured layer—often bright rust red—lying beneath a darker organic surface.

Regosolic order

In southern Alberta, Regosols are restricted to small patches where the appropriate conditions exist. Regosols are characteristic of floodplains, dunes of windblown material, river outwashes and the exposed face of a landslide.

Regosols develop where the surface is periodically and frequently buried with fresh sediments, and mountains are ideal for the purpose. Each year, wind, flooding rivers, crushing landslides and avalanches sweep new material over the established surface, obliterating the thin buildup of biological soil.

Regosols are fresh and pristine for only a short while. If the fresh material is not too thick, hardy seeds will sprout in the buried soil and push through to the surface. Surviving trees and shrubs will send up new growth. In a few years, a great many plants will grow until again buried under a load of fresh sediment.

Gleysolic order

Gleysols are found in wet and boggy places. They are poorly-drained, often waterlogged mineral soils. The water trapped in the soil is poorly aerated, giving the soils a greenish or bluish colour from reduced iron oxides in the soil. Gleysols are often capped with peat beds and water plants. For walkers, Gleysols are a challenge: How to get across them without sinking in mud above the boot tops. As well, they may be rather smelly.

Rockland

The Alpine Ecoregion is mostly rockland. In rockland, there is very little biological soil, if any. If there is soil, it can be in any one of the other orders, depending on exactly how a particular little place is oriented, exposed, drained, nourished and so on.

No matter the type, a slipping foot, hoof or wheel can peel the scant soil down to bedrock, erasing centuries of development. Bare rockland is found mostly in the western mountains and foothills, but patches of exposed rock can be found in many parts of southern Alberta, each sporting a unique rock environment.

Climate

Ian Tyson, an icon of western culture, sang of southern Alberta as a landscape of "buckskin and blue," describing the endless vista of grassland merging with sky. Alberta indeed is a land of clear blue skies and sunshine.

In an average summer, 60 per cent of daylight hours have bright sunshine, and there are only three days in a summer when the sun cannot be seen. About 40 per cent of winter daylight hours are bright and sunny. These are provincial figures, and southernmost Alberta enjoys the high side of the averages—meaning more blue skies and sun.

Continental climate

Alberta is near the centre of North America, and shares Canada's continental climate, a climate conditioned by a continental land mass far from the oceans—long cold winters, short cool summers and low annual precipitation. Generally, summers are hottest and driest far east of the mountains in the Dry Mixed Grass Ecoregion, while summers are cooler in the Montane Ecoregion and quite chilly in the Alpine Ecoregion. Winters are colder and drier in southeast Alberta than in the Fescue Grass Ecoregion, and in the mountains winters are fiercely cold.

The source of weather

Alberta's notoriously fickle weather is the result of large interacting forces, including northern latitude, elevation differences, distance from the ocean, prevailing circulation of the atmosphere and the features of local geography. Differences in any of these factors can result in great local weather variation.

Southernmost Alberta lies between 49 and 50 degrees of north latitude, or slightly north of midway between the equator and the North Pole, and a little west of the centre line of the continent. The region's northern latitude deep in a continental land mass sets the stage for weather. The main features of the prevailing continental climate are tempered by an array of modifying conditions.

The distance is only 600 km from Alberta's boundary with British Columbia, due west of the Crowsnest Pass, all the way to Vancouver on the shore of the Pacific Ocean. Between the western boundary of Alberta and the ocean lie multiple ranges of north-south lying mountains. By directing the force of wind, these mighty mountains play an important part in shaping western Canada's essential climate.

At the finest grain, even the existence of plants can modify local conditions. In early spring, the exposed and dry faces of prairie coulees are spotted with clusters of moss phlox. The plant grows in low, dense cushions, with many overlapping and interlocking stalks of short, soft spines. Each plant protects a patch of soil from drying sun and wind by day, and the cold spring sky by night. Insects spend the night under the plants, where the air may be 10°C warmer than the surrounding air.

Moisture

Alberta, and especially southernmost Alberta, is very dry. The lowest relative humidity in Canada was recorded in southern Alberta—down to about six per cent relative humidity in 1968. The driest parts of the province are encountered in the eastern grasslands, while Waterton Lakes National Park is comparatively moist and well watered. Snowfall accounts for about 35 per cent of precipitation in southern Alberta.

Parts of Space and Place

Wind

In the northern hemisphere, prevailing winds come from the west, including the southwest and northwest. Prevailing winds carry warm, moist Pacific air east across the rising mountains and as they do, the air cools and moisture falls as rain or snow on the western side of the Continental Divide.

Usually, the Pacific air is squeezed of moisture as it rises over the lower and warmer coastal ranges. More moisture falls as snow as the air moves farther east and higher up the mountains. Cresting the Continental Divide, the Pacific air descends the eastern slopes of the Rockies and arrives in southern Alberta as a dry, warm wind—the famous and fabled chinook wind.

Prevailing winds blow from the west, but because the mountains lie north-south, there is no barrier to cold arctic air sweeping down from the north to fill the entire Interior Plains with deepest winter. Neither is there an obstacle to warm masses of air pushing north from the American southwest, and when these two masses of air meet, there is turbulence, cloud, wind and precipitation. Battling air masses are another source of Alberta's notoriously variable weather.

Northern winds are less frequent, but common enough, usually the carrier of cold arctic influences. Eastern and southern winds are even less frequent. Eastern winds carry rain and snow, and southern winds are warm and dry.

Elevation

There are almost 3000 m of altitude difference between the lowest and highest points in southernmost Alberta, and elevation is a major influence on regional and local climate and weather. Generally, the greater the elevation, the lower the temperature.

Temperature

The Dry Mixed Grass Ecoregion has the longest frost-free period, but it is also one of the driest places in Canada. The region suffers chronic shortages of water and cycles of prolonged drought, because air moving into the region is either dry and cold from the north, or the wrung-out remnant of wind passing over the western mountains.

Notorious weather

For visitors, southernmost Alberta's weather means skiers can expect a 25 per cent chance of finding good skiing conditions, and in the summer a 90 per cent chance of good hiking, biking and riding days—not too hot or cold, but with maybe a little rain or snow, or a strong breeze. Delightful for wilderness travel. It's the other 10 per cent of days that make southern Alberta's reputation for unruly weather.

In late 1996, most of British Columbia and the Interior Plains were blanketed in arctic air tracking from the north along the north-south lay of land. A huge low pressure system of moisture-laden air built over the warm Pacific Ocean and invaded the south coast of British Columbia.

Vancouver and Victoria were buried in 70 cm of wet snow. Coastal British Columbia is well adapted to lots of rain, but the cities were immobilized and isolated for four days by the heavy, wet snow. According to the Insurance Bureau of Canada, this very rare event in Canadian history cost over $200 million in property damages.

In the meantime, southern Alberta had weeks on end of very cold weather and lots of snow. Records for cold and snow were set and broken in the autumn and early winter of 1996. In Pincher Creek, at 9:00 in the morning of December 31, the temperature was -20°C. Suddenly, a roll of fog swept over the mountains on the Continental Divide above the near horizon. The fog swept through Pincher Creek and across the montane foothills, plating everything with hoar frost.

Even more suddenly, powerful western winds blew the fog to the east, and carried in a rush of warm air. In less than an hour, the temperature had risen to +4°C, apparently a record for the fastest temperature change in Canadian history.

The landscape of dramatic climate events—colliding continental air masses, mountain channelling, extreme topography—results in equally dramatic weather events, including tornadoes, blizzards, flooding rain, lightning and thunder, truck stopping snow, hail, deep cold and howling winds. And these events can be expected almost anywhere at any time.

Alberta lore is filled with wild stories of rapid weather changes. Visitors must keep alert to the possibilities.

Plants and animals

Naturalists have not completely inventoried the plants and animals in all parts of the province, and in fact naturalists may never know all there is to know about how animals and plants are distributed in southernmost Alberta.

Until 1996, naturalists believed long-toed salamanders were found only in the alpine and subalpine parts of southern Alberta. However, in that year Robin Walsh, a high school student in Longview, discovered a salamander living in her family's farm dugout. The fact that long-toed salamanders lived so far east came as a surprise to naturalists at the University of Alberta. You never can tell....

Ecoregions support "typical" plants and animals, the kinds of things you expect to see almost anywhere in that landscape. Ecodistricts, the special areas in a bigger landscape, have their own unique plants and animals—things you expect to see mostly in those areas. Then, there are species that exist only in very select places, almost lost in the bigger landscape.

The combinations of soils, climate, geology and human actions influence the kinds of plants and animals that survive and perhaps flourish in a particular place. These are representative, or indicator species visitors will find in an ecoregion. Some species are only found in particular landscapes—mountain goats are found, where else?—And some other species are everywhere, for example, mosquitos.

However, there is no simple formula saying that certain plants and animals and only those plants and animals will be found in an ecoregion. There are far more likely to be surprises in terms of the plants and animals a walker might see in any particular place. There are at least three reasons why the lines between communities of plants and animals are blurred.

Specialization and generalization
A few species of plants and animals are found only in certain places and in no other places. These are specialized species that demand a very precise mix of environmental conditions. If those

28

conditions are not present in a place, then neither is the species.

Far more plants and animals, however, are generalists capable of surviving and thriving in a broad range of environmental conditions. Crows, for example, are found almost everywhere there is flyable air, from the most desiccated coulee in the Dry Mixed Grass Ecoregion to high above barren rock in the Alpine Ecoregion.

While few species are as adaptable as the crow, there are others that can tolerate a broad range of soil, climate, moisture, exposure and disturbance conditions. This means many species will be found where conditions approximate the ideal, even if the species' ideal conditions are not met.

Gradients

Maps usually show sharp and clear boundaries between ecological conditions, but in fact there is usually a more gradual transition from the characteristics of one ecoregion or ecodistrict to those of another.

Species typical of a particular ecoregion will continue to exploit the gradient between ecoregions until the balance of conditions is too precarious for their survival. The zones of transition between ecoregions often contain the greatest diversity of species because plants and animals typical of bordering ecoregions are all likely to occupy the space between.

Connections

While southern Alberta is a unique part of the world, it is by no means cut off and isolated. The region is directly connected to the rest of North America, and the nature of these connections has a major influence on the kinds of plants and animals found in any particular place.

The Dry Mixed Grass Ecoregion in the southeastern corner of the province is part of the Mississippi-Missouri drainage system, while the rest of the region drains entirely into rivers flowing east and north. A number of plants and animals have used the connection to the Missouri as a dispersal pathway to move into southern Alberta. Soapweed, a species of yucca, used this route and is found only in a few particularly arid valleys in the Dry Mixed Grass Ecoregion of southeastern Alberta.

There is a moth, the pronuba moth, that only lays eggs on seed capsules of the yucca plant. In turn, the yucca plant needs the pronuba moth for pollination. Because the moth depends on the presence of yucca, the pronuba moth is only found where there are yucca plants, and nowhere else.

On the other end of the region, Waterton Lakes National Park is a gateway to the western side of the mountains, and typically Colombian species of plants and animals use that gate to penetrate southern Alberta.

The Milk River has its headwaters in the eastern slopes of Montana's Rocky Mountains, and animals have used its valley to move far from the mountains and into the grasslands.

The yellow-bellied marmot is a symbol of the Alpine Ecoregion in southwestern Alberta, usually seen and heard by hikers on steep scree slopes and rock falls below towering mountain cliffs. However, this typically mountain species is also found along the Milk River and the adjacent coulees. Perhaps because of declining mountain habitat, increasing numbers or declining predators in the grasslands, pioneering marmots have recently moved out of the mountains and onto the plains or, at least, the rocky valleys of plains rivers and coulees. These animals seem to be doing well in their marginal, but previously unoccupied marmot habitat.

Species lost and gained

Finally, human beings have disrupted patterns of naturally occurring plants and animals. Early hunters in ancient time may have helped eliminate some species of large mammals, including horse, mammoth, mastodon and camel. Thousands of years of improving hunting technologies meant the end for some species as successful humans demanded more and more energy from their environment to feed growing populations.

Human impacts increased hugely with the arrival of Europeans in Canada, followed by the rest of the world.

In some places, entire species were eliminated from their natural habitats, and in other places, alien species were introduced from around the globe. There is no longer any point to looking for naturally occurring bison, bighorn sheep, gray wolf, grizzly bear, prairie dog, swift fox or elk anywhere in the grassland ecoregions; they were eliminated by Europeans many decades ago.

In other places it is equally futile looking for common natural grasses that have been eliminated and replaced with grasses better suited for livestock production. Sweetgrass, for example, long used by aboriginal peoples in their ceremonial and religious lives, was regarded by Europeans as a weed because it formed sod and because cattle do not find it especially tasty. Today, sweetgrass is rare in places where it once was common.

In southeastern Alberta, in the heart of the Dry Mixed Grass Ecoregion, there is magnificent white spruce, the characteristic tree of western wooded ecoregions, especially the Montane and Subalpine ecoregions. Early settlers planted them around their homesteads and along windbreaks. Until humans carried young trees into the grasslands, white spruce never had the opportunity to grow in this apparently hostile environment. Once there, however, the spruce had little difficulty in adapting to their unusual home, in part because of the settlers' ability to supply the trees with water.

Protected places are not immune to human influence. In 1997, two ranchers shot and killed a male and female wolf just outside the boundaries of Waterton Lakes National Park. Apparently, the pair were the Alpha male and Alpha female in a small pack occupying the park. The female was pregnant with six pups. Park naturalists believe the remaining pack of young wolves, now leaderless, would disperse.

By summer of 1997, there were no wolves left in Waterton Lakes National Park. Wolves may be legally trapped, poisoned or shot in Alberta, where they are still designated as vermin.

No doubt, indigenous plants and animals diminished as western Canada was domesticated. Species were greatly reduced in numbers, some species were forced out of their natural ranges, and some were eliminated entirely. Today, the dominant species everywhere is humans. Nevertheless, there are still fine places scattered here and there in all parts of southernmost Alberta where walkers can see and experience the essentials of grassland, foothills, parkland and mountain life. The Special Places are this kind of place.

Humans

The Palliser Triangle, named after Captain John Palliser, which includes most of southern Alberta, has been described as a "cultural pump," because dramatic alternations and oscillations of environmental conditions over the past 10,000 years have promoted cycles of human population and depopulation. In good centuries, people quickly moved into the great grasslands, enjoying plentiful rain, warm summers, mild winters and lots to eat. In bad centuries, people avoided the waterless and starved plains of the Palliser Triangle.

In these cycles of colonization and depopulation, people tried to meet environmental change through combinations of technologies and modes of social organization better adapted to changing natural conditions. Social scientists suggest the long-term trend of adaptive change is toward increasing industrialization, that is the increasing use of technology and social organization as the means to overcome environmental constraints.

Ancient history

About 12,000 years ago, the Ice Age glaciers receded from southern Alberta and the first humans occupied the truly new land. Since that time, there were several enduring cycles of favourable and decidedly unfavourable environmental conditions, at least for humans.

In the first 3,000 post-glacial years, the environment was almost ideal—warm and wet, with lush vegetation and plentiful animals. The first people in this landscape were hunters of large mammals. They worked in small family groups using heavy-duty tools needed to bring down a tonne or more of meat—large-bladed, heavy-hafted thrusting spears and hand axes.

Then, the millennia from 9,000 to 5,000 years ago were too warm. Scarce moisture was sucked up by dry winds, and the new soils first stopped accumulating and then were eroded away. Plants and animals were reduced to dryland species, and rivers were warm and shallow. From time to time, long spells of drought were broken by dramatically colder decades when mountain glaciers came back to life. The record of human life in southern Alberta almost disappears for this entire long part of history.

By 5,000 years ago, the climate had cooled and precipitation had increased, ending millennia of alternating cold deserts and hot deserts. By then, the landscape included most of today's plant communities. The humans who returned to this more agreeable environment came equipped with a greater variety of small tools, suggesting they had moved away from specializing in the hunting of large animals. More likely, their subsistence strategies included a larger variety of small animals taken with lightweight throwing spears and processed with tiny blades and scrapers. Clothing was probably tailored, offering better protection from winter cold.

For several centuries, beginning 3,000 years ago, there was a cycle of cold and wet, resulting in a mini-ice age. Human populations were smaller, but they did not disappear. By then, the aboriginal peoples had learned new ways of living in harsh conditions, including the bison jump and pound, food storage, improved clothing and shelter technology, the domestic dog and trade routes and protocols. Each of these technological advances was accompanied by larger populations and increasing organizational capacity needed to get many people working together, sharing labour, skills, material resources and the rewards of joint effort.

Recent history

Then, there were almost 2,000 years of moderate climate and greater environmental stability, and the landscape appeared more or less as it does today, with the same plants and animals. Humans quickly repopulated southern Alberta and established the rootstock of today's First Nations. Stability is only relative, however, and this paradise was disrupted by alternating decades of drought and unusually cold, wet winters.

A period of severe winters climaxed in the 1880s, and pioneer European and American ranchers were almost driven out of the Interior Plains. Thousands of cattle perished in blizzards that swept across the overstocked ranges. At the same time, white-tailed deer disappeared from southernmost Alberta, starved out of their range. They began to reoccupy select parts of southern Alberta in the 1900s, and even today are scarce in places where once they were common. The cold winters were the final blow for the bison, already hunted to the point of extinction by Canadians, Americans and Europeans.

A moment of success

Once again the environment warmed in the early part of the 20th century and humans poured into the Interior Plains, this time equipped with heavy industrial technology including irrigation, steam and later gasoline tractors and heavy tools of cultivation. Society was later organized on a provincial and national level. This is the beginning of a time when changes in the social environment outpace and dominate changes in the natural environment. This is the present.

Try it!

Even casual travellers in southernmost Alberta appreciate the region's complexity, a fact brought home when the sunlit Crowsnest Highway disappears into a snowy torrent of chinook wind somewhere west of Brocket. Science, history and common experience agree that the many landscapes of southernmost Alberta are as endlessly fascinating as they are complex.

The sheer diversity of southernmost Alberta makes it one of the most interesting landscapes in the world. It would take a lifetime to sample all the variety, but the Special Places were chosen because they well illustrate an important theme in the natural history of the area. They bring to life the principles of science and history. It is time to get out and try it.

From Grassland to Rockland

Pinhorn Grazing Reserve.

Red Rock Coulee.

From Grassland to Rockland

Writing-On-Stone Provincial Park.

Twin River Grazing Reserve.

From Grassland to Rockland

Prairie Townsendia.

Yellow bell.

Apricot mallow.

Prickly pear cactus.

From Grassland to Rockland

Eastern Porcupine Hills.

Fescue grasslands.

From Grassland to Rockland

Upper Oldman River and Beehive Mountain.

Near Whaleback Ridge.

From Grassland to Rockland

Oldman River and the Livingstone Gap.

Blakiston Creek valley, Waterton Lakes National Park.

From Grassland to Rockland

Balsamroot.

White mariposa.

White Dryad.

From Grassland to Rockland

Table Mountain.

Mount Blakiston from Mount Galwey.

3
Dry Mixed Grass Ecoregion

The Dry Mixed Grass Ecoregion seems like an endless horizon of grass, especially to car drivers hurtling along the highways of southernmost Alberta. The marvellous variety of the dry grassland is only seen on a closer look from ground level and at the studied pace of those on foot.

Here and there, slight swells push a prairie crest higher into the grassland heat, light and wind, creating an island of brilliant desiccation. In contrast, coulees and river valleys sink below the hot horizon and fierce winds, creating a refuge of sheltered shade and moisture. Between the rolling crests of the high grassland and the cool waters of prairie streams, every kind of difference in orientation, slope, exposure to the sun, force and direction of winds, and nearness to water give the landscape great and subtle variety.

Dry grassland carved by the Milk River, summer. Pinhorn Grazing Reserve.

A horizon of variety

In the driest places on the flat prairie table land, the soils are desiccated Chernozems supporting grama grass and wheat grass. On the north-facing sides of low hills and shallow bowls, soils are slightly thicker, richer and moister, and grama grass gives way to needle-and-thread grass and June grass.

Here and there, the prairie is pierced by coulees. Most grassland coulees were carved by rivers draining meltwater backed up behind the continental ice sheet at the end of the Ice Age. Today, gentler forces are at work modifying the coulees, and the original bold lines left by the torrent of glacial water are still much as they were thousands of years ago, only now covered with a carpet of grass.

Shrubs sparsely cover the north-facing sides and bottoms of coulees in the Dry Mixed Grass Ecoregion, wherever enough water and protection will support a few larger plants. Closer to running or standing water, where plants have better access to moisture, nutrients and shelter, there are thick shrubs and even huge cottonwoods.

Prairie streams

Prairie rivers and smaller streams usually have a floodplain, a margin that is flooded more-or-less regularly. The shore of the stream will be flooded almost every year, creating freshly disturbed Regosolic soils of water-washed cobbles, sand, silt and clay. The shores and shoals of water-borne sediment support only a few hardy pioneer plants, including seedlings that will probably not survive the next year's flood.

The higher floodplain is not flooded as frequently as the near shore, and plants are much more settled and established. Dense and tall shrublands of willow, saskatoon and wild rose choke the periodic floodplain. In some special places there are groves of cottonwood.

During infrequent floods, stream channels and other depressions are filled with water. The newly-filled ponds and pools have nowhere to drain when the flood recedes. Water lingers in these ponds for months and perhaps even years, creating saturated, muddy Gleysols supporting luxuriant water-loving plants, including sedge, sandbar willow and tall grasses.

Milk River, spring. Pinhorn Grazing Reserve.

In the Dry Mixed Grass Ecoregion, the greatest diversity and density of life is usually found near streams and on floodplains. That, in part, is why the Special Places described in this chapter involve prairie rivers.

Variety and species

There are at least 58 different mammals and 370 species of plants in the Dry Mixed Grass Ecoregion of southernmost Alberta. Only a few of these species are truly unique to the Dry Mixed Grass Ecoregion—rattlesnake, yucca, pale big-eared bat, pronghorn antelope, grama grass, burrowing owl and other species specially adapted to a very dry prairie landscape. On the other hand, mosquitos, juniper, crows and voles are common from the eastern Dry Mixed Grass Ecoregion to the far western Subalpine Ecoregion.

As well, there are some plants and animals you might see in other ecoregions, but that you surely would see in the dry mixed grassland environment—prairie crocus, yellow bell, wild rose, wheat grass, mule deer, Richardson's ground squirrel, prairie falcon, nighthawk, horned lark and meadowlark.

The dry lands of southeastern Alberta are unmatched in diversity of life, even if most species are both small in size and few in number. Walkers will have to keep a sharp eye if they want to enjoy all the offerings of the Dry Mixed Grass Ecoregion.

Humans and the dry grassland

A quick look at southeastern Alberta from a speeding vehicle would reveal few signs of human life, and even a casual look would reveal only a few more signs. The entire region seems built to repel rather than attract human interest, especially in the present era of industrial agriculture. Much earlier, though, the dry grassland had its full share of resident humans.

People may have occupied southeastern Alberta 20,000 years ago and perhaps slightly earlier. By that time, the last of the Ice Age glaciers was melting away toward the north leaving the reshaped surface ready for colonization. No doubt, the landscape would have been cold, wet and inhospitable, but people lived in similar harsh circumstances in Canada's north well into historic times. However, the earliest archaeological remains found in the region date to much later than 20,000 years ago and closer to 10,000 years ago. Perhaps earlier signs of human occupation were obliterated by ongoing forces of erosions after the great glaciers disappeared, leaving only more recent remains for modern archaeologists to find.

The most interesting things archaeologists have found in the region are the great many circles and other shapes made from stones plucked from the glacial debris covering the entire region. Students of the region have called these circles "tipi rings" after what may have been their most obvious use as weights holding down the edges of hide tipis. A typical "tipi ring" was laid out as a near perfect circle 4-6 m in diameter with a gap in the east-facing side of the circle for a doorway, a small stone hearth near the centre, and a floor packed hard by its long-ago occupants. The circles are easily imagined with a cone of poles towering above the rocks, tightly draped with a snug hide covering, the door turned away from the relentless western winds, a wisp of smoke blowing from the open top—home for a family of six or eight people.

However, there are many other circles and shapes that most probably were not "tipi rings." Some shapes are not circles at all—straight lines, small arcs, huge arcs, mounds, eccentric rings, and outlines of humans and animals. Others are circles, but

Dry Mixed Grass

they have no doorway or hearth and there is no packed floor. Instead, the circles are crossed by one or more straight lines of rocks, or have a tall heap of rock in the centre.

Some places where stone circles are found cover several hectares and contain dozens of patterns, only a few of which suggest they were ever occupied. The many others served purposes we shall probably never know. One of the largest concentrations of circles found along the Milk River is just east of Writing-On-Stone Provincial Park. The circles and the famous, mysterious petroglyphs are not necessarily connected, except that both are joined in the Great Mystery of the plains.

Much more recently, the dry grassland was occupied by sometimes cooperating and sometimes conflicting peoples, including the Shoshoni, Kutenai, Pend d'Oreille, Peigan, Cree, Assiniboine, Blackfoot, Gros Ventre, Dakota, Crow and Métis. After them came the traders and trappers, then the whiskey runners and police, then the ranchers and finally the oil and gas industry. There was a modest flow of immigrant farmers into places with water, but the Great Depression and western droughts of the 1930s blew most farmers off the land. There never was another land rush in southeastern Alberta, and it is still under the care of a few ranching families.

The Dry Mixed Grass Ecoregion

Area: 47,299 sq. km or 7.2% of the province.

Topography: Level or gently rolling, broken by river valleys and coulees.

Elevation: 700 - 825 m

Climate: This is one of the driest parts of Canada. It receives the least summer precipitation in Alberta (156 mm) in less than 10 days of measurable precipitation per summer month, and in less than five days in winter. It has the warmest summer temperatures in Alberta (16.2°C). Summer high temperatures reach over 35°C. Summer water deficits lead to drought conditions. The growing season is more than 100 frost-free summer days. Winter snow is scant and winters are cold (-7.2°C). The open landscape experiences strong winds, but there are only a few days of winter chinook warming.

Soils: Mostly rich Chernozems.

Humans: Most of the Dry Mixed Grass Ecoregion is domesticated, and places of preserved natural features are rare. Only the hostile remnants of this ecoregion have been saved from the plough, roads, fences and towns.

1 Pinhorn Grazing Reserve

Mode: foot
Rating: moderate
Time: 4 - 5 hours
Distance: 11 km
Elevation change: 151 m
Map: 72 E/2 Calib Coulee

The Pinhorn Grazing Reserve is a huge, pristine expanse of dry grassland, penetrated and deeply carved by the Milk River. The contrast between the arid undulating grassland, steep badland canyons and the verdant river valley could not be more dramatic. The highlight is the view from the rim of the river canyon, overlooking 75 million years of history exposed in the clear, dry near-desert light. It is hard to believe this desiccated country was once at the bottom of an immense sea.

Prairie rivers are vital reservoirs and conservators of authentic prairie landscape and amongst all the great prairie rivers, the lower Milk River valley is one of the premier landscapes in all of Alberta and, perhaps, in all of western Canada. The river has sliced deep into the bedrock of the Interior Plains where its fine grain may be examined and experienced.

The Pinhorn is public land open to visitors, and is an excellent example of western rangeland management. In some parts of the reserve you can walk an entire day and never see a sign of human impact.

There are no formal hiking trails anywhere in the Pinhorn Grazing Reserve. Hikers must use their routefinding skills to connect a maze of cattle and wildlife trails leading from one place to another. For the most part, this is not too difficult and, in any event, the lay of the land makes it almost impossible to get lost. But, there are plenty of challenges for walkers in the Pinhorn Grazing Reserve.

Across the grassland

Visitors will leave their car or truck on an established road and walk across the grassland to the canyon rim. The stroll across the gently-rolling prairie is a textbook lesson on the composition of the dry grasslands of southeastern Alberta.

The grasses rarely stand above 30 cm in height including blue grama grass, the distinctive species of the Dry Mixed Grass Ecoregion. Along drier and more exposed swells, spear grass is common.

Spear grass has another name—needle-and-thread grass. The seeds of this grass include a very sharp tip containing the seed proper attached to an awn, or long thread of tough fibre. The awn is hygroscopic, that is, it attracts moisture from the air. As the awn picks up moisture, it twists and as it dries, it straightens. This twisting action drives the seed deep into the moist soil for germination.

The twisting of needle-and-thread grass also drives the sharp tip into the

Coulees and canyons, summer.

45

Pinhorn Grazing Reserve

Getting there

This outing explores the Milk River where it flows through the Pinhorn Grazing Reserve, which is in very remote country, even though almost any car or truck can make it right to the rim of the canyon. In dry weather. In wet weather, the silt turns into mud and even four-wheel-drive vehicles are immobilized. Getting there is part of the adventure.

Drive Highway 501 east from the town of Milk River or west from the Saskatchewan boundary. Approaching either way on paved Highway 501, there are very few intersections worthy of the name "road." This is a very sparsely populated part of Canada. The correct turn-off is located between Highway 885 to the west and Highway 887 to the east. Both these highways are well signed.

Between these intersections, look on the south side of Highway 501 for a wide gravel road heading in the direction of the Sweetgrass Hills visible in nearby Montana. On the southeast corner of the intersection there is a large ranch homestead where the barns, sheds and plank fences are all painted red. The correct turn-off for the reserve is not signed, and the red farmstead is the landmark. There are no other farmsteads anywhere near this section of the highway.

Just west of the farmstead, turn off Highway 501 and drive south 3 km on the gravel road to a cattle gate and a large sign identifying the boundary of the Pinhorn Grazing Reserve. Three more kilometres beyond the cattle gate the gravel road splits, with one branch continuing south and the other turning toward the east. The southern branch leads to the reserve headquarters nestled on the floodplain along the Milk River. Drop in and tell the rancher you will be admiring his work for the day. Then take the eastern branch, which continues across the grassland.

The entire reserve is dotted with small tin sheds that protect gas wellheads. The wellheads are serviced with primitive roads and one of these service roads about 3.5 km east of the junction ends overlooking the steep canyon walls. This is the place.

Camping

There are no camping services or facilities of even the most primitive kind within the reserve, and there is no drinking water. The closest campgrounds are at Writing-On-Stone Provincial Park and at the town of Milk River, both a considerable distance from the reserve. Most visitors will endure the driving and make a long day trip to visit the Pinhorn Grazing Reserve.

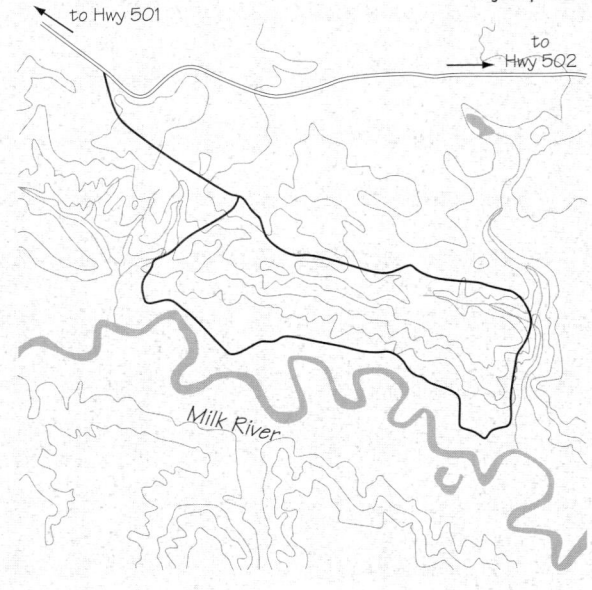

46

Moss phlox, early spring.

Colorado rubber-plant, early summer.

skin of animals. In the 1820s, Lord Selkirk, founder of the Red River Settlement in Manitoba, sent an expedition to Minnesota to buy a herd of sheep. His drovers started back with 200 head, but most died on the trail when spear grass pierced the sheep's skin and infected. Walkers in the dry grasslands will get used to pulling the spears from their clothes.

Amongst the grasses are sage, especially pasture sage, and stunted threadleaf sedge. Moss phlox and dwarf clubmoss struggle to cover the exposed gaps between the grasses and taller plants. These tough, ground-hugging species protect the brown Chernozem soil from wind and water erosion, and when they die their deep roots are an important contribution to the buildup of organic material. The white or pale lavender flowers of moss phlox are a pleasing contrast to the desiccated grasses of early spring.

Flocks of horned lark swoop low over the grass. Every slightly higher point is claimed by a meadowlark and the day is filled with their song. Sharp-tailed grouse strut between clumps of grass and stalks of sage.

At the rim

The first sight of the canyon should leave walkers slack-jawed. The deep, severe walls of the valley are completely unlike any other place in the western prairie.

Prairie Townsendia, spring.

At the point where the level grassland breaks and joins the valley wall, grasses thin out and cactus and creeping juniper take over. Early in the spring, the exposed lip of the canyon may be lined with the delicate blossoms of yellow bell, prairie Townsendia and musineon.

A little later in the season, the more unusual dryland flowering species make their appearance, including cushion vetch, blue beardtongue, butte marigold and Colorado rubber plant. The roots of the Colorado rubber plant contain a milky sap that was explored as a source of rubber during World War II.

The rim of the canyon is marked by the first exposed layer of rust red sandstone, a place free of plants with barbs,

Alberta's Seas

Over millions of years, ancient rivers flowed out of the west and into a series of shallow saltwater seas that ebbed and flowed as the drifting continental plates settled against each other.

The land buckled and broke, and seawater flooded the low, flat plate that eventually became the Interior Plains. The land buckled again, and the water flowed out.

In the early Cretaceous, 140 million years ago, seas encroached from the north to put Fort McMurray on a tropical beach. By the late Cretaceous about 65 million years ago, the sea poured in from the southeast, covering the present Interior Plains almost to the Continental Divide. The Bearpaw Sea, which finally drained away in the middle of the Tertiary less than 50 million years ago, was the most recent sea to cover much of the Interior Plains.

At that time, the Rockies were building in the higher country to the west and were already wearing down under the assault of erosion. Frost, chemical action and gravity broke the surface of the new mountains, and running water and wind carried the finer material far downward and to the east. Cretaceous rivers flowing out of the growing Rockies and into the Bearpaw Sea were much larger than today's grassland rivers and each carried tremendous loads of silt, sand and stone. Eventually, this debris of ground-up mountain covered the Interior Plains from the Eastern Slopes of the Rockies all the way to western Manitoba.

As a result of these growing and shrinking seas, most of the Interior Plains of Canada is underlain with shales or sandstones of Cretaceous and earlier age dating to between 45 and 100 million years ago.

Sediments

Because the seas were shallow—about 50 m in depth—and warm, there was abundant marine life, especially crustaceans. Conifer trees lined the western shores of the sea and the rivers pouring out of the growing mountains. Tree branches and twigs littered the sea floor and woodboring molluscs used the litter for food. The Bearpaw Sea was shallow, warm and full of life, and it was also very muddy, a mix

Iron-rich concretions in sandstone.

of organic debris, clay and silt particles, and exotic inorganic compounds. The mud settled to the bottom and consolidated into soft shales and mudstones.

Here and there, the bedrock yields the remains of dinosaurs and fish, along with a great variety of marine fossils. Most of the dinosaur remains are those of marine animals who spent their lives in the sea. Farther west at Dinosaur Provincial Park, remains are usually of terrestrial and amphibious animals, indicating a waterlogged but not inundated landscape.

Near the ancient western shore of the sea, the great rivers flowing off the higher Rockies deposited huge loads of sand, gravel and boulders near their mouths, forming flats and mounds of debris standing above sea level. As the weight of accumulated river rock and marine sediments built up, the region subsided. Shallow seas then flowed in to cover the river flats with a fresh layer of marine mud.

The ocean came and went at least three times. As the ocean advanced, the river mouths were pushed back into higher ground, and the river sand was covered with a layer of sea mud. Then, when the ocean retreated in front of continental rising, the mouths of the rivers advanced, and the mud was covered with sand.

In this way, much of the vast Interior Plains is underlain with alternating beds and lenses of sandstone and shale. The advance of the ocean was quite rapid, but the retreat was slow and hesitating, resulting in intermingled layers of sandstone and shale.

Hard economics

The middle layers of sandstone are vast water reservoirs in a region desperate for water. The deeper layers of sandstone are reservoirs for natural gas, the centrepiece of Alberta economics. Some marine deposits are ideal for making pottery, ceramics and porcelain. Several enterprises quarry clay and sell it around the world. Medicine Hat was built on a combination of clay, fuel and transportation. Finally, the sandstones, shales, siltstones and mudstones react very differently to erosion, resulting in the weird and wonderful landscape so attractive to visitors.

Freshwater and saltwater

The bedrock under the Interior Plains includes saltwater shales, freshwater sandstones and brackish water siltstones, a blend of shale and sandstone that forms where fresh water and seawater mix. The closer a place is to the Rockies, the more likely the bedrock will include freshwater sandstones. Farther away to the east, where the Cretaceous seas were deepest, marine deposits are thicker than sandstones. In most places, sandstones interleaf with beds of marine shale because the seas rose and fell and rivers advanced and retreated.

In the lower Milk River valley, which was far from the western shore of the Cretaceous sea, shales are thicker than sandstones. In the foothills of southern Alberta, near the mouths of Cretaceous rivers, sandstones are thicker. The Porcupine Hills, for example, are made up almost entirely of sandstones formed at the same time the Milk River shale was being laid down. There are only traces of marine deposits in the Porcupine Hills because the foothills are adjacent to the Rockies and were only briefly flooded with seawater. Each kind of rock, so well exposed by the Milk River, has its special attraction.

Hoodoo towers at the canyon rim, Sweetgrass Hills beyond, summer.

Pinhorn Grazing Reserve

On animal trails through a carpet of grass and sage, early spring.

thorns and spines where walkers can sit and examine the steep descending wall into the valley below.

The way down

The coulees are all interconnected, with higher coulees leading ever deeper toward the river bottom. In principle, pick a coulee and keep moving down toward the bottom of the system. Take your time finding a route to the bottom.

Any route will drop 150 m from the canyon rim to the river bottom. The first 50 m are the most difficult part of the route. Almost everywhere, the terrain is steep and loose. Once in the coulee system you will lose the advantage of a big visible horizon. Some coulees are very steep, or are surfaced with loose erosion debris, or hide a sheer drop over a shelf of sandstone, or bottom out in a narrow, muddy slot carved by spring runoff.

Try to avoid these surprises by following well-used animal trails leading down the coulees. They are easily navigated, but keep in mind mule deer and pronghorn are quite a bit more nimble than humans. Some scrambling and controlled sliding may be necessary. Whenever you stop to catch your breath and take your bearings on the way down, have a close look at the high and steep coulee walls.

Sandstone capping a bed of muddy shale.

Pinhorn Grazing Reserve

storms and year-round winds that continue to refine each sculpture.

The buff sandstones are sprinkled with iron red concretions and fragments of Cretaceous sea shells. A little lower, where some debris has built up, sage brush is the dominant and often the only plant, filling the warm coulees with tangy perfume.

The sides of the coulees sag as the surface soil creeps and slumps under the force of gravity. Clumps and clods are falling all the time, and even huge landslides occur regularly. In early spring, streams carve a little deeper into the coulee, leaving steeply undercut precipices that must be negotiated. All the while, every step is buffeted by strong wind.

The journey down the coulee system is a humbling reminder of the forces of grassland nature.

Hoodoos and wolf willow, summer.

Coulee walls

Near the top are hoodoos, wind and water sculpted columns of sandstone and shale. Hoodoos are weird and wonderful sculpted shapes formed near the rim of a coulee where harder rock covers a layer of softer rock. As the ancient Milk River carved its way toward the valley floor, the softer rock was eroded more quickly than the protective cap of harder rock. Soil buildup is slow in this dry region, so the stone pillars are exposed to the lash of violent summer thunder-

At the bottom

The first 50 m of the upper coulee, where erosion is most rapid, can be very steep. All that loose erosion debris ends up on the bottom of the coulees, forming a pediment below the upper zone of rapid erosion. The gradient below the first 50 m of descent is less steep, and the coulee floors are covered with a meadow of dryland grasses and sage brush. The wind is strong, but

Sand beach crumbling into the Milk River, spring.

nothing like the wind on the prairie high above.

Animal trails cross a series of broad, shallow grassland benches and lead directly to the river. The benches are old shores of the river, formed in an era when the Milk River was much bigger than it is today. The lowest bench is the modern floodplain.

The floodplain

Some parts of the floodplain are occupied by small groves of black cottonwood and willow. Other parts closer to the water are covered with fresh pink sand beaches. Wherever erosion is especially active, the river has a steep bank dropping abruptly into the fast-flowing water. The sound of wind and water is punctuated by the loud splashing of undercut shoreline as it tumbles into the rushing river.

Once on the bottom of the canyon, walk up or downstream as far as you wish. Many more animals occupy the river bottom than the prairie above. It seems every patch of ground is sprinkled with mule deer, pronghorn and hare pellets, and the groves of cottonwood are riddled with beaver-gnawed trees and shrubs.

In one loop of the river there is the stump of a cottonwood dropped by beaver. The stump is a metre across and once supported five huge trunks, each jutting out in a different direction. The beaver had chewed at least 30 cm into the wood before gravity took over. All of the trunks came down, apparently at once, forming a star of dead trees lying on the ground almost 30 m from tip to tip. The beaver along the Milk River are very prodigious animals.

The Milk River loops and twists its way through the canyon, and usually the loops are grown over with shrubs so tightly packed it is almost impossible to penetrate. Fortunately, the many deer and pronghorn using the canyon floor have woven a fabric of trails throughout the floodplain. By connecting trails together, walkers can easily travel many kilometres along the bottom of the valley.

The way up

Finding a way to the top is the reverse of finding a way down. Start with an animal trail heading toward the mouth of a coulee. Eventually, the trail will lead to the prairie, or it will lead to a place where human ingenuity and hands will find a scramble route to the top. Coming at last out of the narrow confines of the upper coulee, the huge and endless grassland sky fills the horizon. The long tramp across the prairie and back to the trailhead is a last chance to experience the wealth of small, sparse life dwelling high above the water of the Milk River.

Fate of the Milk River

Engineers and water managers have identified several places along the Milk River where dams could be built and reservoirs created. The goal is to shape natural water regimes to better suit the needs of agriculture. If any one of the proposed dams is built, much of the lower part of the Milk River will disappear under an artificial lake. These plans are on the books, but managers have yet to find a way of justifying the destruction of the Milk River and until they do the river is likely safe.

A greater threat focuses on access to the grazing reserves, including the Pinhorn Grazing Reserve and the Twin River Grazing Reserve described in the next chapter. Presently, grazing reserves are public lands where travellers have access so long as they do not interfere with the reserves' rangeland functions. The provincial government, however, is contemplating giving the reserves to the ranchers who now put their cattle on the range for the summer. If they do, then these vast public lands will become private lands. Visitors will lose their rights of access and be shut out of enjoying some of the best grasslands left in Canada.

2 Writing-On-Stone Provincial Park

Mode: foot
Rating: easy
Time: 2 - 3 hours
Distance: 5.5 km
Elevation change: 30 m
Map: 72 E/4 Coutts

Writing-On-Stone Provincial Park is one of the few places with easy access to the waters of the Milk River where visitors can browse the rich natural history of a prairie river. Located deep in the dry grassland, Writing-On-Stone Provincial Park is famous for its intimate setting amongst a field of weird and wonderful hoodoos and its sandstone panels of symbolic art recording a millennium of aboriginal thought. Then, there is the river landscape itself, showing the marvellous passage between places without water and places with water.

Trails are scarce, because backcountry is scarce. Access to much of the park is restricted because of sensitive environments. So be it. On the other hand, visitors are more-or-less free to roam amongst the hoodoos nearest the campground, and nobody can resist.

The park's small backcountry is on the south side of the river. The south boundary of the park forms a large, hollow U-shape with the two arms embracing a strip of private land. The western arm takes in most of Police Coulee, a landscape of delicate habitats and even more delicate rock art. This part of the park is off-limits to independent visitors, but the east arm, Davis Coulee, is open for hikers.

Hoodoo interpretive trail

The well-made Hoodoo Trail heading west along the river samples some of the best landscapes in Writing-On-Stone. Everything is close at hand—shrubs lean into the trail, hoodoos loom within reach, birds and animals make eye contact, and the shallow river invites wading. It is a great experience in a rare grassland place.

The Hoodoo Trail begins in the interpretive centre, where visitors will find a trove of pamphlets on the birds, flowers, landforms and human history of the park. There are also detailed topographic maps available for backcountry walkers. A nearby cluster of interpretive signs tells the natural history of the park. The signs are very well designed and the text and graphics effectively describe the things people will see in the park. A path leads from the

Shield-bearers.

Getting there

Writing-On-Stone Provincial Park is south of Highway 501, reached by driving from Lethbridge on Highway 4 to the town of Milk River, then 32 km east on Highway 501, and finally 10 km south. There are large signs all the way. Milk River is the last place to pick up anything important.

Camping

There is a comfortable campground in the town of Milk River, complete with the usual amenities and a very reasonable cost. At the entrance to the campground there is a large stone and mortar cairn erected when the campground was dedicated. The stones in the cairn represent all the kinds of rock found in southeastern Alberta, including petrified wood, obsidian, granite, conglomerate, igneous rock and many kinds and colours of sandstone. Most stones have been sliced with a diamond saw, revealing their inner life. A masterpiece of craft.

There is good camping and RV facilities at Golden Springs Park, 8 km south of the junction of Highways 4 and 501 in Milk River. Road signs direct the way off Highway 4 and east on a paved and gravel road to the campground. The side road crosses fenced rangeland with cattleguards and cattle on the road and a good view of life on the range. The campground is set amongst the loops of an oxbow lake, carved and abandoned by the Milk River long ago, and now fed by a spring. The lakes are managed with dikes and dams, and the result was worth the effort, at least to the numerous geese, ducks, shorebirds, hawks and songbirds nesting and feeding there. A colony of marmots lives under the outhouses and another under a pile of cottonwood logs with a sign reading "Marmot Hotel."

There is very comfortable camping in Writing-On-Stone Park, with more than the usual amenities, including a museum, nature trails and natural history interpreters. All this comes at a steep price by provincial park standards—$18.00 a day for a basic drive-in site.

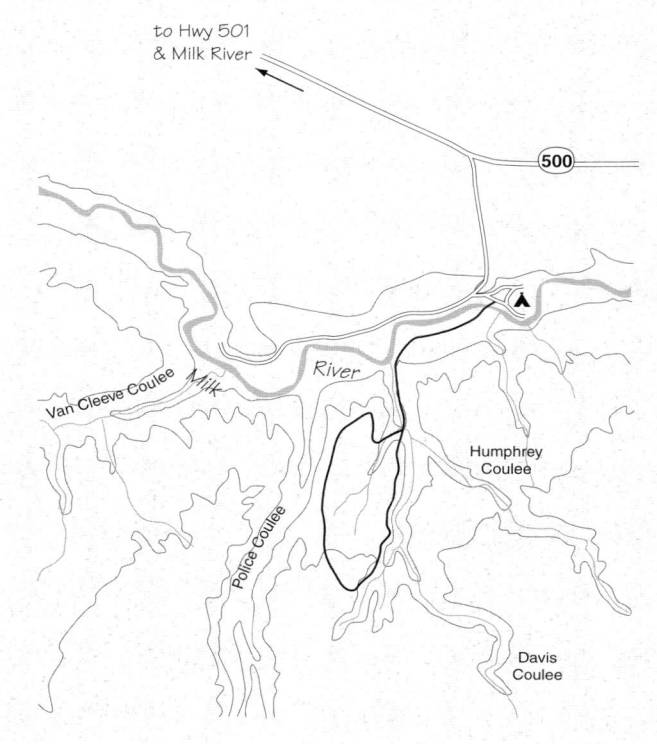

Writing-On-Stone Provincial Park

Floodplain campground and the field of hoodoos.

signs across a groomed lawn to a trailhead kiosk. A pamphlet keyed to numbered posts along the trail provides a detailed natural history of Writing-On-Stone Provincial Park.

Maps, species lists, trail guides, signs and descriptive pamphlets are augmented with guided hikes featuring the park's staff of interpreters. As well, there are many popular and scientific books and journal papers written about the natural history of the region. This park is distinguished by an abundance of information.

Through the forest

From the kiosk, the Hoodoo Trail leads first through the campground set in a forest of western cottonwood and an understorey of shrubs and pools of grass. In places, the trail is overhung with tall water birch, golden currant and even a few exotic box elder or Manitoba maple and spruce. Just beyond the campground, located on a level terrace, the trail leads into the field of hoodoos.

The hoodoos

The entire campground is hemmed with hoodoos on all sides away from the river. Just west of the picnic area, the trail enters a narrow slot-like passage between two towers of fluted rock and ascends the field of hoodoos.

South along Davis Coulee toward the Sweetgrass Hills.

55

Aquifers

Writing-On-Stone is in the driest part of Canada, and access to water sets the limits on most life-forms in the region, including humans. Human economies demand big lands and plentiful pure water. There is lots of land in southernmost Alberta, but very little water, especially surface water—rivers, streams, lakes, ponds, springs and marshes. A fortunate few humans live within reach of surface water, and today most accessible water is committed to somebody's use. The rest must get their water the hard way—from beneath the surface.

Fortunately, much of the region is underlain with a thick bed of Milk River sandstone, the sandstone now carved into hoodoos and canyon walls. Milk River sandstone is permeable and holds a vast reservoir of water. Since the early part of the 20th century, people have been drilling through the overburden of glacial drift and deep into the bedrock to find the water that makes possible human life in the region.

Origin of the aquifer

Milk River sandstone was formed early in the lower Cretaceous, about 100 million years ago. At the time, the Interior Plains to the east were mostly covered with vast seas and to the west the forces of mountain building were at work. As the western lands lifted, the eastern lands sank forming a huge trough. The new mountains were immediately attacked by erosion and the debris moved downhill, toward the east, and into the trough.

Much of this erosion debris came from the Selkirk Range of mountains in British Columbia and included coarse fragments of limestone, dolomite, quartzite and chert. Erosion was so ferocious that debris built up faster than the crust of the earth was sinking. Gradually, the shore of the Cretaceous sea was pushed toward the east behind the vast buildup of tough and resistant quartzite and chert fragments.

The coarsest material quickly fell to the bottom of the sea, but water currents moving parallel to the growing mountain ranges moved the finest sand and silt into long, linear belts lying farther offshore. The deposited material was thickest in the west and south and gradually tapered into nothing toward the east and north. Over millions of years, this material was transformed into Milk River sandstone.

At first, the beds of sandstone lay relatively flat and level. Then, shifting of plates deep in the earth transmitted forces upward to gently fold and wrinkle the beds of sandstone and shale. When the deep plates moved, cracks were opened and about 48 million years ago igneous rock flowed upward, pushing violently through the cracks. The molten material did not actually reach the surface; before there was an eruption, the upper part of the flow solidified and plugged the cracks. As the plugs grew, the flat beds of sandstone and shale were bent and warped up the sides of the swelling igneous mass.

Then, the entire region underwent massive erosion, but the much tougher igneous rock survived better than the softer sedimentary material. Over millions of years, the igneous plugs were exposed and left standing high above the relatively flat and level prairie. The final shaping was done by Pleistocene glaciers, carving away the overburden from the flanks and exposing the underlying bedrock. The results are the Sweetgrass Hills, standing just across the border from Writing-On-Stone.

Tafoni.

Floodplains are the richest part of the dry grassland.

The bed of sandstone underfoot at Writing-On-Stone sweeps to the south and climbs a third the way up the flanks of the hills.

Origin of water

Water enters the Milk River aquifer almost entirely through the exposed and up-tilted beds of sandstone on the flanks of the Sweetgrass Hills. The Sweetgrass Hills stand over 1000 m above the surrounding grassland, and they create their own weather, including much more precipitation than on the plains below. Rain falling on the upper slopes runs downward until it reaches the exposed sandstone. There, part of the water seeps into the aquifer. A much smaller amount also enters the aquifer where the river flows over bedrock near Writing-On-Stone.

There is no better place to charge an aquifer than high on the side of a wet mountain. However, water moves slowly through the bedrock—less than 7 m each year—and it takes a long time to move water from the Sweetgrass Hills to beneath Alberta's plains.

Water economics

Milk River sandstone holds a great deal of water and natural gas. People have been drilling into the sandstone for their water supply since the early part of the 20th century and now most communities, farmers and ranchers get their water from deep wells. Some also get a supply of natural gas, mostly methane, which is dissolved in the water and released when the water reaches the surface.

Most wells are artesian—there is enough pressure in the aquifer to force water up the drill hole to the surface. Artesian wells are a blessing for those who have them because they do not need expensive pumps to get their water supply. However, if the wells are not controlled the water flows freely whether or not it is needed. This is not a problem so long as enough water is entering the aquifer to replace the water that is removed.

In fact, the inflowing water is not enough to meet human and livestock requirements and for almost a century, people have been drawing down the ancient water stored in the aquifer. As a result, the water table has been getting steadily lower. Wells drilled 50 years ago are now dry and new wells must be drilled much deeper before water is reached. Eventually, the aquifer may be drained and there will be even fewer people living in southeastern Alberta than there are today.

Unless, of course, the government of Alberta intervenes with a water management program focused on all that free-flowing surface water. There are already plans on the books for dams and reservoirs on the Milk River. As it is, water must be diverted from the St. Mary River into the Milk River to maintain summer flows. Dams will allow a few people to live well beyond their means in terms of water use and their own impact on the environment.

A caprock barely protects the softer stone beneath.

The hoodoos and cliffs of exposed bedrock tell the story of an ancient riverbed buried under a lobe of a mighty continental glacier and filled with exotic glacial debris. Later, a powerful river of glacial meltwater found the old channel, scoured out the glacial till, and carved into the soft sandstone bedrock. Floods of water poured over the lip of the new valley, engraving coulees into the landscape. The glacier receded, the meltwater dwindled, and the huge valley was left with a much smaller river wandering across a wide bottom. Cold dry wind poured off the toe of the receding glacier, blasting every loose particle of sand, silt and clay over the rim of the valley. Together, water and wind carved the rim into a natural fantasy.

There are signs pointing out the trail. In the first half kilometre amongst the hoodoos there are several places where the trail approaches the rim of the canyon. There are grand views up and down the river and deep into the coulee systems on the other side. In places, the trail is forced upward to avoid deep and narrow slot coulees choked with tall willow and birch. Thick summer foliage prevents more than a glimpse into the coulee, but the thick tangle is an ideal home for small birds, rabbits and rodents that prefer to be out of sight of humans.

Wherever there is the least bit of protection from sun and wind, a little soil has collected and supports tough juniper and bearberry shrubs lying flat on the ground. The hardest sandstones capping each hoodoo are lavishly decorated with orange and gray lichen. The sandstone beneath the caprocks erodes too quickly for lichen to gain a hold.

Willow on the wet margin of the river.   *An alert Canada goose.*

Heading for the backcountry south across the Milk River.

Caprocks overlooking the river are also decorated with Canada geese. The geese nest up there, and in early spring any penthouse property is occupied by a mature goose. If people are below the geese, they will just fix the intruder with a beady black eye to make sure they don't do anything rude. If a human approaches a summit goose, there is a great deal of loud complaint in an astonishing variety of honking voices. The warning echoes off the sandstone cliffs and soon every creature in the park knows humans are afoot. So much for sneaking up on a basking marmot.

The cliffs and hoodoos are also home to pigeons, politely called rock doves. They nest in rounded holes called tafoni. Tafoni result when soft ironstone concretions erode out of the slightly harder sandstone, leaving a cavity just the right size for a nest.

Riverside
At other places, the trail leads downward toward the river. The lower alleys are filled with several metres of erosion debris washed and blown off the ever-shrinking hoodoo towers. The fine, sandy mineral soil is thinly covered with a brown Chernozem soil and clumps of needle-and-thread grass, sage, buckbrush and wild rose. The trail levels on a floodplain standing less than a metre above the surface of the river. The richest soils in the region are located at the highest reach of the floodplain, including layers of Chernozem soil over 40 cm thick in places. A narrow crescent of tall water birch and treelike willow thrives on this soil between the sandstone pillars and the regular high waterline. The dense shrub belt is penetrated only by rabbits, hares, prairie chickens and other animals moving very close to the ground.

The soils found closest to the river are Regosols, developed almost every year on fresh river deposits of fine and medium sands. The wettest soils near the river support cottonwood. The lower floodplain is thick with slender willow, grasses and sedge. These grassy areas are the delight of early-arriving geese and ducks. In spring and after a rain, the muddy soils along the river make walking a bit sticky and slippery.

Grassland
After wandering more than a kilometre through the twisting and turning alleys between hoodoos and cliffs, the trail ascends a last time and emerges on the high sunlit grassland above the river canyon.

Most of the small prairie included in the park was once cultivated, then sown into tame haylands, and is now slowly reverting to something more

Writing-On-Stone Provincial Park

The mouth of Davis Coulee, summer.

like the wild grassland of a century ago. However, by some estimates it took 3,000 years for yesterday's grassland to evolve into the shape first seen by Palliser, the North-West Mounted Police, and the earliest ranchers and settlers. Since then, much of the dry prairie was domesticated and now the park's grassland contains crested wheat grass, smooth brome and farm weeds.

Near the rim of the canyon and beyond the reach of plows, the grassland still flourishes with many of the arid prairie's hallmark plants.

As usual in the dry grasslands, the best place to see flowers is on the desiccated rim where prairie and canyon meet. Most of the rim is exposed, shattered rock seared by summer sun and blasted year-round by relentless wind. Few numbers of plants actually grow on the brow of the canyon. Although few in number, the variety of flowering plants is not matched on the level grassland only a few metres away.

By early April, some of the earliest spring flowers in all of grassland Canada are blooming along the rim of the Milk River canyon, including yellow bell, golden bean, prairie Townsendia, chickweed and crocus to brighten a drab and weathered grassland. Cactus show some more green and moss phlox is ready to bloom. Silvered sheaths of last year's needle-and-thread grass glint over the new colours. In a month the grassland will shimmer with growth, grasses and flowers, attracting birds, mule deer, pronghorn and other wildlife.

From the brow of the hoodoo field the trail follows a set track across the grassland and toward a viewing platform complete with detailed natural history panels. On a hot day, the trail across the grassland is a stern reminder of the importance of water in an arid environment. To take the walker's attention away from thirst, the trail and approach road are lined with a superb collection of Pleistocene erratics. Every kind of far northern igneous rock is represented along the trail and road.

Prickly pear cactus.

The writings

Writing-On-Stone has been a Special Place for at least 4,000 years and millennia of visitors have left their mark.

The famous writings, engraved and painted long ago by aboriginal peoples on sheer sandstone cliffs, are part of the grassland's great mystery and will likely never be understood as they were meant to be understood. Still, they are a powerful reminder of an ancient human presence equipped with a separate system of knowledge and expression. A guided tour takes visitors to the best of the writings with interpreters telling their story.

The entire region along the Milk River is rich in ancient human presence, including some of the largest and most interesting fields of stone cairns, crescents, animal shapes and tipi rings. They are a separate mystery.

Frontier history lies directly across the Milk River opposite the writings where the North-West Mounted Police established an outpost at the mouth of a large coulee appropriately named Police Coulee. In 1886 to 1918, this was near the middle of nowhere, but it had water, wood and game animals and it was on the route of travel across the western plains. From here, the police could intercept tribes, trappers, traders and travellers.

Ranchers came later, followed by gas extraction, and now tourism. There are no manufacturers anywhere around Writing-On-Stone and no industrial intrusions besides agriculture.

Humans are present, but in such small numbers that the park abounds with plants and animals, including over 100 species of birds, 22 mammals, 16 species of fish, 265 species of plants, and a dozen species of reptiles and amphibians. Some species are very rare in Canada, including several that are found only along the Milk River. The abundance of unusual and interesting plants and animals makes sure Writing-On-Stone Provincial Park remains popular year after year with local people and distant visitors.

Three generations of human figures.

3 Davis Coulee

Mode: foot
Rating: difficult
Time: 3 - 4 hours
Distance: 7 km
Elevation change: 125 m
Map: 72 E/4 Coutts

Crossing the Milk River

The entrance to Davis Coulee is reached by wading the river near the Hoodoo Trail kiosk. In early summer runoff season the water is less than a metre deep and the riverbed is a mix of smooth cobbles and sand. The river is about 15 m wide and flows with a moderate current. There is a faint footpath leading from the south bank into the coulees beyond.

Coulees

The backcountry takes in most of Davis Coulee and Humphrey Coulee. The larger of the two is Davis Coulee and it can be followed almost 4 km until a fence and private land is reached.

The trail enters Davis Coulee between two high walls of sculpted sandstone cliffs deeply drilled with holes where soft ironstone concretions eroded out of the sandstone. American kestrel and rock doves have filled the holes with their nests, and smooth walls of stone are liberally decorated with swallow nests. The trail wanders along the coulee bottom following the course of thin stream that dries up by late spring leaving a muddy trench thickly overgrown with rose and willow shrubs and tall grasses.

In less than a kilometre, the trail reaches a slot canyon 4 m deep and barely wide enough to admit passage. Walkers may be forced out of the coulee and onto the grassland above.

Grassland

The grassland in the southern part of the park is much larger than that on the northern side, and in much better condition. The mix of grama grass and needle-and-thread grass is richly coloured with blooming prickly pear cactus, golden aster, blue and yellow flax, umbrella plant, prairie rose and prairie groundsel.

From the high grassland the entire wall of hoodoos and park across the river is in clear view. Looking south, the rolling prairie gradually merges with the Sweetgrass Hills in Montana.

The flat, upper grassland offers delightful strolling under a hot prairie sky. The journey back across the Milk River is an opportunity to cool off and the shade of the park's tall trees will be very welcome after a few hours of blazing heat in the backcountry.

Slot canyon in Davis Coulee.

4 Red Rock Coulee

Mode: foot
Rating: easy
Time: 2 - 3 hours
Distance: 6 km
Elevation change: 50 m
Map: 72 E/10 Bulls Head

Red Rock Coulee, southwest of Medicine Hat, is a little known and little visited patch of dry mixed grassland at the head of a coulee system carved by the receding meltwater of glaciers at the end of the Ice Age. The landscape is dominated by native grasses—needle-and-thread grass, grama grass, bluegrass and indigenous wheat grass. The grasses are liberally sprinkled with dozens of flower species, especially in the spring and early summer.

Coulees etched into the grasslands of the Canadian West have proven very difficult to domesticate. At Red Rock Coulee, ploughed land comes to within a few metres of the coulee rims, but here and there on islands and peninsulas of prairie surrounded by coulees there are still sizeable spreads of untouched grassland. Amongst and between the effects of dryland farming, this Special Place contains most of the animals, plants and landforms you would expect to find in a dry grassland setting. Though there are numerous and plentiful plants carpeting the arid soil, even in the height of summer no grassland plant stands higher than mid-calf.

Red Rock Coulee reveals a deep slice of history in southern Alberta. The exposed bedrock is 75 million years old, the coulee was created about 13,000 years ago, the flat table land has supported mature prairie for less than 3,000 years, and a collapsing settler's farmstead dates to the late 1920s. All this history is contained in the single jewel of Red Rock Coulee.

There is no trail as such, but the great rocks are right there in front of the parking area and the slope of the coulee leads into the badlands beyond.

Red rocks on a field of Bearpaw shale.

Red Rock Coulee

Getting there

Red Rock Coulee is easy to find. Turn south off Highway 3—the Crowsnest Trail—and onto Highway 887, just west of Seven Persons. Nailed to a post in the ditch is a very small green sign pointing south for Red Rock Coulee. Highway 887 is paved.

Where the paved road makes a sudden turn toward the east, a kilometre of good gravel road continues straight south, marked by another small sign, pointing to the site. The gravel road ends exactly where the Red Rock Coulee system begins.

The first part of the site is a small parking area equipped with a sign and a stile passing through a strong four-wire fence. On the other side of the fence, two wooden campground tables are settling elegantly into the turf of a peninsula overlooking the coulee system.

A last small sign says the coulee is unique because of its exposed Bearpaw Shale and the world's largest sandstone concretions, and warns against cutting down trees!

Camping

Follow the gravel road a few hundred metres to a turn-around loop. This is the camping area. Again, a few tables and two pit toilets are on the other side of the fence. There is no water, no fire pit, no fire wood, no garbage cans, no fees, and the whole area is neat and tidy.

The loop is near the summit of Bull Head Butte, at 1075 m above sea level the highest point for far around. This seems an insignificant elevation, but it is just high enough above the surrounding terrain to give a commanding view of the grassland all the way to the green and snow-capped Sweetgrass Hills, 110 km away to the southwest in Montana.

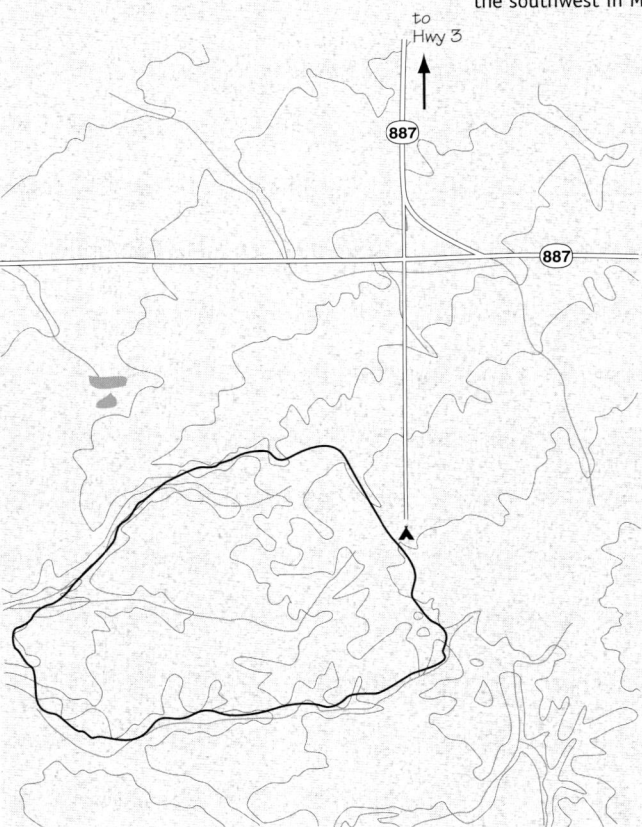

Red Rock Coulee

By early summer, the ground is dry enough for walking, and not yet baked like a biscuit under the full summer sun. Spring and early summer are the best seasons for flowers and by mid-July the grassland growing season is over.

Coulee structure

All routes into the coulee system pass through the field of rocks. From there, one coulee joins with another, and by connecting them walkers can make a long and exotic trip of it. But, travel is strictly routefinding; there are no trails other than animal trails.

It's hard to get lost. Almost everywhere, trails laid down by wild animals are good for human travel. In the harsh environment of southernmost Alberta, animals do not waste energy strolling around and admiring the view. They move efficiently from one place to another and people may as well take advantage of their routefinding. If you find a good animal track heading where you want to go, stay with it.

If you are at the bottom of a coulee and wondering where to go next, climb to the prairie above and find a landmark, if only the pit toilets perched near the high rim of the coulee system. If there are no recognizable landmarks, head for the next highest point on the horizon, probably to the southeast. The highest point won't be all that high, 10 m at most, but from there you can usually find your way home or anywhere else in the coulee system.

To the west just beyond the red rocks, the coulee system opens up, leading deeper into a badland country of erosion and weathering, miniature hoodoos and balancing rocks, wind

The largest red rocks are two metres across.

Glacier-born granite cobbles washed down to the coulee floor.

Concretions

Red rock and orange lichen.

Red Rock Coulee is famous for its huge, red rocks. But the coulee is also unique in a landscape of undulating grasslands, because the shale and sandstone bedrock beneath the western prairie is so well exposed. Elsewhere, except along rivers, most bedrock is covered by a deep blanket of glacial deposits. Because glacial debris is so thick, many coulees carve through the glacial debris without reaching bedrock.

At Red Rock Coulee, the layer of glacial debris is very thin and the coulee walls are cut into the soft bedrock itself. The grey and buff shale and contrasting red sandstone bedrock lies exposed. Scattered across this weathered landscape are the great red rocks.

The red rocks

The red rocks are huge and beautiful sculptures more than 2 m across and composed of relatively coarse-grained red sandstone. The rocks sit exposed on an abrupt face of the coulee, near the top where the brown Chernozemic soil and thin gravel are cut away to expose the underlying Bearpaw Shale. The soft shale has broken down and eroded, leaving the red rocks free of their matrix.

Some rocks are balanced on small pedestals, undercut by erosion, and some have their base stuck in a layer of muddy shale. The shale has a soft, even dusty appearance, but right under the loose surface lies harder rock, as yet untouched by erosion.

Historic rocks

Similar sandstone spheres are found throughout the Cretaceous sediments of the Interior Plains, including the Bearpaw Formation. Some are quite small and some are very big and they are made of either clay, silt or sand. Some are grey and bleached of iron, and others are the robust orange of concentrated iron oxides. Some are coated with a layer of gypsum. Some are glued together with calcium, and some are not. Some are formed around a nucleus of fossil shell, but others have no obvious nucleus.

In 1857, Henry Youle Hind described globes of rock showing in the Qu'Appelle Valley of Saskatchewan. His rocks were over 2 m across; they had a nucleus around a fragment of seashell; and they were coated with dull gypsum, totally unlike the red rocks of Red Rock Coulee.

Glaciers and the red rocks

The red rocks are frozen in the posture of balls rolling downhill. At the end of the Ice Age, the receding glaciers formed dams that backed up meltwater into huge lakes. When the ice finally melted enough to release the dammed-up lake, water rushed in tremendous rivers along the available drainage channels. These rivers tore through the loose mantle of glacial debris and gravel, and then started to work on the soft Bearpaw Shale.

The rivers were powerful, but short-lived. As soon as the lakes drained, perhaps in a few decades, the rivers dwindled to what they are today. The pouring water had enough life and power to carve deeply into the shale, but the harder sandstone spheres resisted. Instead, they were pushed bodily toward the bottom of the growing coulee.

Most of the red rocks never made it to the bottom in the short life of torrential Ice Age rivers, and they are poised as though ready to continue their journey. Eventually, under the slower but no less relentless forces of erosion, the red rocks will disappear downhill.

But are they concretions?

There is still something of a mystery about how the red rocks were formed, and even if they are concretions. Concretions are formed when particles gather around a nucleus and are bonded together into a single entity. In a sense, pearls are biological concretions. Concretions have a nucleus and layers like an onion. There are concretions at Red Rock Coulee, but they are much smaller—about the size of a big potato. The smaller rocks break and peel apart in shell-like layers, showing that they are real concretions.

Some of the huge red rocks also seem to match this description. The shale slope is littered with red rocks that are split from top to bottom, revealing faint concentric layering, and perhaps these are also real concretions.

Some of the red rocks have very fine parallel layers rather than concentric layers. This suggests the red rocks are blocks of ordinary sandstone, perhaps broken up and shaped by the receding glacial lakes and rivers. Or they may have eroded in place when the thin layer of sandstone cracked under the weight of rock, glacial debris, ice and water above, and allowed the torrent to scour through the open cracks. No matter their origin, the experience for walkers is undiminished.

There is plenty of evidence the red rocks have been where they are for a long time. All are quite worn, with little mounds of sandstone dust heaped where rain washes it off the rocks' eroding backs. Some are split from water and frost action. Some sport crowns of established plants and bugs. Most are covered with various species of crust lichen. Blazing orange patches of Xanthoria lichen are 25 cm across. Even smaller patches of lichen have dead centres, indicating great age for a lichen patch in a semi-arid, soft-rock environment.

The red rocks overlook the coulee system and the grasslands beyond.

Red Rock Coulee

A fan of ironstone nodules washed out of a wall of soft shale.

and water dunes, and blown out rough cobble pavement. Deep and narrow water channels disappear underground. Small springs bleed a vein or two of water down a clay incline.

My friend and I followed a deer trail down the main coulee until we met a four-wire fence, usually a sign of private property beyond. From there we took a circuitous route to the north winding our way along the bottom of the connecting coulees for a total of about 6 km of walking and three hours of looking at this and that.

Upper coulee

The walls of the upper coulees are V-shaped and grown over with prairie and coulee plants. In these older, more stable coulees the soils change gradually from the rich brown prairie soils near the top of the coulee system to leaner grey soils more heavily loaded with stone and sand near the bottom. If there is water at the bottom of the coulee, soils are muddy springtime clays.

The V-shaped coulees all lead quickly down to U-shaped coulees with broader and flatter bottoms, perhaps 20 m wide, covered with boulders, gravel, sand and clay, and resting on a harder layer of rock. These broader coulees in turn lead to the main bottom, 70 m across. North-facing slopes try to support a few shrubs, especially sparse buckbrush and rose, but the south-facing slopes are usually bare of shrubs.

Main bottom coulee

The walls of the main bottom are often sheer and undercut, clearly showing the recent geologic history of the place from Chernozemic soils of today, through glacial till laid down 11,000 years ago, and into the Cretaceous bedrock of 70 million years old. The main bottom and some of the broader coulees are laced with ribbons of water that carry on the task of eroding the coulee deeper into the soft sandstone and shale.

The recent history of erosion is perfectly preserved. In spring, it is all pristine country, with every carved and sculpted edge and plane sharp and untracked.

Along the coulees

The narrow deer trails leading to the valley floor may at first be damp, then muddy where a spring almost makes it to the surface. Oval-shaped pods of flattened grass show where deer lay down to rest, even though the thick grass and sedges shelter many biting insects. Mule deer and humans retreat from biting insects on the windy grasslands above. The biting insects rarely venture into strong prairie winds.

Dropping back down from the windy rim of the coulee, another faint deer track leads to a shoal of fine white and silver sand trapped below a few ancient cottonwood logs almost rotted out. Some time in the past, the upper coulee was moist enough to support trees, but there are no trees anywhere near Red Rock Coulee today.

Prairie rose.

Water and life

Wherever there is, was or might be water there are fairly lush growths of grasses and sedges, mosquitos and deer flies. At the margins of waterways, bunch grasses take over along with wildflowers. There is no water humans would think of drinking.

As the trail drops into the coulee's wind shadow, the environment changes. There are more succulent flowers, including the first plains prickly pear cactus bloom of the season. On the steeper and drier clay slopes, various sages have dug in to survive in their weird and wonderful shapes, scenting the cool air.

By early summer, there are some last golden beans, but most have set their pods; three-flowered avens are past the seed stage, and the season's last crocuses are withered around the edges. Milk vetch, wild blue flax, northern hedysarum, mouse-ear chickweed and clusters of yellow small-flowered rocket are in their prime. Very pale, exquisite prairie roses proliferate on the upper curves of the coulee.

The main coulee, formed when glacial meltwater scoured the soft bedrock.

Red Rock Coulee

Water and fate

The place was once probably much more important to animals in the past. In wet times, in the last century and earlier, the coulee was a green oasis, attracting animals with water and lush plants—horses, cattle and before them, bison and deer. Some time in the recent past the upper coulee supported stands of sizeable cottonwood.

Today, there are no trees and little evidence of animals living in the higher reaches of the coulee system. There may be a few adult and infant mule deer tracks, a line of coyote tracks, a pair of mourning doves, a hare, a few overhead hawks, nighthawks, spiders, beetles, ants and loud crickets enjoying the calm on the lee side of the rocks.

Bison bones are washing out of the coulee walls: the heavy and durable leg and foot bones, parts of a scapula, and a few rib bones. More delicate deer bones were scattered here and there.

The small coulees connect to the big coulees, and eventually to Forty Mile Coulee and real water. No doubt, the density and variety of plants and animals is much higher there, closer to water, than at the arid head of the coulee system.

Humans

At the bottom of one coulee, beneath a bank of marine clay covered with glacial gravel beds, there is a midden of settler debris including a piece of tin stovepipe, the shards of a pickling jar made in Red Wing, Minnesota, soldered tin cans, and other signs of settlers from the early part of the century.

On the prairie 20 m above the garbage tip stands a thicket of caragana, clear evidence of a settler homestead. The caragana thicket is impenetrable except by smaller animals and there is plenty of evidence of hares and rabbits using the hedge for shelter. On the shaded and sheltered side of the hedge were one or two places where deer lay down.

The frozen grip of winter.

A slumped and sodded basement pit faces east-west and a large flat granite rock marks the threshold on the south side of the house. The midden is thin and scanty, and the whole sad site is once again undomesticated, except for the caragana hedge and the large, flat rock. These settlers did not last long deep in the Palliser Triangle.

Red Rock Coulee in winter

In winter when windblown snow drives visibility down to 100 m and windchill up to 2,200, Red Rock Coulee looks like a miniature alpine landscape—cornices, snowslide slopes, exposure glazing and lee-side banks.

The red rocks are even less animated than in summer, frozen into the least action, hibernating. The wind and snow represented all the action, carving the land into a smoothed cartoon of the rough summer face. Winter wind and snow reflect the summer landscape, in white. Wherever there is lush green in summer, there is deep white snow in winter. Winter uses a heavy hand to shape the Dry Mixed Grass Ecoregion.

5 Canoeing the South Saskatchewan from Grand Forks to Medicine Hat

Mode: canoe
Rating: moderate
Time: 4 days
Distance: 101 km
Elevation change: 21 m
Maps: 72 E/13 Grassy Lake, 72 E/14 Bow Island, 72 L/3 Suffield, 72 L/2 Medicine Hat

The South Saskatchewan River is one of the last great prairie paddling rivers, flowing through a valley deeply incised into the flat table of the Interior Plains. In most places, human intrusion makes it to the very lip of the valley, but not beyond. Humans and their works are safely out of sight. The valley with its steeply sculpted walls and lush bottomland is in a different world dominated by works of nature. The best way to experience and enjoy the great river is by canoe, floating on the swift current through some of the most unusual landscape in the region.

The route, of course, follows the broad back of the river. This reach of the river from Grand Forks to Medicine Hat covers a distance of almost 100 km and strong paddlers can cover the course in two long days. Most paddlers will take a few more days, especially if they intend to actually see some of their surroundings. Either way—fast or slow—canoeists will have to execute some refined plans to make their trip a success.

Resting on a beach of glacier-born quartzite pebbles.

Logistics

The South Saskatchewan River is fed by streams originating high in the Rocky Mountains, and the river's seasons are very much determined by the flow of spring meltwater. In winter and early spring, the rate of flow drops off to less than 50 cubic metres per second and in most places the water is only a few centimetres deep. From April to June, the rate of flow rapidly increases, reaching a peak of about 600 cubic metres per second. By August, flow has dropped back to early spring levels.

These are average, long-term flows, but in 1995, the year of the One Hundred Year Flood, the river peaked in early June at slightly less than 4500 cubic metres per second, bringing devastation to low-lying lands and city streets in Medicine Hat. Because of its flow habits, the best season for canoeing the South Saskatchewan is the summer months from late May to early July.

Getting there

The entire length of the South Saskatchewan is navigable by canoe, from its source in southern Alberta to its mouth near Prince Albert, Saskatchewan, where it joins the North Saskatchewan River. Most canoeists will tackle the river in sections, though some truly intrepid canoeists might take a month or so to do the river's entire length. The section described here is conveniently accessible, long enough for a three to five day expedition, and packed with all the features for which the river is famous.

The route begins at Grand Forks where the Oldman River and the Bow River join to form the South Saskatchewan River, and ends 96 km downstream at Medicine Hat where a successful river expedition can be celebrated in fine style.

The put-in point is at Grand Forks, just north of the town of Grassy Lake on Highway 3. At Grassy Lake there are a few small signs pointing the way to the Forks. Take the gravel road heading north through town and across the railway tracks. About 5.5 km north of town, the road makes a turn to the west for about a kilometre and then heads back north across the flat, cultivated prairie until it reaches the valley above the river. The point where the road dips down to the river is marked by a large sandstone boulder painted white with the legend "Grand Forks" in red.

The road curves down the valley, past a few oil and gas wellheads, and onto the bottomland. Where the road crosses a cattleguard there is a nice handmade sign warning of the presence of rattlesnakes. Follow the road right to the edge of the water. Canoes and gear can be unloaded directly on the shingle shore. The biggest challenge at this point will be finding a stopping place near the shore and between the fishers who park their pickups as close to the water as possible. From a lawnchair parked in the shade of their vehicles and within easy reach of the beer cooler in the back, the fishers try their skill on sturgeon, sauger and pike.

The end of the journey is inside the city of Medicine Hat, where there are several good places for a take-out. The first place is the Kiwanis Park just below the bridge where Highway 1 crosses the river. Pickup vehicles can be parked here or on nearby city streets.

Camping

There are basic camping facilities at the put-in point near Grand Forks, including a pit toilet and a few fireplaces set under the spreading branches of tall plains cottonwoods. Nothing fancy, but entirely adequate for canoeists expecting to spend several days on the river.

There are no other campgrounds on this stretch of the river, but there are abundant exquisite places to set up a tent and relax for a night.

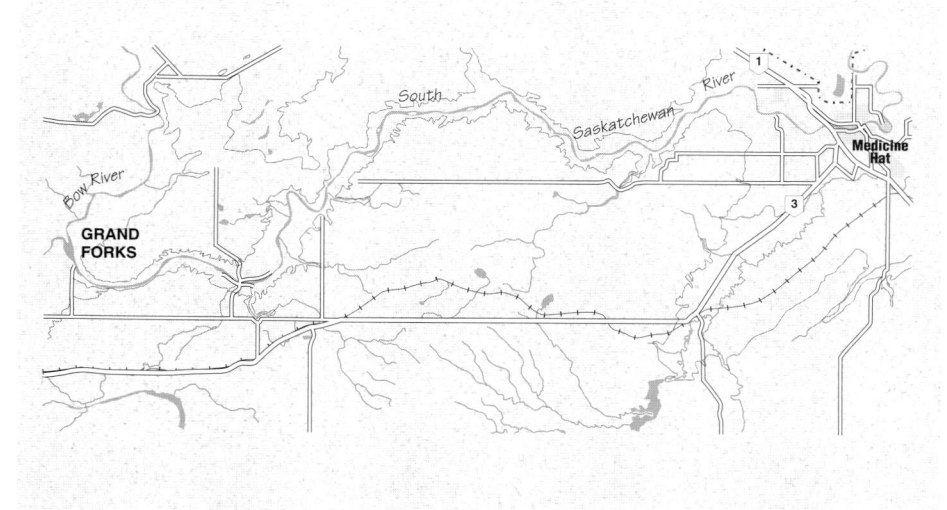

South Saskatchewan River

Grand Forks at the start of the South Saskatchewan River.

Even in peak flow, the water shows little turbulence although the current can be quite powerful. The section of the river described here is rated as Class I canoe water. With an average gradient of 0.6 metres per kilometre of length, the current will help move canoeists along at a leisurely rate of 2-5 km/hr., depending on the season.

However, paddlers cannot just sit back and let the river do the work because much of the valley is exposed to strong winds, and the winds tend to flow along the valley course. It may take a great deal of hard work to get around a windy stretch and into a lee curve of the river.

Nevertheless, compared to any other non-motorized way of getting around in the backcountry, canoeing allows for many luxuries that cannot be carried on human or horse back—commodious tents, thick mattresses, lawn chairs, a cooler of exotic eats, and all the guidebooks and other toys you want. But, leave plenty of room for water, because the South Saskatchewan River is undrinkable thanks to intensive dryland and irrigation farming on the table lands above the valley, livestock farming on the floodplain below, and community sewage outflows.

There are places where canoeists will practise their turning skills while dodging large, horned cattle wading about in the shallows. One look at the water downstream of a herd of milling Herefords will discourage swimming in the river, much less drinking the water. In other places, visitors will scrape cow patties away from suitable campsites, and shoo cattle out of their tents.

Don't count on firewood. There are few trees and every dead branch is needed by a more deserving species than the canoeist. Take your own cooking technology. A small gas-fired stove or barbecue fits nicely into a canoe.

A granite kitchen.

The joy of canoeing—lots of everything.

73

Rattlesnakes

The South Saskatchewan River is the northern limit for prairie rattlesnakes, creatures usually associated with deserts much farther south in the United States and Mexico. They are just as much at home along the parched shores of southern Alberta's largest river.

We had been paddling downriver for about two hours after leaving Grand Forks when we decided to put ashore for a break. The bow of the canoe touched the sand and I stepped from the rear of the canoe and went forward to pull it a little ways onto the beach. I grabbed the front rope and headed for a dead cottonwood log lying below the riverbank that would serve as a tie up. I barely entered the taller grass along the shore when the silent air was pierced by a sharp rattling sound. I had never heard a live rattlesnake's rattle before, but a deep natural awareness must have kicked in because the next thing I knew I was in mid-air on my way back to the canoe. I caught sight of the snake as it departed just as rapidly through the grass in the opposite direction.

Actually, people are at little risk from rattlesnakes who prefer not to keep company with humans. Most bites occur when people try to kill or capture a rattlesnake. However, the South Saskatchewan River is well-known rattlesnake habitat, and canoeists should review what to do in case they are bitten. Take them into account, pay your respects and keep alert.

The moist floodplain was cleared of cottonwoods to grow hay.

South Saskatchewan River

The thick burden of glacial drift deeply scored into cliffs and coulees.

Push off

With everything loaded in the canoe, push off and stroke toward the middle of the river to avoid the inevitable shallows near the shore.

From Grand Forks to Medicine Hat, the South Saskatchewan flows through a landscape of steep, heavily-eroded cliffs and broad flat river terraces. Very often, there is a cliff on the one side of the river, usually on the outside bend, and a terrace on the other inside curve of the bend.

Ice and water

The cliffs and intruding coulees were formed when huge volumes of glacial meltwater at the end of the Ice Age scoured down through 50 m and more of glacial debris and began to carve into the underlying bedrock. The bedrock is entirely sandstone and shale of Cretaceous origin, laid down when ancient shallow seas invaded the Interior Plains over 100 million years ago. Because the Interior Plains escaped the devastation of mountain building farther west, the beds of stone lie as flat as the river itself. Canoeists will be thrilled with the close-up view of towering walls banded with multicoloured strata of bedrock.

Today's landscape

Debris continues to tumble down from the heights and accumulate as a small slope at the base of the cliff, finally melting into the water. Most of these slopes are scoured by spring ice and floodwater, so there is little opportunity for the development of biological soil or colonization by plants. Slopes that have avoided a regular spring cleaning might have a few sprigs of sage and grass sprinkled across their face, but most are barren of plant life.

The sheer south-facing valley walls are the best testimony of the river's geological history, as there are few plants to obstruct a clear view of finely layered pastel rock and glacial debris.

Dry grassland immediately above the river.

North-facing walls, protected from the relentless summer sun and winter wind, are lightly clothed with sage, buckbrush, grass, moss phlox and a crust of lichen.

The terraces were formed when the much reduced post-glacial river wandered from side to side of its steep-walled valley, moving erosion material from here and placing it there. As the river continued to dwindle over the 15,000 years since the end of the Ice Age, it filled less and less of the valley. Each reduction left behind the bottom of the old river, and these are the terraces marching across the low floodplains bordering some parts of the river.

The margin of the river up to the contemporary high water line—usually a strip less than 5 m wide—is grown over with a lush mat of water-loving grasses and sedges. Slightly higher above the moist foreshore sage, willow, buckbrush and prickly rose help stabilize the bank of the first terrace. Immediately behind the brow of the terrace, there is a flat expanse of dry grassland—cactus, sage, needle-and-thread grass, blue grama grass, yarrow, vetch and many other plants characteristic in the Dry Mixed Grass Ecoregion.

Cool shade beneath a western cottonwood.

Cottonwood on the inside of the river's curve rarely form more than a fringe.

Other terraces support thick stands of willow and young plains cottonwoods, where long-past floods drenched the zone with water and fresh mud needed for propagation and proliferation of these species. In time, these thickets of shrubs and young trees may grow into majestic groves and meadows like those found on the more stable terraces.

The mature trees occupy a position near the water, but just high enough to avoid most floods, usually on a placid part of the river where shoreline erosion

White pelicans and gulls on a sand bar against a layered cliff of sandstone and shale.

is subdued or where deposition may be occurring. The tall cottonwoods are rarely more than a fringe two or three trees deep away from the terrace rim. Beneath the shade of the trees, and sharing their moisture, is an exceptional growth of grasses and flowers.

As the river approaches Medicine Hat, the landscape becomes more domesticated. Irrigation pumps suck up the last of the runoff, roads come close to the river, houses with marketable views perch on the high bank, and power and gas lines pass overhead. Finally, manicured trails and lawns, a golf course and the city comes in sight. The end of the trail is under a towering concrete bridge on Highway 1, carrying people from one side of the continent to the other.

Experiencing diversity

All these different niches—river water, dry foreshore, moist foreshore, grassland, cliff, terrace, immature cottonwood grove, mature grove, urban centre—sustain a great variety of plant and animal species.

The waters contain fish and many other organisms and the surface is home for graceful white pelicans. The muddy foreshore is covered with the tracks of Canada geese, white pelicans, ducks and wading shorebirds. The barren, sheer cliffs of till, sandstone and shale are completely devoid of plants, but they are places favoured by hawks, golden eagles, cliff swallows and even Canada geese, honking loudly from their arid penthouse perches, contrary to every popular image of goose habits.

The terraced grasslands attract rattlesnakes, pronghorn, mule deer, ground squirrels, coyote, ground-nesting birds and hawks. The young groves of shrubs and small trees attract beaver, mule deer and tree-nesting birds. The moisture and protection of the trees and shrubs makes this a breeding ground for insects and animals that consume insects. The mature groves are home for owls, flickers, eagles, hawks and other species needing tall, old, hollow trees.

These are the predictable features of the South Saskatchewan River, but there are lots of exceptions to the rules—special places within a Special Place. There are springs and creeks, hoodoo rocks, meandering coulees,

South Saskatchewan River

Settler's homestead abandoned to the sun and wind.

sand dunes, spotless pink beaches, islands, wetlands and isolated backwaters waiting for appreciation. With good luck and good planning, canoeists can see it all.

Reminder

People canoe this stretch of the river in two days, but should allow two whole extra days for exploration and contingencies. Let us say a four-night expedition, including reaching the trailhead and launching before the first night of camping. There are endless places to camp along the river. When the hour arrives, simply pick a likely looking place and pull in for the night. Remember, places you prefer—a grassy bed, leafy shade and out of the wind—are also preferred by other species, including rattlesnakes, insects and cattle. Deer, coyotes, owls and nocturnal rodents will snuffle and scuttle through the night. Coyotes appreciate a good view of the moon as much as the next wilderness soul and they will likely be just behind your tent, celebrating the reflection off the water. This is as good as it gets.

A cool evening camping on the beach.

Special Places for a Quick Visit

Sandy Point Park

Where Highway 41 crosses the South Saskatchewan River, just before it heads east into the neighbouring province, there is a fine little park perched on a terrace immediately above the river water. Sandy Point Park is an excellent place to see the details of a prairie river landscape without venturing onto the water. The surrounding valley is steeply carved into millions of years of geology.

Sandy Point Park is 101 km north of Medicine Hat. Don't worry about getting lost. You won't cross any other rivers; in fact, you won't see any surface water all the way north unless it is raining. The tallest objects are likely oil and gas works and pronghorn. There are few cattle because this dry landscape cannot tolerate high concentrations of livestock.

Suddenly, the wide smooth highway begins a long curving drop to an iron bridge spanning the South Saskatchewan River. The entrance to Sandy Point Park is on the west side of the bridge and marked with lots of big signs.

The campground is set in a small grove of western cottonwood, willow, rose and buckbrush. The growth is natural, situated just above the first terrace, but the cottonwood grove and surrounding grassland are manicured to accommodate the campground. Each campsite is screened from the others by a cottonwood or two and a shrub hedge. All sites face onto the river over a low, steep bank. Heavily eroded coulees and badlands are out the back door.

The land on the north side of the river is lease land, or public land. As well, the foreshore of the river is public land. Between the river edge and the lease land there is lots to explore outside the fenced confines of the park.

Cross the river on the bridge. Keeping close to the river, the way upstream first crosses a broad coulee adorned with hoodoos carved from soft buff

The flat grassland, once the bottom of a vast glacial lake, now etched with coulees.

Special Places

The blue iron bridge over the South Saskatchewan adds colour to the sun-baked landscape.

sandstone capped with iron-rich red sandstone. Scattered amongst the hoodoos are boulders of granite and basalt carried from the far north on the back of the Continental Glacier of the last Ice Age. One huge boulder of quartzite the size and shape of a sailboat is smooth and slick after a thousand kilometres of churning in the belly of a glacier.

On the other side of the coulee, the trail drops closer to the river. The trail is obviously used by every other creature visiting this place, including deer, coyote, hare, beaver and cattle. The trail follows the foot of a tall bank of hills on the outside curve of the river where the forces of erosion are greatest. The river is still pressing on this shore and the first terrace is only a few metres wide from water's edge to ascending slope.

Here and there, a minor coulee adds enough landfill and water to sustain a small grove of cottonwoods and shrubs. Looking to the north, the rich geology of the great river is laid out in plain view. Towering stacks of sandstone, shale, volcanic ash and glacial till are the record of 100 million years of history.

Trails in the campground are good for wheelchairs, but the river edge and coulee require some nimble movements.

If you want to see Sandy Point in its near-natural state, you had better hurry. In 1998, the Meridian Water Management Association, a group of farmers and municipalities, proposed to dam the river and create a single reservoir 140 km long, from near the Saskatchewan border and Sandy Point in the north to just below Medicine Hat in the south. The main obstacles to the dam are a federal military reserve, a national wildlife area and an ecological reserve. In the past, the federal government might defend national interests in the area, but in early 1998 the federal government all but surrendered its voice in environmental affairs to the provinces. The larger decisions will probably be made in Alberta.

Special Places

Police Point Park

Like the Lethbridge coulees, Police Point is built into a major city, in this case Medicine Hat. The park occupies most of a floodplain on the inside of a broad bend in the South Saskatchewan River. Opposite the park, on the outer side of the bend is a high wall of exposed glacial drift and bedrock, a splendid backdrop for a grove of very old western cottonwood. These trees are at least 300 years old and scattered amongst the living trees are the standing and fallen remains of an even earlier generation of cottonwood. All the trees, living and dead, are hollow and made into living space by owls, porcupines, skunks, and many rodents and insects.

Just behind the grove of venerable cottonwood is a band of much younger cottonwood towering above thick clumps of willow, golden currant, rose and saskatoon. Patches of grass and flowers spread between the trees and shrubs. Farther from the river and above the usual level for floodwaters, the last corners of the floodplain are thick with tall willow and saskatoon.

At the exact place where the valley wall surges above the floodplain, all trees and shrubs disappear. The grassland covering the valley wall merges with the dry grassland reaching endlessly away from the river. Grasses in-

Dead western cottonwood tower over new growth.

clude grama grass, June grass and needle-and-thread grass, growing in sparse clumps between dozens of kinds of flowers.

The entire landscape is ideal habitat for a large variety of plants and animals. Over 200 species of birds have been found in the park, and 80 species nest there in the summer. There are 30 species of mammals, 23 species of fish, and many species of plants, reptiles, amphibians and insects.

Police Point Park is the place to see and casually explore an exemplary prairie river. Trails are designed for wheelchairs and easy walking. There is a staffed interpretive centre and all kinds of maps, guidebooks and pamphlets. It is only minutes away from urban comfort.

The cobble shore is fringed with a band of willow, then tall cottonwood.

Mixed Grass

Coulees, cottonwood and the Oldman River in the Mixed Grass Ecoregion.

4
Mixed Grass Ecoregion

The Mixed Grass Ecoregion emerges as an arc surrounding the outer boundaries of the arid Dry Mixed Grass Ecoregion to the southeast. At the western edge of the Mixed Grass Ecoregion fescue grasslands take over, and the northern limit merges with the aspen parkland. The transition from the drier grassland to the east is quite gradual, revealed by slightly taller grasses and flowering plants, a few more shrubs wherever water collects, and an occasional grove of trees. The best indicator of the transition lies hidden just below the surface—a thicker and richer layer of soil.

Pavan Park, Lethbridge, autumn.

Mixed Grass

The shallow Oldman River sustains fish, waterfowl and shorebirds, summer.

Richer soils

The Dry Mixed Grass Ecoregion and the Mixed Grass Ecoregion share many species of plants, but in different blends and proportions reflecting the slightly greater elevation, greater annual moisture level, richer soils and milder winter temperatures prevailing in the Mixed Grass Ecoregion. More grass covers the land surface, along with fewer of the tough species common in the Dry Mixed Grass Ecoregion. Blue grama grass is restricted to the driest places in the Mixed Grass Ecoregion, needle-and-thread grass grows in dry and moderately watered places, and wheat grasses and June grass are more common everywhere.

The thicker and more luxuriant growth of grasses and other plants in the Mixed Grass Ecoregion means that each year there is abundant dead plant remains to incorporate into the top layer of humus. This, in turn, means better soil. Most soils in the Dry Mixed Grass Ecoregion of southeastern Alberta are arid brown Chernozems with relatively shallow topmost layers supporting sparse vegetation. To the west and north in the Mixed Grass Ecoregion soils are dark brown and black Chernozems.

More water

The richer soils of the Mixed Grass Ecoregion also receive more precipitation than does the dry region to the east and south, and this allows plants to take better advantage of the soil. In the Mixed Grass Ecoregion, the moister and

Mule deer against a slumped bank of glacial debris, early autumn.

richer soils are clothed in luxurious grasslands, and even north-facing slopes support thickets of shrubs and trees growing in Chernozemic or Brunisolic soils. The landscape includes streams and small rivers, where soils are typically muddy and stony Regosols sporting aspen and willow. On river floodplains, there are splendid stands of huge cottonwood that depend on periodic flooding to propagate.

More animals

The Mixed Grass Ecoregion and the Dry Mixed Grass Ecoregion share wildlife species, but in the north and west where grassland gives way to woodland, forest animals have penetrated the grassland.

White-tailed deer are more plentiful in the northern part of the Mixed Grass Ecoregion where it joins the Aspen Parkland Ecoregion, than in the western part where the Mixed Grass Ecoregion flows into the Fescue Grass Ecoregion. White-tailed deer favour deciduous woodland and are not usually found on the open grassland. Instead, they are found in wooded river bottom ecodistricts scattered across the Interior Plains.

There are few unique species in the Mixed Grass Ecoregion. Rather, the landscape is more like a better-nourished version of the drier lands to the southeast. Walkers expect to see savannah, western and Baird's sparrows, long-billed curlew, mule deer, yarrow, golden bean, wild rose, garter snakes, white pelicans and, in the springtime, in the right places, there are swans. There are also more extensive wetlands in the Mixed Grass Ecoregion than in the Dry Mixed Grass Ecoregion, along with more waterfowl and shorebirds.

Humans

Almost all the Mixed Grass Ecoregion is domesticated, especially the part of it in southern Alberta. Farms, fences and fee simple titles blanket all but a few select sites. Even at its pristine best a century ago, the transition from the Dry Mixed Grass Ecoregion to the Mixed Grass Ecoregion would have

Cottonwoods along the Oldman River, late summer.

Mixed Grass

been difficult to detect, but it is much more difficult now that the plow has been everywhere.

Walkers will be hard put to see much in pristine condition. The place to look is along creeks and rivers and on floodplains—wherever the plow and pivot irrigation system cannot reach. There are extensive pristine places on the Blood and Peigan First Nations reserves, but these are sovereign aboriginal lands and cannot be entered without permission.

The region is permeated with humans and human influences. Vast areas, seen in hour after hour of monotonous driving, are cultivated beyond recognition. Between the fences, highways and backroads every passing kilometre is dominated by cultivated crops. The crops are fed with mountain water. As well as thirsty crops there are thirsty humans and livestock.

The Mixed Grass Ecoregion has a good share of long-abandoned homesteads, given up because there was no access to water, but by the end of the 20th century, problems of water distribution had been solved. Today, extensive systems of canals deliver water where before there was no water. The Oldman, St. Mary, Belly, Waterton, Milk and South Saskatchewan rivers are dammed and impounded in reservoirs to feed southernmost Alberta's insatiable demand for water.

Here and there, a visitor on the backroads may find two adjacent properties where on one side of the fence the land has water rights and is irrigated, and the land on other side of the fence has no water and may only be grazed by a few cattle. The contrast is quite startling. The irrigated land is tall with barley, canola, alfalfa, sugar beets, corn and a score of other market crops. The nearby dry land is blanketed with short, tough grasses and shrubs.

The grassland is rich and, once tamed through irrigation, humans settled in numbers, including some of the most exotic settlers of the Canadian west—Hutterites, Mennonites, Mormons and ranchers, scattered amongst the Peigan, Blood and Blackfoot peoples. Their communities are scattered across the grasslands of southern Alberta.

The Mixed Grass Ecoregion

Area: 29,924 sq. km or 4.5% of the province.

Topography: Undulating in the eastern part, more rolling in the west closer to the mountains, cut by extensive river valleys and coulees.

Elevation: 800 - 1100 m

Climate: The climate is similar to that of the Dry Mixed Grass Ecoregion, but less extreme. Higher elevation and closer proximity to summer storm tracks assures about 20 per cent more rain in the whole year, and more precipitation in any month of the year. Summer temperatures average about 15.2°C, and winter temperature averages -5.5°C, about 2°C warmer than in the Dry Mixed Grass Ecoregion. Summer water deficits (drought conditions) are less common and less severe. Snow cover is deeper. The Mixed Grass Ecoregion experiences over 30 days of chinook wind each winter.

Soils: Mostly richer Chernozems.

Humans: Almost the entire Mixed Grass Ecoregion is domesticated.

6 Lethbridge Coulee Trails

Mode: foot, bicycle, horse
Rating: easy
Time: 3 - 4 hours
Distance: 5 km
Elevation change: 151 m
Map: 82 H/10 Lethbridge

Compared to Red Rock Coulee in the heart of the Dry Mixed Grass Ecoregion, the Lethbridge coulees are prairie oases. No badlands here; in five minutes you can walk from a downtown cappuccino patio to the closest trailheads; the "remote" trails are groomed red shale paths and those closer to the city centre are paved and wheelchair accessible; there are drinking fountains and heated washrooms and toilets. You will never be more than minutes away from everything a modern city has to offer.

But the Lethbridge Coulee trails should not be overlooked as an excellent place to see a remnant of Mixed Grass Ecoregion and the intricate landscape of an Interior Plains river bottom—coulees, floodplains, cottonwoods and the Oldman River.

Origin of the river valleys and coulees

Like most of the grasslands east of the Rocky Mountain foothills, the Lethbridge area is built on layers of shale and sandstone laid down during the late Cretaceous 70 to 75 million years ago. Outcrops of bedrock are rather rare near Lethbridge, because most of the bedrock is thickly covered with layers of clay, silt, sand and rounded rock deposited during the glaciations of the late Cenozoic era. Exposed rock is seen mostly along rivers and road cuts.

Two sides of a coulee—dry south facing and moist north facing. Alexander Park, summer.

Getting there

Finding Lethbridge is no problem and neither is finding the trailhead. Almost any avenue from the city centre has its western end poised above the coulee system, and the trailheads are all well marked and clearly mapped.

Camping

Every kind of overnight lodging is available in and around the city. There are only two commercial campgrounds in the city where a tent can be pitched, but both are best suited for RV vehicles. The Henderson Lake Campground is on the table land, just south and east of the city centre. The Bridgeview Campground is on the floodplain where the Crowsnest Trail crosses the Oldman River. Both campgrounds have every kind of camping facility.

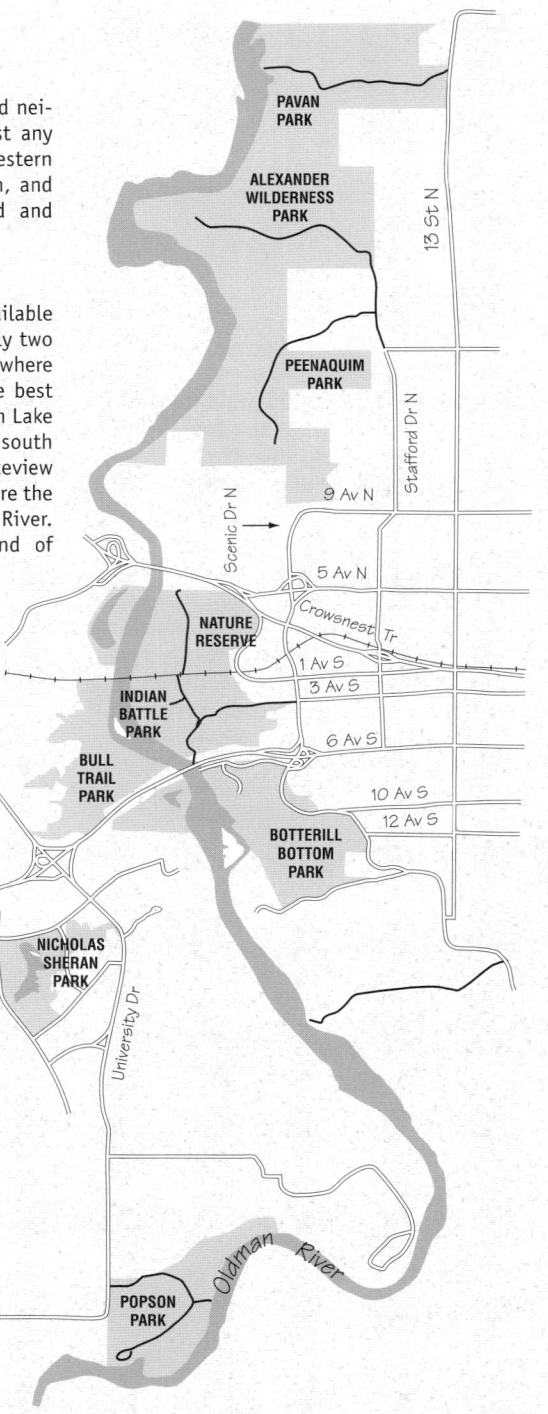

Western cottonwood fringe a floodplain meadow below steep cliffs of river-cut debris and bedrock.

There are two kinds of trails. Urban trails have a trailhead directly off a downtown avenue. The suburban trails are slightly away from the city centre. All trailheads are road accessible, and the urban trails are thoroughly domesticated—paved parking and trails, elaborate cooking and partying facilities, heated washrooms, drinking water, shelters. Fort Whoop-Up, a historic interpretation centre, and the Helen Schuler Coulee Centre, a nature centre, are at the bottom of one urban trail near the heart of the city. The suburban trails also are served with just about everything, only at a very slightly less comfortable level.

The trails can be travelled on foot, bicycle, in-line skates, and there is an excellent horse trail at Pavan Park. You can launch a canoe at Popson Park, the southernmost suburban trail, and drift nine pleasant kilometres downstream on Class I water to Pavan Park, the northernmost trail. If you travel all the trails connecting the rolling grassland

Along an arid upper ridge. Beyond is an irrigated loop in the Oldman River.

above to the river below, you will go a distance of 36 km and lose and gain more than 700 m descending and ascending the river valley. A stiff jaunt by most standards. All the trails are through similar landscapes, but each has its own unique features.

From top to bottom

At Lethbridge, the looping course of the Oldman River has carved out a steep and wide valley with flat dry lands above and flat moist lands below. Between the high and low flatlands there are steep-walled coulees.

The Great Ice Age

Humans like to call the most recent glaciation the Ice Age, because it had an impact on us humans. In fact, the last glaciation was routine in the history of glacial events, and humans were unimportant anywhere near the vast sheets of ice.

In the two million years of the Pleistocene epoch, ending when the last continental glaciers melted back to a few remnants in the western mountains and the Arctic, glaciers advanced into Alberta several times. Until a few years ago, geologists believed southwestern Alberta was inundated three, four and even five times. A recent re-examination of the evidence along with new evidence from thousands of exploratory oil and gas wells now suggests the continental glacier reached southwestern Alberta only twice. Both times, the glaciers were on their last legs by the time they reached the vicinity of Lethbridge, and they stalled completely just across what is now the border with the United States.

The ice flowed in massive sheets from the northwest and the northeast, meeting on the Interior Plains of today. The greatest of the recent ice sheets, the Laurentide, flowed from Hudson Bay and the Northwest Territories and eventually covered 13 million sq. km extending into the northern United States. Virtually all of Canada was encased in unbroken ice. From time to time, corridors of ice-free land flanked the western mountains into Alaska and across the Bering Straits into Asia. Through this corridor, the Americas got humans and Asia got horses.

Ice Age lakes and rivers

The continental ice sheet began to melt and recede toward the northeast about 18,000 years ago. Because the Interior Plains also slope downward to the northeast, water from the melting glacier was trapped between the wall of melting ice and higher land to the west. At one time or another almost all the prairie provinces were covered by lakes much larger than any of the Great Lakes. About 14,000 years ago, Lethbridge was lakefront property.

The lakes were probably shallow, murky and cold, but with enough life to facilitate widespread distribution of aquatic plants and animals. Everywhere else, the landscape was littered with glacial debris ranging from huge boulders to fine clay, and split by raging rivers.

Far to the north and east, air above the glacier's thickest dome cooled and began to flow downward into warmer, lighter air. By the time the air reached the lakes and lands far below, it was howling. On the way down the slope of the glacier, the air compressed and warmed up a little, and while the wind was not deeply cold, it blew a relentless gale across the lakes and piles of rubble. The wind was strong enough—averaging over 100 kilometres an hour—to create vast sand dunes in eastern Alberta and western Saskatchewan, and to cover much of the Interior Plains with "loess," the fine silts and clay particles that blow so well in a strong wind. In these conditions, dust storms may have lasted months.

As the climate warmed in the late Pleistocene, glaciers in the Rocky Mountains also melted, feeding rivers that were broader, deeper and carried much more water than they do today. These torrents carried huge amounts of debris out of the mountains and far into the vast lakes that flooded the Interior Plains.

Together, the water-borne lake, river and glacial materials, covered by a film of wind-blown dust and soil, is what we see around Lethbridge today.

Steep coulees carved by a flood of glacial meltwater.

Big coulees

In preglacial times, the western rivers were broad, shallow, slow and fairly straight. The advancing glaciers first crushed the gentle walls of the river valleys and then filled them in with debris. Lakes grew as the ice shrank, until the water was deep enough to escape the toe of the glacier. The lakes that covered southern Alberta drained to the south and east toward the Missouri River. The torrent of water had no trouble carving a valley into the loose glacial debris, and some huge lakes were drained completely in as few as 10 years. While one lake drained, the glacier receded farther, leaving the drainage channel high and dry. Another lake would form until it too carved a way out.

Southern Alberta is contoured with at least 10 broad and deep trenches across the flat lands of southeastern Alberta marking the channels of the now dry rivers. Red Rock Coulee, for example, is an uppermost finger of the Forty Mile Coulee system that once drained glacial lakes to the south and east of the Cypress Hills.

In only a few thousand years ending 10,000 years ago, the glacier melted, the lakes formed and drained, and the crust of the earth rebounded from the lost weight of ice. Together, these forces decide where rivers flow today, and often they occupy beds first established by glacial rivers. Today's rivers, however, are tiny in comparison to Pleistocene rivers, and they meander around in the vast, ancient river bottom.

A small glacial lake grew between a continental lobe of ice near Lethbridge and higher land to the west, where the upper Oldman River flowed out of the mountains filled with meltwater. At first, the lake drained to the south until the ice opened a channel along its present course. The lake drained in a rampage. The rush of water carved into the lip of the river valley, reaching the river through layers of sand, silt, clay and rock. The channels draining the table land formed the splendid coulees we see today.

Even though much smaller than their ancestors, the rivers are always working to make their courses straight, and in 1995 the Oldman River showed how this is done. The once-in-a-hundred-years flood of 1995 almost closed off roads to the west of Lethbridge, and filled the Oldman and South Saskatchewan rivers to overcapacity, sending floods raging everywhere in southwest Alberta. The Oldman River inundated Alexander Wilderness Park in Lethbridge, and swept away a developing foreshore beneath a cliff of glacial debris. The river undercut the cliff, causing the cliff to collapse, and shortening the river's long trip to Hudson Bay by about 5 m.

The coulees drop steeply below the flat plain in a series of curving ridges.

Lethbridge Coulee

The trip from top to bottom leads from parched and patchy grasslands, through shrublands, luxuriant grasslands, forests, and ends near waterfowl nests.

All trails from top to bottom lead through a belt of domesticated grassland where the prairie near the coulees has been seeded with alien grasses, especially crested wheat grass, smooth brome and bluegrass. Close to the rim of the valley where ploughs cannot go, native grasses and other plants take over—fescue, needle-and-thread grass, June grass and northern wheat grass. Unexpectedly, the places to find the greatest variety and largest number of flowering plants is right on the driest and most severely exposed leading edges of the coulee ridges. There, grasses are quite sparse and even nonexistent, leaving plenty of room for flowers.

The most spectacular ridge flowers are the iridescent scarlet blooms of the cushion cactus and the liquid yellow of the prickly pear cactus. Spaced carefully around the long cactus spines are golden bean, northern bedstraw, northern hedysarum, numerous vetches, Colorado rubber plant, yarrow, white beardtongue, wild blue flax, bluebell, brown-eyed Susan and the delicately coloured apricot mallow. There is hardly a square metre of ridge top that does not contain a dozen or more species of flowering plants. The exact mix and blend of flowers changes over the summer season.

Flowers compete with sage on desiccated ridge tops exposed to fierce chinook winds, filling the air with a heady mixture of perfumes. The view from the rim of the valley is always spectacular, revealing the full sweep of the diverse landscape below.

Inner slopes

The steep south-facing slopes of ravines and coulees exposed to the fierce summer sun sport bunch grasses, cactus, sage and little else. North-facing slopes protected from the heat of summer have a bigger mix of grasses, flowers and shrubs. The descending slopes end in a belt of treeless grassland and a flourishing mixed grass community. Beyond is a long, narrow forest of cottonwoods and associated understorey plants, ending at the edge of the Oldman River.

Apricot mallow.

Brown-eyed Susan.

Winter, after a chinook wind has removed all the snow.

Cottonwoods

Cottonwoods are members of a large family of trees including poplars and aspens. Collectively, the genus *Populus* tends to dominate any landscape in which they grow, so they have attracted the attention of people who live amongst them. One result is a wealth of popular names for the five species of *Populus* native to southern Alberta.

Between them the five species enjoy 14 different and often contradictory popular names. For example, in books describing the trees of Alberta, *Populus deltoides* is called western cottonwood, eastern cottonwood and plains cottonwood. Another text gives *P. trichocarpa* the common name of plains cottonwood, but also black cottonwood. *P. balsamifera* is called black cottonwood in some books, black poplar in others and balsam poplar in a few more. The most common member of the genus, *P. tremuloides*, is also known as aspen, aspen poplar, trembling aspen, quaking aspen and white poplar.

All the confusion justifies the use of scientific, Latin names. This book uses the common and scientific names for cottonwoods and poplars set out in Kathy Tannas' *Common Plants of the Western Rangelands*, published by the Lethbridge Community College and listed in the Recommended Readings. Her book is very recent and it was written from the perspective of southernmost Alberta.

Tannas on *Populus*

P. trichocarpa: black cottonwood
P. angustifolia: narrow-leaf cottonwood
P. balsamifera: balsam poplar
P. deltoides: western cottonwood
P. tremuloides: aspen

Making a certain identification of a particular tree can be a challenge. They hybridize with ease, and they are delighted to occupy the same kinds of habitats. The authoritative text on the subject, *Trees in Canada*, says that determined walkers might have to visit a particular tree three times to identify

Lethbridge Coulee

Porcupine dining on cottonwood.

it—when the tree flowers in the spring, when it is in fruit and just before leaf fall in autumn. Each season reveals subtle differences in flower, fruit and leaf shape that, together, make for a confident identification.

Coulee plants and animals

On any trail, urban or suburban, you can expect to see many characteristic plants, animals and birds dwelling in this landscape, each in its favourite habitat.

Ground squirrels, prickly pear and cushion cactus, golden bean, locust, killdeer and partridge occupy the rim of the valley. On north-facing slopes, the descending ground has saskatoon bushes, vetch, brown-eyed Susan, yarrow and wild rose. Horse flies and face flies appear wherever there is protection from the wind. On the terrace at the bottom of the valley, the grassland appears primeval and most of the plants typical of mixed grass prairie are present. The majestic cottonwoods offer a cool embrace away from the towering sun, and a retreat into a completely different environment—well watered, humid, sheltered, luxuriant, subdued, protected. The trees are full of birds—by 1996, over 250 species had been counted in the coulees around Lethbridge, including everything from hummingbirds to eagles and pelicans. Fewer than 50 species of birds live on the grasslands above.

The cool evenings erupt with insect life under the cottonwoods, first biting insects and then dragonflies. Later in the evening, bats arrive to pick off any lingering insects. Coyote, fox, ground squirrel, hawks, magpie, crow, beaver and numerous rodents can be seen almost anywhere. More exotic occasional visitors include raccoon, moose, rattlesnake and black bear. All the mixed grassland mammals are likely present somewhere in the Lethbridge coulees, including mule deer and white-tailed deer.

White-tailed deer and mule deer are very similar in appearance, especially when seen in failing light. In white-tailed deer, the eye orbits are angled forward, giving better depth perception in a wooded landscape. In mule deer, the eyes are angled to the side for better peripheral vision in open country. Mule deer are called "jumpers" and for good reason. Their high, leaping style of running is ideal for covering broken, open grassland. White-tailed deer are more straight-line runners with an ability to leap obstacles encountered in their wooded habitat.

The most obvious difference between the two species is the relative size of their ears. Mule deer are well named—they have long, wide ears that are in constant motion. However, there are hybrids of the two in which characteristics of either species are blurred. Both deer are in the Lethbridge coulees.

Water's edge

The cottonwood forest continues right to a bank dropping into the river. From the bank, the force and power of prairie rivers is revealed in the shape of the water's current. Birds abound on and near the water—ducks, geese, white pelicans, blue herons, gulls and many species of shorebirds.

At water level, grasses are at their best, almost a metre tall. There is willow, sedge and, in backwaters, bulrushes. There are blackbirds and mosquitos. There is never a dull moment in the life of a coulee.

The Lethbridge coulee trails in winter

The coulee trails are little used in winter, at least by humans. Birds and animals, on the other hand abound, taking advantage of sparse human intrusion, protection from winter's cold winds, access to open water and more food for at least some species.

Shrubs on the north-facing coulee walls trap a lot of snow, and drifts may measure more than a metre deep. Cottontail rabbits sit just at the edges of the densest thickets of shrubs, where they nibble and keep an eye out for foxes and coyotes. If a red fox approaches the thicket, the rabbits disappear in the impenetrable hedge. Rabbits can move much more quickly inside the shrubbery than can a fox. Anyway, magpies fly about and mark

Pavan Park's broad floodplain forest of cottonwood, summer.

Lethbridge Coulee

Open water below Alexander Park after a snowfall and before a chinook.

the fox's progress through the shrubs by landing on branches over his head, all the time calling noisily.

Apparently, magpies do not have the tools to open a dead animal and so they rely on coyotes, foxes, wolves and other predators to make the kill and leave some scraps they can handle. Perhaps the magpies were cheering the fox on, but their racket must distract even the stealthiest fox. Or the magpies were just having fun.

Where there is not too much snow, the sides and bottoms of the coulees are covered with deer, rabbit, hare, fox, porcupine and coyote tracks and droppings. Herds of 15 and more mule deer can be seen in the suburban parks most winter days. Wherever a chinook melts the snow off the grassy areas closer to the bottom of the coulees and the river floodplain, intricate rodent runways are exposed.

Larger trees near the river are home to great horned owls sitting immobile on cottonwood branches trying not to attract the attentions of magpies and crows. More exotic birds wintering in the river valleys are the belted kingfisher, downy woodpecker and hairy woodpecker, bringing flashes of light and sound to the hushed cold forest.

In the coldest weeks of winter, much of the Oldman River freezes over, but here and there are large patches of open water. Most of the year a long and wide patch of water stays open on the upstream side of Alexander Wilderness Park. Lethbridge's sizeable resident flocks of geese and ducks cover the surface, and beaver are seen crossing the open water.

In winter, the coulees are far more active than the grassland above. Birds and animals that don't migrate or hibernate gravitate to the advantages of the sheltered trees, shrubs and tallstanding grasses. Because humans rarely wander about in the coulees during winter, animals are easier to find and see.

The Lethbridge coulees get really cold in a strong winter westerly wind, but there is a cappuccino bar at the trailhead.

7 Twin River Grazing Reserve

Mode: foot, bicycle
Rating: easy
Time: 4 - 5 hours
Distance: 10 km
Elevation change: 38 m
Maps: 82 H/1 Milk River, 82 H/2 Shanks Lake

The Twin River Grazing Reserve might confirm your impressions of Canada's western grassland—vast, almost featureless expanses of rolling grass, a hill or two on the horizon, and few plants growing taller than grass. In fact, the region is much more diverse.

Located in the southern part of the Mixed Grass Ecoregion, right along the United States border, the northern part of the reserve captures the rolling upland prairie of the Milk River Ridge. The southern part is cut through by the Milk River and its lesser tributaries. Unlike the lower part, with its dramatic canyons and arid badlands, the upper part is set in the softer Mixed Grass Ecoregion without the harsh beauty found farther east.

The rivers transform the grassland monotony into a landscape full of life and vigour. Here and there on the upper grasslands are sentinels of bright coloured rock, seeming out of place in a landscape of grass and sky. These tall boulders are erratics and, in a sense, they are out of place.

There are trails everywhere in the reserve. The trails are created and maintained by cattle and sheep grazing over the summer, and by herds of mule deer and pronghorn. The animal trails are ideal for foot, bicycle and horse travel. The best route lies on the south side of the second fence. The land between the fence and the river has cattle on it infrequently, so the grassland is quite pristine.

There are animal trails on the prairie above and the floodplain below running the length of the Milk River through the reserve. Use these trails to cycle, hike or ride for 20 km on the dry prairie in easy view of the river valley. Shorter routes can be put together to include an outward trip on the prairie, then descend the valley and pick a way back along the maze of trails near the river.

As it once was—bison on the winter range below the Milk River Ridge.

Getting there

From Lethbridge, take Highway 5 south to Magrath and there turn onto Highway 62 to continue south as far as Del Bonita, near the United States border. Turn east on Highway 501 and drive 21 km to the grazing reserve's western boundary. At that point, the highway takes a turn toward the northeast and then after 5.5 km in that direction, another turn back toward due east. At this last turn from northeast to due east the highway bisects the fenced-in grazing reserve. There is a sign and a Texas gate on the north side of the highway and a four-wire gate on the south side. This is the trailhead.

The north gate is decorated with a large sign, weathered so much it is almost unreadable. Careful study of the sign reveals that the grazing lease is open to the public, and sets out a few basic rules for visitors—no driving off the established roads, no fires and no molesting of livestock.

Before parking and setting out, go and tell the range manager your intentions. Turn back to the reserve's western boundary where Highway 501 makes an abrupt jog from due east to northeast, about 5.5 km west of the trailhead. At the jog, take the gravel road heading south to the grazing reserve's neat headquarters. The range boss is your best source of information about current conditions.

Back at the trailhead

The gate to the south leads to a primitive road that eventually reaches the bank of the Milk River. The river may be reached from the paved highway on foot or bicycle without taking a vehicle into the reserve.

Cross the wire gate at the highway and travel 3 km to a second wire gate. The road disappears on the south side of the second gate, so cattle and wildlife trails are used from here on. Be certain to leave the gates exactly as they were found.

The gate to the north of Highway 501 crosses a cattleguard and leads toward the North Milk River. The road ends in the yard at the herdkeeper's shack and sheep corral.

The Twin River Grazing Reserve is very well managed from a visitor's perspective. The sensitive areas near the valley rim and all the way to the water are fenced off. There are few signs of cattle south of the second fence. There are cattle to the north of the fence, but the prairie is only lightly grazed. Wildlife and indigenous plants abound. There is no litter, and there are few off-road tracks. It is a great place to enjoy the mixed grass prairie.

Camping

There are no camping facilities of any kind in the grazing lease. There is a simple campground on Highway 62 just north of Del Bonita on the bank of the North Milk River. There is a better campground at the town of Milk River on Highway 4 to the west. Either one is about a 30 minute drive from the grazing reserve gates.

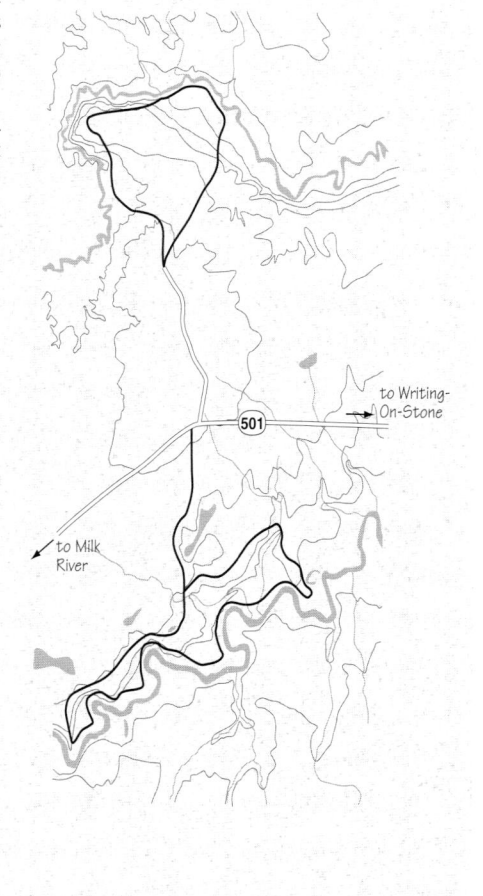

The upper grassland

The gently rolling prairie is covered with stands of needle-and-thread grass, wheat grass, June grass and pasture sage. The grass and sage are dotted with prairie crocus and golden bean in the spring, and yarrow and pussytoes later in the summer. Keep a sharp eye open for pronghorn fleeing across the prairie. Sharp-tailed grouse, meadowlark and horned lark are everywhere.

There are 75 species of lark in the world, but the horned lark is the only one in North America. This lark has two dark stripes of feathers that cross from just behind the bill and between the eyes to the back of the head. These feathers can be raised erect, especially as a courting display.

Horned larks are never found in treed areas, but they are common in the grasslands and, oddly enough, high above the tree line in mountain tundra landscapes. Horned larks favour open ground and seem to have a preference for roadways and highways. They have not learned to avoid vehicles, and drivers will be playing dodge-'em with horned larks anywhere they drive in the grasslands.

The valley walls

The panorama opens up near the lip of the river valley. In most places, the valley walls slope gently down to a broad floodplain. The south-facing slopes are parched and sparsely covered with grasses. Here and there, a shallow basin in the prairie tips water over the edge of the valley in a short-lived streamlet feeding a small clump of shrubs and taller flowering plants—a micro-habitat for species preferring concealment, shade and protection. On north-facing slopes on the other side of the river where more winter snow is trapped, there is a profusion of buckbrush, silverberry, saskatoon and rose shrubs.

In sharp contrast to the lower Milk River valley in the Pinhorn Grazing Reserve, there is no exposed bedrock. The two parts of the river had quite different geological histories: one making the Pinhorn Reserve harsh and jagged, and the other making the Twin River Reserve smooth and softly shaped.

In the Twin River Grazing Reserve, the Milk River is almost lost in its wide, shallow valley.

Erratics

Most of the grasslands of southernmost Alberta are underlaid with a bedrock of Cretaceous sandstones and shales, while most of the rock in the Rocky Mountains is a combination of limestone and dolomite. Rock that originated as molten material is very rare. Nevertheless, there are boulders of igneous rock scattered throughout the region. These boulders are erratics, or rocks of very different composition than the underlying bedrock.

Moving ice

During the Pleistocene and the end of the last glacial age, southern Alberta was covered repeatedly with glacial ice. A few isolated places escaped glacial innundation, including the summits of the Porcupine Hills, the Cypress Hills and western summits called "nunataks" high enough to thrust above the mountain glaciers. Everywhere else was covered with ice. The main continental ice sheet was born far to the north and east, in the vicinity of Hudson Bay and the Northwest Territories. Smaller glaciers were born in the high valleys of the Rocky Mountains.

As the continental glacier grew, it pushed its way toward the south and west, carrying with it a huge load of broken and crushed rock plucked from the surface of the Canadian Shield almost 1000 km away. Eventually, the progress of the great ice sheet stalled just south of the United States border, the ice melted and disappeared, and the load of imported rock was left exactly where the glacier died. Any place where these colourful, extremely tough and hard rocks are found scattered on undisturbed soil was under the last great continental glacier until about 12,000 years ago.

The mountain glaciers, on the other hand, carried material quarried from the tops and walls of the Rockies. These glaciers flowed out of the mountain valleys to join with the continental glacier on its irresistible journey southward. One mountain glacier in particular created a most curious feature—a train of slightly pink or purple quartzite boulders reaching from the Athabaska Valley near Jasper and all the way into the United States.

Erratic train

The train of boulders is narrow—about 10 km in width—and parallels the eastern front of the Rockies. Geologists think a massive landslide down the side of a mountain deposited millions of tonnes of rock on the top of the Pleistocene glacier that filled the Athabaska Valley in the northern Rockies. The glacier carried the debris east beyond the foothills, where it was deflected toward the southeast by the edge of the continental glacier. Because the erratics rode on the top of the glacier, they were not ground, rounded and polished as were rocks embedded in the ice itself.

Eventually, the mountain glacier stopped moving, stagnated and then melted away, dropping the rocks where we find them today. The most famous of these erratic rocks is the Big Rock a few kilometres west of Okotoks, measuring about 6640 cu. m and estimated to weigh almost 17,000 tonnes. The erratics at Twin River Reserve are not part of this string of Rocky Mountain material, and none of them are as big, but they are just as distinctive. Over the past 10,000 and more years, weathering has split and reduced these rocks, but they are still an impressive and curious part of the landscape.

Precambrian granite.

The gentle river barely disturbs the burden of glacial debris.

Bedrock

Like the rest of the region, the Twin River Grazing Reserve is underlaid with sandstones and shales. At creation between 100 and 65 million years ago, the bedrock was flat and level, but subtle shuffling of continental plates and the last dwindling forces of mountain building in the west reached far enough inland to very gently warp the bedrock into domes and arches. One of these, the Sweetgrass Arch, ends near the border with the United States and close to where the Twin River Grazing Reserve is now located. As the ancient Cretaceous seas receded and finally disappeared, the exposed surface was attacked by the unrelenting forces of erosion—wind, water, frost and gravity.

The layers of soft bedrock were peeled back, ground up and eventually redeposited far to the south and east. Because the layers of sandstone and shale were slightly arched, rather than lying perfectly flat, erosion revealed the underlayer of bedrock as a series of concentric rings. The oldest Cretaceous rocks were exposed at the centre of the arch, surrounded by huge rings of progressively younger rock. The effect is rather like taking a slice off the side of an onion. The exposed surface at the centre of the cut is deeper in the onion than are the outer rings. The bedrock under the Twin River Grazing Reserve, near the apex of an arch, is much older than bedrock exposed at the Pinhorn Grazing Reserve, due east, or at the Kimball Campground on the St. Mary River, due west.

Mountain rivers

The exposed Interior Plains were subjected to millions of years of erosion, especially erosion by flowing water. Then, as now, rivers flowed out of the higher lands to the west and the shape of the land decided where the water would flow. In what is now southernmost Alberta, mountain rivers were forced to flow north and south of a long and wide strip of slightly higher land emerging from the foothills and extending a third of the way across the province.

This higher land is the Milk River Ridge, in clear view to the north of the Twin River Grazing Reserve. The Milk River Ridge was probably a stream divide more than two million years ago, just as it is today. Today, the Milk River Ridge rises to an elevation of 1272 m. This is about 130 m above the trailhead at the reserve gates, 180 m above the Milk River, and 300 m above the surrounding prairie.

Sandstones and shales are very soft and rivers raging out of the new-forming Rocky Mountains had little difficulty carving channels around the Milk River Ridge. About 25 million years ago in the middle of the Cenozoic era, mountain building caused a slight uplift of the Interior Plains.

Uplift in turn increased the rivers' rate of flow and as rate of flow increased, so did the rate of erosion. The powerful rivers cut deeply into the burden of debris washing out of the Rocky Mountains, and began to carve into the bedrock.

The Ice Age

Then, the great glaciers of the Pleistocene epoch first scoured the surface of the plains clean of rock eroded out of the mountains, carved deeper into the hump of the Sweetgrass Arch, filled in the ancient river valleys carved through the sandstones and shales, and finally covered the entire region with metres of glacial debris. The result is the rolling and hummocky land surface walkers can enjoy today.

The great sheet of ice stagnated and then melted away, releasing a torrent of water that carved a new river channel directly over the top of the ancient riverbed. The glacial river had only a short lifespan and did not succeed in carving all the way through the debris to expose bedrock.

The floodplain

The broad, shallow valley of the middle Milk River was filled with water during the glacial meltdown. Then in its youth, the river carved into hills of glacial drift and now the prairie ends at a sheer cliff dropping into the valley below, a viewpoint to enjoy the great feel of the place. The flat river bottom was laid down about 13,000 years ago when a glacial lake finally found a channel draining east and south. When the lake was drained in a decade or so, the dwindling flow left a last token cover of finer material sorted on the bottom of the valley.

The modern river has plowed the river bottom with determination, but comparatively little effect. There are abandoned channels, ox bow ponds and secondary channels, the signs of an "underfit stream" or a small stream wandering around in a bigger river's valley. In comparison with the mighty streams that carved the broad valley, the Milk River is a low volume and low speed stream, with little power of erosion. It will be many years before the river uncovers the ancient bedrock lying metres beneath a mantle of glacial debris.

Since the disappearance of glaciers, gravity is the main force of erosion and many of the river valley walls are slumping slowly down toward the valley floor. Some of the most severely eroded cliffs are now occupied by large colonies of cliff swallows and they have no fear of losing their homes to erosion.

Cliff swallow nests.

Twin River

The Rocky Mountains to the west, and the source of the Milk River.

Valley descent
The descent from prairie to floodplain is less than 70 m. At the bottom of the slope, where the soil is moist, grasses are much more luxuriant and include water-loving species like hair grass and bluestem. In contrast to the steeper valley walls, which are only thinly dotted with clumps of plants, the surface of the floodplain is almost entirely covered with plants. Not only are they thicker, they are greener and taller, the advantages of more water, richer soil and less wind.

In the larger loops of river, the grassland extends unbroken for several hundred metres. Then, closer to the river, there is a broad thicket of waist-high shrubs. The belts of shrubs are hatched with animal trails making travel on foot easy, but cyclists will probably push their wheels through the stiff and close-packed branches. The shrubland ends just above a narrow beach of sand or gravel that gets progressively wetter toward the water's edge.

The zone where land meets water is crucial habitat for wildlife. In the spring, the river edge is alive with nesting geese and ducks, and early-season visitors must be careful not to disturb them. There are also many herons, hawks and eagles. Mule deer and white-tailed deer graze the taller grasses.

Cone flower.

When you are done wandering around on the floodplain, pick a straight-line route up to the prairie. The quick transition from muddy shoreline to parched plains reinforces the drama of a river set in a near-desert landscape.

North of Highway 501

The road through the north part of the Twin River Grazing Reserve ends about 3 km from the highway. A small herder's yard and cabin are perched on a slight rise overlooking the North Milk River. Across the river is the gentle rise of the Milk River Ridge.

The banks above the shallow creek are liberally sprinkled with large and small rounded and polished erratics of granitic rock. They were polished to a high gloss by generations of hairy, itchy hides, first by bison and perhaps mammoth and much later by domestic cattle and sheep. The taller and heavier rocks are surrounded by a depressed ring of completely bare, trampled soil.

Just beyond the herder's cabin is a collection of ancient seeding and hay cutting equipment, and in the meadow below is a wooden gantry used long ago to pick up piles of hay and place them on a horse-drawn wagon. The gantry is unused today, except as a nesting site for golden eagles who have built upon it a large disorganized nest of twigs and branches. Below the nest, the ground is littered with hair pellets and the whole bones of Richardson's ground squirrels, which are plentiful in the grassy soils near the stream.

There are between 100 and 500 breeding pairs of golden eagles in Alberta. They were once much more plentiful, but ranchers, with the encouragement of government, shot them as predators on domestic livestock. In fact, hoofed animals make up only five per cent of their diet, and most of this is in the form of carrion. They do, however, eat many ground squirrels, the rancher's and farmer's archenemy.

There are excellent animal trails and crude no-vehicle roads leading everywhere in the north part of the grazing reserve. The rolling texture of the landscape keeps the horizon unrolling from one discovery to another. The details of this landscape are mostly very small and few, but splendid. The ground is littered with gem-like pebbles of quartz, chert, basalt and many other souvenirs of the last Ice Age glaciation. Slight folds in the land give and take away habitat advantages, revealed in changing communities of plants and animals. The landscape is dry, windy, hot or cold, but gentle underfoot, and a strong hiker could spend a day exploring the north part of the reserve.

Twin River Grazing Reserve in winter

Winters are fickle in the far south of Alberta. In most winters, the reserve gets sparse snowfall regularly swept away by chinook winds. In most winters, the landscape is presented in the traditional colours of southernmost Alberta—buckskin and blue.

In March of 1998, southern Alberta was covered with a record dump of snow. Calgary and Lethbridge received over 50 cm of heavy, wet snow. The foothills got 75 cm and the mountains received over a metre. The Cypress Hills were covered with 30 cm. Transportation, power, communications and other vital services were interrupted, but within hours visitors had penetrated most of the new snow.

Twin River Grazing Reserve received a fresh fall of 15 cm of snow, outlining every feature of the landscape in white and shadow. For this dry Special Place, thick snow was a windfall of moisture. The following days were sunny, but cool, resulting in a slow melt. In only a few weeks the meltwater was put to work sustaining a rich community of new prairie plants and animals.

Special Places for a Quick Visit

Taber Provincial Park

Taber Provincial Park is a small pocket of well-preserved river bottom nestled on the bank of the Oldman River and surrounded by intensive dryland and irrigation agriculture.

The park is equipped with secluded camping sites, kitchen buildings, washrooms, fire pits, drinking water and RV dumps. The resident park ranger has maps and natural history guides.

Nearby is an immense assembly of over 200 stone circles and shapes, created by the first people to occupy this land. After them came Mormon settlers from Utah in the late 19th century, then the railroad, natural gas, Highway 3, and an increasing focus on intensive agriculture and transportation.

The floodplain is underlaid with thick beds of Cretaceous sandstone, shale and coal. Earlier in the 20th century, small coal mines operated west and south of the park. The first coal was used to power a large pump that lifted water up to the thirsty railroad locomotives 60 m above the surface of the river.

Because the park is an island of diversity set in a sea of grass, it attracts many species that may not be seen elsewhere. The main attractions include some of the largest western cottonwood in Canada. In summer, the huge trees, some well over a metre across at the base, are filled with nesting birds and in winter they offer a secure perch for owls.

The park is quite small, and most of the flat land is groomed for camping, picnicking and recreation. The main trails are wheelchair accessible, and there are informal trails leading down to the river's edge through tall thickets

The park nestles on a floodplain in a grove of western cottonwood at the edge of the Oldman River.

Special Places

A still pond is home to wetland birds and insects.

of willow and sedge. The muddy shore is speckled with clam shells and brightly coloured pebbles and cobbles left behind when the great continental glacier melted.

About midway between Lethbridge and Grand Forks, Taber Provincial Park is a fine base for canoeists. The section from Lethbridge starts at Pavan Park, which has a boat launch. Lethbridge is at 820 m elevation, and in 83 km drops to 770 m at Taber. The section from Taber to Grand Forks is 64 km long and drops to 700 m at the start of the South Saskatchewan River. The grade is gentle, with no more than a few Class I riffles over boulders and shoals. There are many idyllic camping places all along the river, and good vehicle access at all ends.

Even though the lower Oldman River flows through a vast belt of industrial agriculture, there are still long stretches that show little human impact. Here, the valley abounds in white pelicans, golden eagles, waterfowl, shorebirds and beaver. The occasional cottonwood groves offer shade to visitors and shelter to mule deer, tree-nesting birds, rodents and insects.

Head-Smashed-In Buffalo Jump

Head-Smashed-In is a United Nations World Heritage Site offering one of the best views of ancient aboriginal life in western Canada. The site was first explored by archaeologists in the 1930s, but it was not until 1979 that the government finally recognized the site's historic significance and made it a Provincial Historic Site. By 1981, it was declared a a site of international importance and plans were underway to construct the $10 million interpretive centre now occupying the site. Construction of the centre began in 1984 and was completed in the summer of 1987.

The centre preserves one of many places on the Canadian prairie where aboriginal people drove herds of buffalo over a cliff in their efforts to supply all the food supplies and materials for clothing and shelter needed by a band of grassland hunters for several months. The buffalo jump represents a technical advance needed to sustain large populations in a hostile environment.

The interpretive centre is the main attraction, with its meticulous displays and dioramas and its even-handed treatment of western history. The jump itself is just outside the centre's upper-level doors, fully accessible by a system of trails. The trails lead along the brow of the jump. The jump took advantage of a cliff formed where glacial ice carved into the flat layers of Cretaceous sandstone. The viewpoints are an excellent place to examine indigenous grassland species up close. Nearby is a spring feeding a narrow slot in the bedrock and supporting a profusion of shrubs, flowers and species that like a wetter habitat.

The lower trails curve along the base of the jump cliff and cross the place where ancient peoples butchered and processed the bison meat. The entire area has been thoroughly explored by archaeologists and there are several viewpoints where their findings are placed in context.

All the public access trails are wheelchair accessible. The building has elevators and wide doors and walkways. The centre has a restaurant and gift shop.

Tipi camp at the annual Head-Smashed-In Buffalo Jump powwow.

Special Places

Oldman Reservoir

In the early 1990s, the Oldman River was the centre of local, national and international attention as competing interests battled over the construction of the dam and reservoir. The project went through all the stages of contest, including a wealth of conflicting technical data and information, elaborate economic arguments and emotion-laden political rhetoric.

Petitions, parades and protests followed the decision to proceed with the project. Then came litigation, civil disobedience and armed violence. The Lonefighters, a clan in the Peigan community living directly below the dam and reservoir, occupied part of their reserve where there was another river control structure, and began to dig a diversion to prevent the filling of the reservoir. In RCMP action against the Lonefighter camp, a shot was fired.

The camp was routed, one man went to prison and the last effort to save the middle Oldman River was over. The dam was built and the reservoir flooded by the time federal environment agencies decided the project broke federal law. Too late. The reservoir was full, and nobody is about to take it apart.

Most accounts say the installation is well managed and what we have today is a superb campground, and a designer canoe and kayak challenge course about a kilometre below the main dam. The riverbed was sculpted to reduce erosion. As a bonus, the sculpted section was implanted with massive boulders creating Class II to IV+ water, depending on the rate of discharge below the dam.

The roads around the reservoir are perfect for bicycling—flawless pavement, broad shoulders, not too much traffic and plenty of pull-offs with information signs and splendid views in every direction. The roads are over rolling hills with little elevation gain or loss.

Off Windy Point.

Windy Point, so well named, is the best place to view the montane, southern parkland, subalpine and alpine delights that lie to the west. Windy Point is where the windsurfers put in. The setting is spectacular—paved access, pebble beaches, smoothly curved shorelines, lots of open water and the Livingstone Range on the horizon. And, there is chinook wind to challenge the best surfers, frequently blowing over 100 kilometres an hour.

Tucked here and there amongst these technological marvels are the downstream remnant of the Oldman River, exposed bedrock and till geology, a floodplain filled with western cottonwood, shrubs and a broad grassland. Cottonwood Campground occupies the cottonwood groves, offering every amenity with a view across the river of Cretaceous sandstone beds tipped on edge.

The campground trails in the cottonwood groves are good for wheelchairs. There are several roadside viewpoints and interpretive plaques that are smooth, level and wheelchair-ready. The highways are superb, with wide paved shoulders. Wheelchair athletes, highway ski-boarders and cyclists work out on the hilly highway in the spring and autumn when road traffic is light.

5

Fescue Grass Ecoregion

The Fescue Grass Ecoregion is a very narrow strip of grassland squeezed between the eastern Mixed Grass Ecoregion and the Montane Ecoregion to the west. The change from the dry mixed grass prairie to the richer Fescue Grass Ecoregion is subtle, but it would have been more noticeable before the transition was completely blurred by agriculture and human activity in general. The grasslands attracted a rush of ranchers and settlers near the beginning of the 20th century and are now almost entirely domesticated. There are only 12,294 sq. km of fescue grassland in the entire province, and the largest area of pristine fescue grassland on public Crown land is less than 30 sq. km in size.

The fescue grasslands are rich and inviting compared to the drier and harsher grasslands to the east. Gently undulating prairie gives way to more dramatic hilly country, broader and deeper river valleys, more wetlands.

There are still plenty of opportunities to experience the fescue grassland. Several of the Special Places discussed elsewhere in this book include well-preserved fescue grasslands—the fescue grassland is part of what makes them special. Some pockets of remaining fescue grassland are at Beaver Creek, Whaleback Ridge and Carbondale Hill in montane country, the Wishbone Trail and Mount Galwey in the east part of Waterton Lakes National Park, and directly below the heights of Table Mountain, Thunder Mountain and the upper Oldman River. It won't be too hard to imagine rolling hills of stirrup-high grass disappearing on the horizon, but sadly there is no place left where the expansive fescue grassland may be enjoyed.

The richest soil

The most distinctive difference between the fescue grassland and grasslands to the east is the difference in the quality of soils. In the Fescue Grass Ecoregion, soils are thicker and darker in colour, indicating a richer bed for rooted plants. As well, these soils are somewhat older and better developed than soils farther east.

Like the rest of the Interior Plains, the fescue grassland was inundated with ice during the last Ice Age glaciations. However, because the western grasslands are at a higher elevation than the eastern grasslands, the blanket

Fescue Grass

of ice thinned as it approached the mountains. When the ice began to melt about 20,000 years ago, the thin ice went first and the first land surface was exposed just east of the Rocky Mountains. Because the region is at a higher elevation, no large lakes formed as the ice melted. Because it was free of ice first and never flooded with icy lakes, the western region was available for plant colonization much earlier—perhaps several thousand years earlier—than regions to the east.

Immediately, the incessant strong winds that blasted along the front of the receding glacier began to blow soil onto the newly exposed surface. The soil arrived from the south where the glaciers had not reached, and provided a rich seed bed for the first pioneer plants to invade the land.

At first, the newly exposed land surface resembled tundra—a wide band of grass, sedge, willow, juniper, buffalo berry, silverberry and other shrubs, dotted with mounds of rocky rubble and cold, clear ponds. As the ice receded and the landscape warmed, forests of white spruce and lodgepole pine advanced over the tundra and covered most of the Interior Plains. As long-term warming continued, the western forests dried out and were replaced by grasslands.

Ever since, the higher western grasslands have enjoyed more precipitation, cooler summers and warmer winters, great conditions for plant growth. The remains of generations of grassland plants is what built the rich soils of the fescue grassland.

Add water

The richness of the fescue grassland is, in part, the result of proximity to the Rocky Mountains. At a higher elevation than eastern grassland ecoregions and closer to the Rocky Mountains, the Fescue Grass Ecoregion has cooler summers and warmer winters. This

A modest remnant of fescue grassland along the St. Mary River.

Fescue Grass

The rocky foreshore, freshly scoured by the St. Mary River's spring floods.

may explain why the fescue grasslands form only a thin strip immediately to the east of the southern Rockies. The beneficial influence of the mountains is at its best near the foothills, dwindles across the mixed grassland, and virtually disappears in the dry grassland.

The organic Chernozems of the Fescue Grass Ecoregion are deep and rich enough to make the entire region more productive than the rest of the grassland in southern Alberta. Over a good summer, sites in the Fescue Grass Ecoregion produce about 950 kg of native plants per ha, compared to 475 kg in the Mixed Grass Ecoregion, and 350 kg in the Dry Mixed Grass Ecoregion.

The Fescue Grass Ecoregion is also closer to the storm tracks through southwestern Alberta, and receives more precipitation than the rest of the grasslands, especially as snow in the winter. While enjoying more moisture, summers in this ecoregion are much cooler than in the drier grasslands to the east, resulting in a shorter growing season and greater threat of frost later in spring and earlier in autumn. Winters, however, are the warmest in all of Alberta, thanks to frequent chinook winds.

Grasslands luxury

As in the other grassland regions, there is plenty of variety within the general landscape. Soils range from thick floodplain blacks to starved, thin Regosols where mountain rivers spill their load of erosion debris onto the prairie. Some places feel the wind's teeth and other places are sheltered in the arms of a protective hill. Some places collect a little moisture and other places are desiccated.

The moist and moderate conditions promote much more luxurious growth of grasses than in either the Dry Mixed Grass Ecoregion or the Mixed Grass Ecoregion. Common grasses include various fescues, June grass and Parry oat grass. Even though the Fescue Grass Ecoregion enjoys better conditions for growing grass, the lack of moisture is still the limiting factor on the region's productivity.

Fescue Grass

Other common fescue grassland plants include pearly everlasting, sticky geranium, silvery lupine, golden bean, balsamroot, pasture sage, yarrow, wild licorice and fleabane. The wind blows snow into deep piles on the lee sides of hills and drainage channels, and this snow melts slowly in the spring. In these more protected and moister areas buckbrush, saskatoon and wild rose proliferate. Along the rivers, Bebb willow, smooth gooseberry, golden currant and huge cottonwood spread over the floodplain's wild growth of water-loving plants.

There is more water in the fescue grasslands than in the rest of the grasslands, and more water adds more variety to the landscape. There are more natural ponds and lakes, especially in the glacially sculpted landscape of the extreme southwestern grassland.

The western margin of the fescue grassland gradually merges into either a montane landscape, an aspen parkland landscape or a subalpine landscape, sharing species of plants and animals with the neighbouring ecoregions.

Bulrushes and sandbar willow line the river's muddy shore.

Fescue Grass Ecoregion

Area: 12,294 sq. km or 1.9% of the province.

Topography: Rolling in the eastern part, hilly in the west closer to the mountains; river canyons and valleys, but no coulees.

Altitude: 1000 - 1300 m

Climate: Most rain falls in May and June, but not in much greater quantities than in the other grassland ecoregions. Winter precipitation, however, is more than 50 per cent greater, and total annual precipitation is almost double what falls elsewhere on grasslands farther east. With more moisture, the Fescue Grass Ecoregion is not as subject to drought as the rest of the grasslands, but a combination of modest precipitation, high temperatures and strong dry winds results in localized water deficits. Summer temperatures average about 1.5°C lower than in the eastern grassland ecoregions, but the Fescue Grass Ecoregion has the warmest winter temperature in all Alberta, largely because of chinook winds. This ecoregion experiences more days of chinook winds per year—up to 35 days—than any other part of Alberta. Where not blasted with frequent warm chinooks, snow builds to considerable depths.

Soils: The richest Chernozems in the grasslands of southern Alberta.

Humans: Most of the Fescue Grass Ecoregion is domesticated—dry land farming, irrigation farming or livestock grazing.

8 Exploring Kimball Park

Mode: foot
Rating: easy
Time: 2 - 3 hours
Distance: 3 km
Elevation change: 30 m
Map: 82 H/3 Cardston

Kimball Park is a small campground tucked away on a bend in the St. Mary River near the United States border. It is a sampler of the ecoregion rather than a representative, a place where grassland meets a thick riverside forest. In a landscape where many forests have been eliminated with the advance of the agricultural frontier, remaining woodlands are especially important.

There is no trail. Kimball Park is simply a convenient place to have a close look at river diversity embedded in a domesticated fescue grass landscape. First, explore the extensive campground floodplain and the surrounding area.

Narrow-leaf cottonwood

The cottonwoods in Kimball Park are not just any cottonwood; they are *Populus angustifolia* or narrow-leaf cottonwood, easily mistaken for a hugely overgrown willow of some kind. The narrow-leaf cottonwood stands straight and slender, between 15 and 30 m tall. The tree's upper branches droop gracefully under a thick cloak of slender leaves, flowers and seeds. The narrow-leaf cottonwood is rather uncommon in Canada and only grows in a few river valleys in southernmost Alberta and isolated places in western Saskatchewan.

There is also black cottonwood in the Kimball forest, *Populus trichocarpa*, the largest of the balsam poplars in Canada, up to 35 m in height. The trunks are mighty and straight with a division or two in the upper third. The leaves are large and round. Black cottonwood grows mostly in British Columbia, but extends over the Rockies as far east as the Fescue Grassland Ecoregion.

Aspen and cottonwood crowd an old shoreline slightly above the active floodplain.

Getting there

The destination is Kimball Park, a small picnic and campground set right on the edge of the St. Mary River. From Lethbridge, take Highway 5 to Cardston and turn south on Highway 2. Drive south 5 km to the junction with Highway 501, heading southeast. Seven kilometres later on Highway 501, Kimball Park is on the west side of the highway.

From Waterton Lakes National Park, take Highway 5 east to Cardston, and then turn south toward the park. From the United States, cross the border at Carway on Highway 2 and drive north to Cardston and from there to Kimball Park.

If you are coming from Milk River after visiting the Special Places in the drier grasslands, take Highway 4 south for 3 km and then head west on Highway 501 for 78 km until you reach Kimball Park on the west side of the highway. It is a fascinating journey across some of the most diverse grassland landscapes in the west.

Camping

Kimball Park is a secret gem of a municipal campground, not even indicated on provincial highway maps. The campground is spotlessly maintained—even the roadside sign gleams with fresh paint.

There are secluded tent and camper sites nestled in a floodplain grove of cottonwood and roses. There is a cookshack, pit toilets, picnic tables, garbage tanks, fire pits and drinking water. It is about as good as it gets at $5.00 per day.

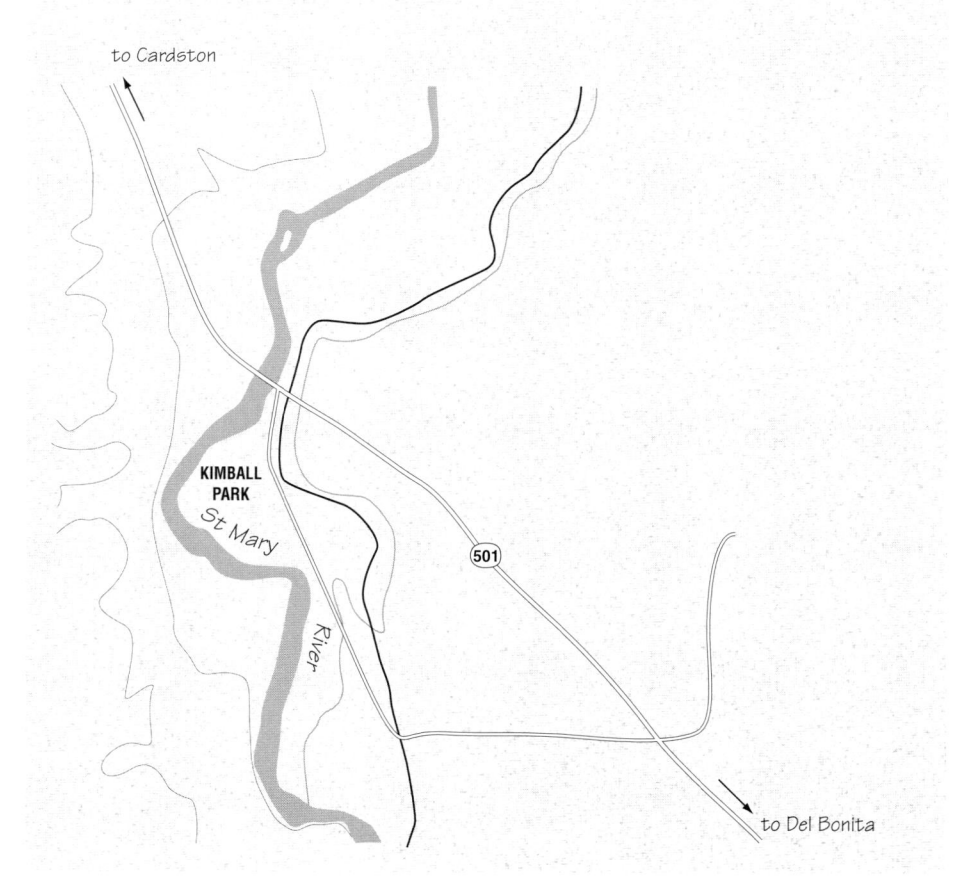

Narrow-leaf cottonwood.

As usual, the two cottonwoods hybridize, and determining the exact kind and degree of hybridization in any particular tree is a matter for tree geneticists. However, in Kimball Campground there are trees with mighty trunks sporting slender leaves and there are trees with slender trunks sporting mighty leaves. All in the life of a cottonwood forest.

Beneath the trees

Beneath the cottonwoods is a tangle of willows and roses, and beneath them is a layer of fescue, crested wheat grass and June grass. Wildflowers grow wherever there is space in their preferred habitats—especially yarrow and brown-eyed Susan.

The thick stands of cottonwoods are split by infrequent drainage channels. Trees do not grow in the wet Regosols and Gleysols along the bottom of these channels, but willow and grasses that can tolerate frequent flooding love it there, shaded from the burning summer sun and desiccating winter wind.

River's edge

The Great Flood of 1995 transformed the lower parts of the floodplain. Much of the mature prairie river bottom's collection of soils, young trees, shrubs, grasses and flowers were crushed to fibre and swept downstream in the ancient way of the world. Left behind is a fresh, new foreshore paved with fist-sized cobbles.

Other places are covered with fresh new silts and mud, burying the older layer of soil and entombing a mat of broken vegetation. Here and there, a quirk in the preflood riverbed preserved a few parts of the mature foreshore. A mat of rootbound Chernozemic soil hangs over an undercut bank of river cobbles. An undisturbed cottonwood forest occupies the foreshore directly above the active floodplain.

The floodplain is covered with young and fast-growing sandbar willow interspersed with tufts of tall fescue grasses. Even closer to the water's edge, hardier plants capable of withstanding moderate and severe flooding

St. Mary River

Narrow-leaf cottonwood over a thick understorey of grass, flowers and shrubs.

The St. Mary River arises in the great mountains of northern Montana, and is filled with meltwater from glaciers high in the shadow of Mount Logan in Glacier National Park. The St. Mary River and other mountain streams fill the two St. Mary lakes that occupy a glacially carved valley, like the one occupied by Waterton Lakes straddling the border.

The river flows north and east and crosses the international border just to the east of Carway, Alberta. The river then flows about 40 km until it reaches the St. Mary Reservoir, northeast of Cardston. From the reservoir, the river continues northeast to just south of Lethbridge where it joins the Oldman River.

The St. Mary River begins as a high elevation mountain stream, then enters a long stretch of montane foothills, crosses the narrow southern fescue grassland and ends in the mixed grasslands. The last 80 km is carved into a deep canyon of water-carved glacial drift and sandstone bedrock.

The whole river can be canoed on Class II to III+ water, offering an exciting opportunity to experience the changing landscape up close. There is a 12 km reservoir just above the lower canyon, and ranch operations—including range cattle and fences—reach right into the water. Canoeists should treat the cattle as pylons to try their slalom skills. Of course, the river water is entirely undrinkable.

Birds in the bush

Birds and trees seem to go together, and many walkers may be surprised by the variety and number of birds in the grassland ecoregions of southernmost Alberta thanks to riverside ecodistricts.

The Atlas of Breeding Birds in Alberta divides the entire province into a grid of 6,623 squares, each measuring 10 km by 10 km. The atlas identifies the number of bird species observed in each of these squares. This information identifies the 10 squares in the province where the highest numbers of bird species were observed. Four of these 10 squares are located in the southern grasslands, in each of which were counted 160 or more species of birds.

Grasslands, however, are not simply lands covered with grass. The grasslands of southernmost Alberta are very diverse at the fine grain, as walkers traversing a straight line from the edge of a stream directly onto the prairie will quickly discover.

Such a walk would move away from the water's edge, through a fringe of water-loving sedges and rushes, into a stand of tall willow or water birch, across a flat of shrubs, through a cottonwood forest, and finally onto the prairie. Each part of the landscape represents a habitat that appeals to different species of birds. The number of breeding birds found in each part of a grassland landscape is astounding.

Furthermore, each habitat is capable of supporting and sustaining larger or smaller numbers of breeding birds, simply because some habitats contain more bird resources than do other habitats. The results of a bird survey in a single place in the grassland landscape are summarized in the table below. Quite clearly, the cottonwood forests along prairie rivers sustain the greatest diversity of bird species and the greatest number of nesting birds.

Trees at risk

Cottonwoods propagate by seeds and every spring the riverbanks, bars and shoals are covered with the cottonwood's floating white fluff. To germinate, the seeds must be covered with floodborn silt; if not, they simply bake in the sun. Mature trees need a regular feeding of flood debris to flourish and set seed.

Unfortunately, cottonwoods are the first to suffer when prairie river regimes are disturbed. Wherever there are dams on prairie rivers (and there are many dams on Alberta's prairie rivers), the downstream cottonwoods begin a gradual decline and disappearance. As wooded places shrink and disappear, the number and variety of birds depending on treed habitat also decline. The remaining patches of treed land like the one at Kimball Park become even more important as places where birds can thrive.

Breeding bird density and diversity in grasslands habitats

Habitat	Bird density (pairs/40 ha)	Breeding species
Plains	32.0	10
Rolling prairie	38.3	4
Eroding badlands	69.6	17
Natural channel	58.3	11
Irrigation channel	364.0	26
Sagebrush	255.6	10
Shrubland	549.9	32
Cottonwoods	706.8	31
Willow	294.0	9

Kimball Park

Sandstone, soft mudstone and glacial debris cut by a shallow coulee.

take over from willow. The very edge of the water is occupied by rushes and sedges, rooted in muddy soils.

The cottonwoods in Kimball Park were also early pioneers on freshly exposed gravels and sandbars and by late 1995 seedlings were sprouting up everywhere. By late summer 1996, most of the seedlings had perished, but there were still many over a metre tall. By 1998, there were fine young trees almost 2 m tall, but not many of them. If people would stop cutting them for hot dog sticks, the existing forest may be able to sustain itself off the benefits of the Great Flood of '95.

St. Mary River sandstone.

Bedrock

Directly across from the campground is a low wall of sandstone of the St. Mary River Formation, exposed in the side of a shallow coulee. Originally, the sandstone was laid down flat on the bottom of freshwater over 65 million years ago. Now, the exposed bedrock is a jumble of dark sandstone slabs broken and tilted steeply on edge when the Rockies were made.

Quite possibly, today's St. Mary River at Kimball Park follows the same channel it occupied before the Ice Age. Rivers have flowed out of the Rockies since they were created less than 60 million years ago. These first rivers carved channels in the soft disrupted bedrock. Much later, glaciers ground over the landscape and filled the ancient river valleys with stony debris. When the glaciers began to melt 18,000 years ago, the free water followed the same course as the preglacial rivers. The melting torrent scoured the old valley clean and once again filled it with water.

The exposed rockwalls of the St. Mary River were probably carved out of the Cretaceous bedrock before the Ice Age glaciers arrived. At that time, the flatlands above canyon walls would have been exposed bedrock, or bedrock covered with a thin layer of soil. The glaciers may have entirely filled the old canyon with debris, but when the ice receded new drainage channels simply occupied the old channel and scoured out the loose material. The main difference is that the flatland above the canyon is now covered with a thick layer of gravel, sand and silt left behind by the glacier.

The river shore is paved with fresh-scrubbed cobbles and pebbles. Sprinkled with river water, they gleam in the sun. None of them are granite, the calling card of the Canadian Shield far to the north and east: the continental glacier did not reach as far west as Kimball Park.

Instead, the shore rocks are local St. Mary Formation sandstone mixed with fragments of ancient red shale and argillite. Opposite the campground, the river has carved into a wall of bedrock topped with a thick layer of glacial drift. The loose material is tinted pink by the distinctive chalky red fragments pushed by glaciers and washed by rivers out of the mountains of Waterton Lakes National Park.

A remnant landscape

Kimball Park has a great deal to offer within its few hectares. In only 100 m, from standing in the middle of a dense cottonwood forest to walking the water's edge, the remembered variety of fescue grassland river bottom can be enjoyed at leisure.

Sandbar willow quickly colonized the new shore exposed in the Flood of '95.

Special Places for a Quick Visit

Woolford Provincial Park

Woolford Provincial Park lies inside the fescue grassland, just east of the boundary with the aspen parkland, and so the grassland aspect of the park is mingled with characteristics of the parkland. Being close to the mountains and at a slightly higher elevation, the middle reach of the St. Mary River receives more moisture than fescue grasslands farther east.

Most of the surrounding land is thoroughly domesticated, especially for irrigation agriculture. Here and there, however, near the edge of the park there are still a few fragments of traditional fescue grassland. The banks near the river are notoriously unstable and plows have not been brought too close. When the North-West Mounted Police established a post about 1.5 km upstream of the park, their land survey showed that the site of the park was once an island. Each year at breakup and spring flood the island was eroded and the river channel was carved anew. In 1964, a major flood drove the river channel almost 120 m east destroying park buildings and equipment. The Great Flood of 1995 did it again, sluicing over the main built-up recreation area in the park. What remains are fine groves of narrow-leaf cottonwood, western cottonwood and aspen towering over a layer of shrubs and taller flowers.

Woolford Park is a popular place to watch birds. Like prairie forests elsewhere, Woolford's groves attract a large number of nesting birds, and the wetlands near the river attract ducks, geese and shorebirds.

The park has all the amenities and is especially popular with local families wanting a safe place for swimming, fishing and strolling. Wheelchair access is limited because of the ever-changing trails.

The nearly spent forces of mountain building, St. Mary River, early spring.

Spring Glen

Like Kimball Park, Spring Glen Campground is a micro landscape that manages to capture the essence of a riverside lined with fescue grasslands. In addition to a superb campground embraced in a loop of the St. Mary River, the tiny space includes an excellent exposure of sandstone and shale bedrock sliced through a covering of glacial debris, and near-perfect examples of narrow-leaf cottonwood, western cottonwood, and most of the shrubs common in the fescue grassland, including golden currant, Bebb willow, pussy willow, rose, buckbrush, wolf willow and saskatoon.

The groves of mature trees and shrubs are groomed to garden-like perfection in a thick lawn of mowed native grasses amongst park buildings and campsites. If you ever wondered how fescue grassland plants would take to taming, this is the place to find out. Judging from the growth and vigour of the park's resident plants, they don't mind at all.

Every road, lane, trail and campsite is outlined with massive rounded boulders of polished granite and other igneous rocks. These are all erratics, carried by an Ice Age glaciation all the way from the Canadian Shield far to the north. Spring Glen is an ideal place to compare the hard and tough rocks of the far north and the soft rocks of the Interior Plains.

Directly opposite the campground is a water control dam, forcing the water of the St. Mary River into the service of irrigation agriculture. The structure itself is interesting, and shows exactly how many similar dams on prairie rivers work. The dam spans a narrow, steep-walled slot carved through the bedrock, an ideal place for efficient dam building.

Narrow-leaf cottonwood and erratics transported by glaciers from the far north line the park's roads.

From the broad top of the dam, there is a grand view of river-polished sandstone, shale and coal beds laid down in late Cretaceous times. In some places the beds lie perfectly flat and level, and in others the beds are crushed, broken and tilted near-vertical. This is a place where the forces of building the Rocky Mountains finally dwindled to nothing.

In a few hours, walkers in a hurry can explore a prairie river, a floodplain forest, a fringe of grassland, exemplary geology and a major human impact on the Fescue Grass Ecoregion.

Most of the campground trails and the surrounding roadways should be wheelchair accessible, depending on rain. If the trails are wet, they can be tricky even on foot.

Aspen Parkland

A remnant of the Aspen Parkland Ecoregion.

6

Aspen Parkland Ecoregion

The Aspen Parkland Ecoregion is the smallest, least represented ecoregion in southernmost Alberta. Most of the aspen parkland is located in central and northern Alberta. In the south, there are only a few isolated pockets of aspen parkland intermingled with montane foothills and crowded between mountains to the west and grassland to the east.

Maps, maps, maps

Some biogeographers have recently chosen simply to include these pockets of southernmost aspen parkland as part of the dominant landscape in which they occur—the eastern remnants are mapped as part of the fescue grasslands and those to the west as part of the montane foothills.

Others have mapped the southern aspen parkland as a separate and distinct landscape. The apparent differences of scientific opinion are the result of different approaches the geographers took to the task of classifying Alberta's landscape. The differences are also the result of the purpose for which the maps were created.

Maps and mandate

The earliest biogeographic map, drawn in 1981, was intended for use by Alberta Energy and Natural Resources. At that time, the province's resources were administered by one government ministry, and the ministry needed a broad map for its equally broad mandate. The goal was integrated planning and management of a spectrum of natural resources. In this scheme, landscape has a complex definition intended to satisfy scientists working in numerous fields and disciplines. This especially complex map provides so much detail that the aspen parkland is clearly distinguished from its surroundings.

By 1992, the Ministry of Energy and Natural Resources had been organized into separate departments including Alberta Forestry, Lands and Wildlife. The new department's mandate was narrower and maps were more closely tailored to the department's narrower mandate. With the reduction of complexity, the southern aspen parkland disappeared from the map.

123

Aspen Parkland

In 1994, Alberta Forestry, Lands and Wildlife was merged with Alberta Recreation and Parks in the Department of Environmental Protection, now in charge of almost everything of interest to walkers and many other users of lands and resources. The 1994 map again takes more things into account than the climate-based 1992 map and aspen parklands can be distinguished from foothills and grasslands, and once again appears on the map.

Close-up

The close-up perspective of the walker settles the issue. When confronted by a landscape filled with aspen and few other trees, the differences between parklands, foothills and grasslands are obvious. Walkers can see and experience the differences for themselves.

Because the distinctive nature of the aspen parkland is obvious close up, the 1992 and 1994 maps are merged in this book to show walkers where there are Special Places set in the remnant Aspen Parkland Ecoregion in southernmost Alberta.

Aspen parklands

In the central part of the province where most of the aspen parkland is found, deciduous trees, especially aspen, form an almost continuous cover.

In the south, however, aspen forms only three per cent to 15 per cent of the ground cover, with the rest of the space taken up by grasslands and shrublands. The southern parklands are at a higher elevation and on steeper and more rugged hills than the parklands in central Alberta. Neither is the southern parkland as moist as the parkland nearer Calgary and Edmonton. The aspen parkland in southern Alberta is typically sparser and harsher than parkland farther north.

Fescue meadow, Maskinonge Lake, aspen forest, subalpine forest and Sofa Mountain. Waterton Lakes National Park, summer.

In the south, the much reduced Aspen Parkland Ecoregion is a transitional zone between the Fescue Grass Ecoregion to the northeast and the Montane Ecoregion to the northwest, and shares the characteristics of the two larger, dominant ecoregions. If a particular patch of parkland is embedded in a fescue grassland context, it will share the climatic features of the surrounding grassland, and if it is in the montane foothills, it will share that ecoregion's climate.

Southern aspen parklands

Southern aspen parklands usually occupy some of the richest soils in southern Alberta—deep black Chernozems. These soils are capable of supporting healthy growths of trees, shrubs and grasses differing in proportions depending on the exact mix of all other important ecological factors.

In the south, groves of aspen clones are often widely separated by expanses of grassland. The aspen crowd into places where moisture is trapped and available during the aspen's critical spring growing season—in catchment depressions, on the north-facing slopes of hills, and near seepages and streams.

The associated grasslands are typically fescue grasslands and may include June grass and needle-and-thread grass. The most common flowers include three-flowered avens, sticky geranium, western Canada violet and northern bedstraw.

In more rolling landscapes where there are plenty of places to trap snow, there may be dense growths of shrubs, especially saskatoon, prickly rose, buckbrush, snowberry and silverberry or wolf willow. In even wetter places where soils are saturated most of the year, Chernozems give way to muddier soils, and aspen, shrubs and grasses yield to willow and sedges.

Because parklands occupy rich, well-watered and sheltered soils, the Aspen Parkland Ecoregion is home to many species of plants and animals including most species found in the adjacent grasslands to the east and foothills to the west.

The Aspen Parkland Ecoregion

Area: 52,148 sq. km or 7.9% of the province.

Topography: Undulating to rolling hills.

Elevation: 1000 - 1300 m

Climate: In the southern extreme range of the Aspen Parkland Ecoregion, climate is very similar and perhaps identical to the climate of the surrounding foothills and grasslands.

Soils: Rich, deep black Chernozems.

Humans: Because the soils are so rich, most of the aspen parkland has been cleared and cultivated: Less than five per cent of the entire parkland of Alberta is still in pristine condition. Mere remnants remain wherever roads have been unable to reach, including the few small remnants found in the south.

9 Wishbone Trail

Mode: foot, bicycle, horse, ski
Rating: moderate
Time: 6 hours
Distance: 16 km
Elevation change: 60 m
Map: 82 H/4 Waterton Lakes

The Wishbone Trail, close to the gate of Waterton Lakes National Park, winds through the most extensive spread of aspen parkland in the entire region. It is one of the few places in southernmost Alberta that is completely immersed in aspen. There are many other places where groves, even large groves of aspen may be found, but few species of trees other than aspen are found along the Wishbone Trail.

The experience is completely unlike travel in the grasslands, with their endless skies and far horizons. Even on a hot summer day, the tunnel-like trails are cool and shaded in contrast to the sun-seared grasslands only a few kilometres away to the east.

The trail is ideal for bicycle and foot travel, and it is one of the few trails in Waterton Lakes National Park where horses are allowed. In winter, the trail is best skied in lightweight gear.

There is a sign at the trailhead, but it is tucked away amongst the aspen and hard to spot. On Highway 6 south of Highway 5, the best landmark is the heavy steel winter gate. It is about 350 metres south of the turn-off onto Highway 6. The trailhead is on the west side of the highway and a large pull-off is on the east. Park here to unload packs, bicycles and horses.

Aspen parkland fills the flat between lake and wetlands and the subalpine mountains.

Getting there

Waterton Lakes National Park is an international landmark and the easiest Special Place to find anywhere in southernmost Alberta. There are huge signs everywhere that point the way. The description of the Goat Lake and Avion Ridge route, in Chapter 8 on the Subalpine Ecoregion, gives complete directions to the park.

The trailhead is south on Highway 6, immediately east of the park gate. This is the highway leading to the Chief Mountain border crossing and Montana.

Camping

There is first-rate camping in the national park. However, the trailhead is at the eastern edge of the park and a more easterly campground would make a better base.

The fine Belly River Campground on Highway 6 near the border crossing is also a Parks Canada campground. It has fewer facilities than the campgrounds near the town, but it has everything needed for a comfortable stay.

There are private campgrounds a few kilometres east of the park gates, offering good basic facilities in splendid parkland settings. The Crooked Creek Campground, just to the east of the park on Highway 5, is managed by the Waterton Natural History Association. These are the nearby campgrounds, and there are plenty of others a few kilometres away in every direction.

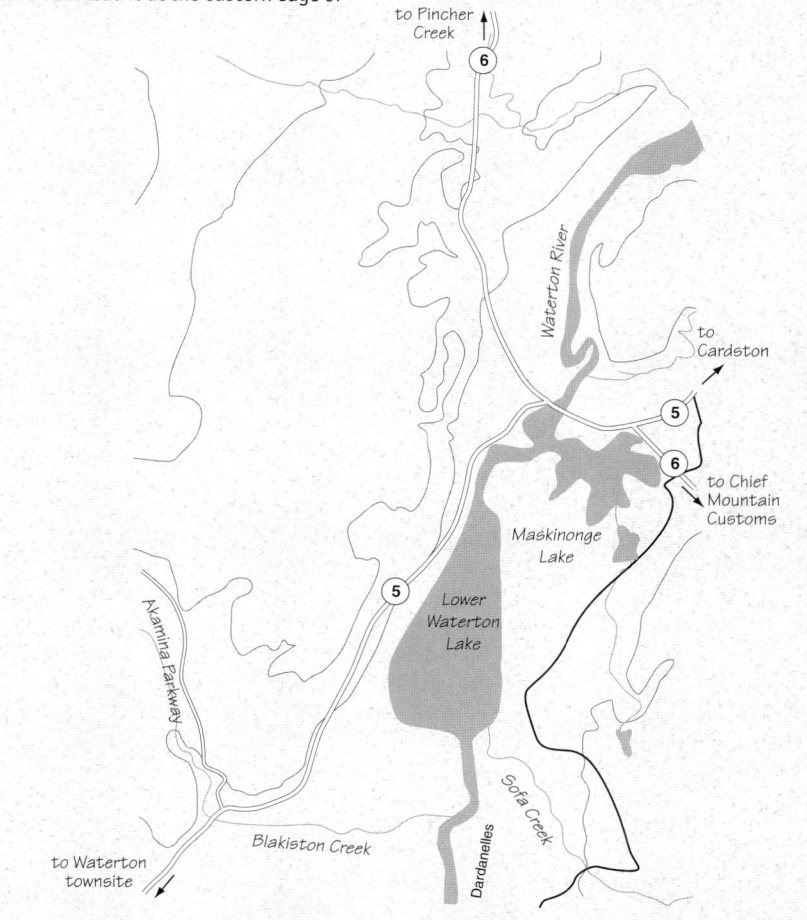

Wishbone Trail

Snow collects under the aspen, assuring a good start on spring's growth.

The first few kilometres

The landscape slopes gently toward the south and west, offering a low impact departure from the trailhead. On bicycle, the trail plunges smoothly into a dense pack of aspen trees along an old double-track, offering plenty of elbow room and a flat surface, but no view of what lies ahead.

Small aspen conceal everything and reveal nothing. They are so close together they form a solid wall only a few metres away from the trail, cutting off visibility and readiness. Walking in the aspen parkland is not at all like in the mountains or grasslands.

The aspen are 3 or 4 metres high and, after a cool moist summer, sport a crown of green tongues speaking for the wind. The undergrowth beneath the trees forms an impenetrable jungle of grasses, shrubs and flowering plants. The plants mostly look familiar from the grasslands and montane Special Places, but these ones are huge. Timothy, brome and fireweed grow to eye level, and cow parsnip towers above the trail. Saskatoon shrubs reach the status of small trees, with their thin branches bowed under the weight of ripe fruit.

The first part of the trail passes through small grassy meadows and the difference in humidity under the shady trees and in the sunny meadows is striking. The moist air and soil account for the luxuriant growth in the aspen parkland.

The trail soon reaches a larger meadow and descends west and south toward a pond and bog emptying into Maskinonge Lake. The pond is heavily fringed with black cottonwood, willow, and tall rushes and sedges. The margin of the pond is alive with insects and small birds.

After the first few kilometres, the trail reverts to a single track carved into the soil by horses and kept clear by all the animals in the forest. The track is barely wide enough to accommodate a bicycle without catching a pedal. Between the narrowness of the trail, protruding rocks and roots, and many piles of bear droppings, the ride will challenge most cyclists to keep their wheels under them.

The next few kilometres

The foot trail then crosses a plank bridge over a small stream. By midsummer, the stream is very low. Water is trapped in a series of quiet pools filled with insect larvae and small fish and the fish have attracted a resident great blue heron. The pool beneath the bridge is fringed with hair grasses that favour wetter and muddier soils.

Farther south, the trail passes in and out of large aspen groves separated by broader meadows. Some of these meadows on south-facing hills are more typical of drier grasslands to the east. Few plants stand more than knee-high, and include a mix of fescue grasses, oat grasses, yarrow, bergamot, bearberry, wild roses, shrubby cinquefoil, bluebell, brown-eyed Susan, sticky geranium and aster. In the drier meadows, the saskatoon bushes are less than half a metre tall.

Sofa Creek

The trail soon reaches Sofa Creek. In the past, strategic boulders offered a dry-footed crossing, but the floods of 1995 ripped a new channel and now the creek must be splashed across. The water is only ankle deep in the summer, but expect to get wet feet.

The creek is fringed with a few black cottonwood and wolf willow growing on a film of soil covering a bed of waterworn boulders, gravel and silt. The trail picks up on the south side of the creek and heads downward toward the Dardenelles, the short section of the Waterton River connecting the Middle and Lower Waterton lakes.

Sofa Creek is perched on a huge delta formed by debris washing out of the mountains to the south and deposited on the bottom of the Waterton lakes. A

Sofa Creek's new bed across the erosion delta and past a surviving cottonwood.

Aspen

Aspen—*Populus tremuloides*, also called trembling aspen, quaking aspen, aspen poplar and white poplar—is the most common deciduous tree in southernmost Alberta. Each aspen grove seems to keep its own annual schedule. In spring, an entire grove may become green at exactly the same time, and in autumn all the trees in a grove may turn golden at the same time. However, other groves nearby may leaf out and turn weeks earlier or later. This is because aspen most frequently propagate along their roots rather than by seed. All the trees in an isolated grove may be clones of a single original root. All would have inherited the exact same genetic response to changing seasons.

A clone grove of aspen in the Uintah Mountains of Utah may be the largest, heaviest organism in the world. The grove includes 47,000 individual trees weighing a total of six million kilograms, all descended from a single ancestral tree. Because they propagate by cloning, aspen groves are effectively immortal so long as even an individual survives catastrophe. Some groves in the American west may be over one million years old. They would have survived the Pleistocene glaciation and spread north behind the retreating ice.

Aspen clone grove near the margin of the subalpine forest.

Useful aspen

Aspen, although classed as a hardwood, actually has quite soft wood and was widely used by aboriginal people and early settlers to make all kinds of carved wares, including paddles, toys, bowls, furniture, scoops, cups and saddle trees. Just as important were the aspen's potent medicinal properties. Wherever aspen grew in the Americas, aboriginal people used the wood, leaves, bark and roots in remedies for a wide spectrum of diseases and injuries in humans, horses and dogs. Amongst many aboriginal peoples today, aspen is still an important source of raw materials for traditional medicines and crafts.

Aspen in the market

Throughout the last century or so, the market treated aspen like a weed, occupying space and consuming nutrients better used by plants with money value. They are easily uprooted, piled and burned, and by the early 1900s most of the southern Aspen Parkland was under the plow.

Until the last third of the 20th century, most pulp and paper was made from softwood fibre, but then a way was discovered to make paper from hardwood fibre, especially aspen. By the last part of the 20th century, Alberta's northern Aspen Parkland Ecoregion was assigned to pulp and paper interests, mostly Japanese.

Aspen will not suffer complete oblivion at the hands of progress. They are too widespread, prolific and too adaptable for progress to destroy them all.

Waterton River and the Dardanelles.

similar delta has built up at the mouth of Blakiston Creek and the two deltas meet in the middle. The Waterton River has kept a channel open, but eventually, the lower lakes will fill with mountain debris. In the meantime, the delta offers cyclists a long and easy glide across dry meadows all the way to the river's edge. A side trail to the Dardenelles leads to the point where horses are waded or swum across the river on their way to Sofa Mountain. The riverside crossing is dense with black cottonwood groves, sandbar willow, nodding onion and tall rushes.

The delta is carved over with old and new channels. The new channels are clean of any soil, revealing a jumble of pastel boulders typical of the mountains in the park. There are no granite rocks, indicating that continental glaciers of the Ice Age did not reach here.

Last few kilometres

The trail moves off the grassy Sofa Creek delta and again drops into the dense forest of aspen. If anything, the undergrowth is even more luxuriant. Gradually, white spruce trees appear to mark the end of the Aspen Parkland Ecoregion. In a little more than another kilometre, the trail forks and the east branch heads toward Vimy Ridge. The west branch of the forest trail carries on toward the Wishbone Campground perched on the shore of Middle Waterton Lake. The westerly trail continues through the last of the aspen parkland before merging with spruce forests close to the Bosporus, the narrows between Upper and Middle Waterton lakes. Both trails are worth exploring, but if your goal is to see and experience the aspen parkland, the fork in the trail is a good place to start back for the trailhead.

Here you can take a rest and contemplate the faster downhill return trip. The waiting aspen groves are liberally mixed with saskatoon bushes and by July the shrubs are hanging with fruit. The trail is also liberally dotted with mounds of bear droppings consisting almost entirely of saskatoon berry pulp. Walkers are all-too-obviously in somebody else's pantry. The overripe fruit attracts wasps who don't take kindly to cyclists whipping through the berry-laden branches. Between the potential threat from bears and the painfully real threat from wasps, the otherwise mild Wishbone Trail achieves hard travel status.

10 Trout Creek Ridge North

Mode: foot, horse, bicycle
Rating: moderate
Time: 4 - 6 hours
Distance: 11 km
Elevation change: 400 m
Map: 82 J/1 Langford Creek

Trout Creek occupies the valley of a small watershed etched in the eastern flank of the Porcupine Hills. There are several routes to and through the creek's compact valley, ascending hills along old roads through groves of aspen and willow and dense forests of spruce, pine and fir. The view from the highest points on the hilly ridges takes in the entire Front Ranges of the Rockies from Chief Mountain in the south to Mount Head in the north.

Trout Creek flows into Willow Creek, and Willow Creek flows into the Oldman River. Willow Creek is the main stream draining the east side of the Porcupine Hills and Trout Creek is a delightful example of streams connecting the eastern Porcupine Hills to the Oldman River.

The clear, spring-fed headwaters of Trout Creek are high up the end of a coulee near the hillcrest in a heavy forest of tall spruce, pine and fir. The middle part of Trout Creek flows across a broad floodplain dense with willow and aspen leaving little room for small, lush meadows of fescue grassland. In less than 15 km the creek leaves the Porcupine Hills and enters the much drier mixed grassland on the east side of the hills. There it turns from a rushing mountain brook into a narrow muddy stream wandering more-or-less downward and to the east. The entire course of Trout Creek is traced with a fringe of willow, all the way to its mouth.

The summit of Trout Creek Ridge looking across the aspen foothills, montane foothills and mountains to the west.

Trout Creek Ridge

Near its mouth on Willow Creek, Trout Creek is a tiny wandering prairie stream.

The north trail

Once away from the highway and across the fence into the forest reserve, there are lots of alternatives for ad hoc wandering and exploring. One of the best routes follows an old road to a low pass between the Ward Creek watershed and the Trout Creek watershed. Ward Creek flows west and Trout Creek flows southeast. The waters in both streams eventually reach the Oldman River and from there Hudson Bay, unless they are lost to water management somewhere along the way.

From the pass, the road branches with the left branch heading eastward and upward onto the crest of Trout Creek Ridge. The right branch leads southward and downward to the headwaters of Trout Creek. The big view is found at the summit of the ridge, but the trail down Trout Creek is also a delight.

To the fork in the road

For both destinations, the trail begins at the side of Highway 22 and follows an old road into the meadow on the other side of the fence. There is a gate, and all gates should be left exactly as they are found. The road passes through a small patch of stunted aspen and into a fescue meadow before curving slightly to avoid the edge of Ward Creek. Heading uphill, the creek is hidden beneath the spreading branches of very large white spruce and a tangle of willow and other shrubs.

The creek is small, but even in winter it keeps up a steady flow a bare metre wide and 10 cm deep, with many small patches of open water. The lower section just north of the highway is crowded closely with tall, old white spruce and big willows approaching tree status. The muddy soils in the gloom of the streamside grove barely support mosses and spindly green plants.

Getting there

Trout Creek is approached from two directions, north and south, toward trailheads over 9 km apart, as the crow flies. Northern access leads directly into high country and a big view. Southern access ascends the valley toward the headwaters. Both lead into the Bow-Crow Forest, part of Alberta's great public lands. The two approaches lead to very different places, and they might be treated as separate adventures.

Because the north and south approaches lead to quite different adventures, they are treated separately in the access and trail descriptions.

The north approach

The northern trailhead leads to the crest of the Porcupine Hills and from there either along a high ridge above Trout Creek or downward toward the creek's headwaters. Finding the trailhead is a little tricky.

Highway 533 from Nanton intersects with Highway 22 opposite the entrance to Chain Lakes Provincial Park. In the 1900s, this area was home to a herd of Przewalski's horses, released there by the Calgary Zoo as part of their herd management program. This is probably better ancient horse habitat than they had in their Eurasian homelands thousands of years ago. Nevertheless, the Zoo posted prominent signs pointing out to hunters the differences between elk and ancient horses.

The trailhead is 13.3 km south on Highway 22, measured from the park gate. At that point, tiny Ward Creek passes near the highway before turning south and through a culvert under Highway 22. There is good parking on a widening in the paved shoulder leading to a country road passing through a stout barbed-wire fence.

The fence straddles a gas pipeline and the corners of the fence and gate are painted red and white. Just beyond the fence is a steel stake with a plaque showing the exact location of the buried pipe. There are no other painted fence posts in the immediate vicinity of the trailhead.

Camping

There is excellent, year-round camping at Chain Lakes Provincial Park with all the amenities for a first-class RV home. The Chain Lakes were once a string of small spring-fed ponds and wetlands connected by a creek running along the bottom of a shallow valley. The valley was heavily used by bison, and settlers later turned the well-watered grassland into a hayland. In 1939, a fire burned away the grasslands and the valley was quickly invaded by the willow and aspen that surround the lake today.

In 1967, dams were built on the north and south ends of the string of springs and ponds. The result is a single reservoir almost 13 km long, half a kilometre wide and 10 m deep. The chain of lakes are gone and now live only in the park name. The lake was stocked with trout in 1970 and the park is popular year-round with ice and boat fishers.

In all seasons, Chain Lakes Park is crowded with birds, each in their preferred wetland, shrubland and grassland habitat. An evening of strolling or cycling is a good introduction to many of the shrubs and flowers common in the aspen foothills.

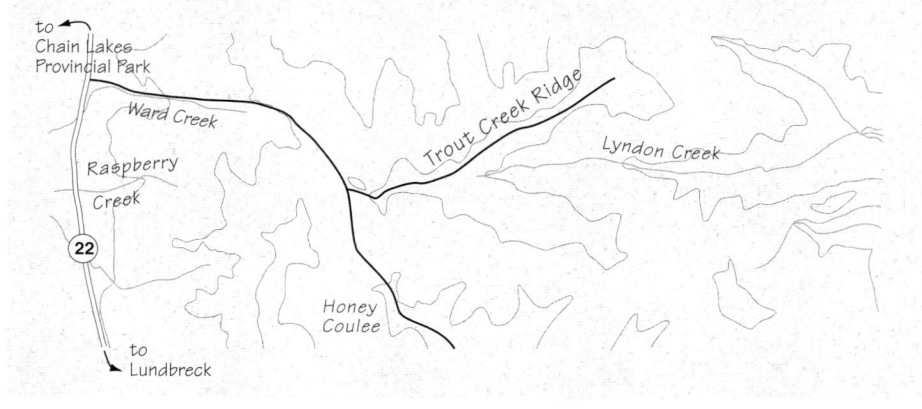

Near the ridge top stunted aspen give way to white and Engelmann spruce.

A few metres away from the water, however, and all spruce trees and shrubs disappear, replaced by a clone grove of identical aspen. Beyond the aspen the south-facing hills are covered with grassland. The north-facing hills are covered with aspen and spruce.

The fescue meadows are left behind as the trail begins the climb toward the ridge. The lower section of the road is lined with stands of huge Engelmann spruce, towering over a forest of immature spruce, fir and aspen. Though scarred, these majestic specimens escaped generations of earlier fires that repeatedly levelled the Porcupine Hills forests. They must be amongst the largest and oldest trees in the hills.

Near the top of the ridge, road-builders cut into the hillside, revealing a thin layer of dark Chernozem soils covering a sandy parent material littered with blocks and chunks of sandstone. Even higher up are patches of exposed sandstone bedrock. These surface exposures are tormented by spruce and fir sending roots between the sandstone beds and prying them apart.

The trail crosses a south-facing hillside covered with spruce and fir sprinkled with large patches of aspen right to the top of the ridge. The north-facing slope on the other side of the creek valley is almost pure spruce, reflecting cooler and moister conditions away from the direct force of the sun and wind.

The road reaches the summit through a last patch of stunted aspen and curves onto a pad of exposed sandstone barely covered with a thin mat of soil and grasses. The last trees at the crest of the ridge are limber pine, widely spaced to allow a great view to the west.

Here, the road divides. The upward branch passes through a thick grove of aspen, a last belt of mature spruce and fir, and then wanders along the length of the ridge. The lower branch descends through the forest along the headwaters of Trout Creek.

Trout Creek Ridge

The turn to the left rises from the pass into a fringe of aspen and a crown of pine on the crest of the ridge. From there, the clear trail wanders between the ridge crests. Here and there, in saddles and on the highest crests the forests of pine, spruce, aspen and willow give way to open meadows and a great view.

To the south and east, classic montane landscapes merge into the aspen parkland. To the west, the view takes in the north ends of the Livingstone Range and Whaleback Ridge, and the lake beyond South Twin Creek is in sight. To the east, the view is across grassy slopes melting into the vast, distant grassland.

Willow

Willows best express the differences between the southern montane foothills and more northerly parkland foothills. In the south, slightly taller grasses and a few more flowers mark any pocket where there is a little shelter from wind and sun, and where a little moisture might collect. In the north, those same places are filled with willow and other small shrubs. As soon as willow can find a small advantage in the landscape, they immediately move in, and the thick clumps of willow show how much moister the northern hills are than the southern hills.

There are more than 30 species of *Salix* or willow in the prairies, and all grow as shrubs or small, gnarled trees. All willows are very nutritious. They contain more protein and phosphorus than grass, and less crude fibre. Some kinds of livestock and wild herbivores find willow very palatable. Moose, for example, are browsers, that is they make their living eating shrubs and trees and in winter eat almost nothing but woody plants. Willows, with their slender, easily-digested branches, thick and juicy bark, and lush foliage are preferred moose food. As a bonus, most willows are in easy reach for a moose so little energy is spent getting a meal. Of all Alberta's wild ungulates—white-tailed deer, mule deer, caribou, elk, moose, pronghorn, mountain goat, bighorn sheep and bison—only bison do not eat willow.

Humans also find many ways to use willow. Aboriginal people used willow bark to make nets, twine, saddle blankets and dyes. Dried, shredded willow bark was an ingredient in kinnikinnick, a ceremonial smoking mixture. Thin branches went into baskets, pipe stems, arrow shafts, flutes, whistles, eating implements and backrests. Thicker branches were used to make lodge supports, tipi pegs and snowshoe frames. The largest branches were used like lumber wherever a tough, flexible wood was needed.

The sap was made into glue and waterproofing for vessels. The bark is rich in tannin, used for tanning hides into a subtle yellow colour. People also ate young willow buds, which are 10 times higher in vitamin C than an equal weight of oranges. Willow root was mixed with fat and used to treat scalp sores and dandruff. A tea of boiled bark was administered for fevers, rheumatism, arthritis, headaches and pain relief.

Almost everywhere, people discovered that willow contained salicin. When eaten, salicin becomes salicylic acid, the active ingredient in aspirin. Because salicylic acid was first isolated from willow, it shares willow's Latin name.

For many species of animals, including humans, willow are a welcome feature of the Aspen Parkland Ecoregion.

Willow mark the wet places in the north Porcupine Hills.

Trout Creek Ridge

At the summit, pine and the Livingstone Range.

With early summer, balsamroot.

Trout Creek headwaters

The turn to the right leads downhill through Honey Coulee to the tiny, spring-fed headwaters of Trout Creek. The first part of the trail is through a thick forest of alternating spruce and aspen groves. In about 4 km, Honey Coulee levels out a little and the bottom near the creek is covered with fescue meadows.

The view is from within a bowl of parklands foothills, with flowing water on the one side and on the other the wave of grassy summits marking Trout Creek Ridge. Protected from the wind, and enjoying plentiful water, upper Trout Creek abounds in wildflowers and signs of deer, moose, coyote and hare.

11 Trout Creek Ridge South

Mode: foot, horse, bicycle
Rating: moderate
Time: 4 - 7 hours
Distance: 16 km
Elevation change: 185 m
Map: 82 J/1 Langford Creek

Again, there are alternative routes from the meadow at the end of East Trout Creek Road. One alternative is a good logging road heading northeast and upward toward a ridge connecting with Trout Creek Ridge. Another road heads northwest on the floodplain bordering Trout Creek with occasional rises over valley spurs. Both are excellent on foot, bicycle, snowshoe, ski and horse.

Across the montane landscape, the summit view takes in Chief Mountain far to the south in Montana.

The high ridge

From the fescue meadow the road is carved into the glacial and erosion debris burying the rising valley walls. At one point the road intersects a flat-lying bed of Porcupine Hills Sandstone, laid down less than 60 million years ago and still quite soft.

Just beyond the exposed late Cretaceous bedrock the road enters a towering forest. The view back along the road toward the southeast lavishly displays parkland foothills anatomy—stream side, wetland, shrubland, grassland, woodland and rocky summit.

Any hillside in sight leading from water's edge to exposed rock can display at least 30 species of flowers at a time. Each species is finely tuned to certain conditions, and the changing trail is decorated with changing regimes of flowers. Towering cow parsnip grow with their roots in wet

Getting there

Highway 520 crosses the middle section of the Porcupine Hills between Highway 22 in the west and Claresholm in the east. A little over 2 km east of the turn off of Highway 22 and onto 520 the good gravel road reaches the height of the hills and begins a hairpin descent toward the eastern grasslands. At the height there is a large sign pointing the way to East Trout Creek Road. This follows the crest of the Porcupine Hills north for about 3 km before descending toward the middle part of Trout Creek.

Just before the road descends toward the creek, the pine and fir forest thins into a dry, windswept and exposed meadow. The horizon is clear of trees, revealing a stupefying view of the foothills and Eastern Slopes all the way from Plateau Mountain in the north to Chief Mountain and Montana in the south, with Mount Gass above the Oldman River's headwaters, Whaleback Ridge, Livingstone Gap, Thunder Mountain, the approach to Crowsnest Pass and summits of Waterton Lakes National Park in between. At least six map sheets are needed to identify the landmark Special Places in sight, including the entire range of the Montane Ecoregion in southernmost Alberta.

East of the clearing there are a few old clearcuts grown up with willow, rose, saskatoon and small aspen offering a great view of the entire valley of Trout Creek almost to its mouth. Looking east, the transitions from aspen parkland foothills through fescue grasslands and then mixed grasslands are easy to sort out.

In 13 km the road ends in a grassy meadow lining Trout Creek, and from that point there are several alternative walking routes.

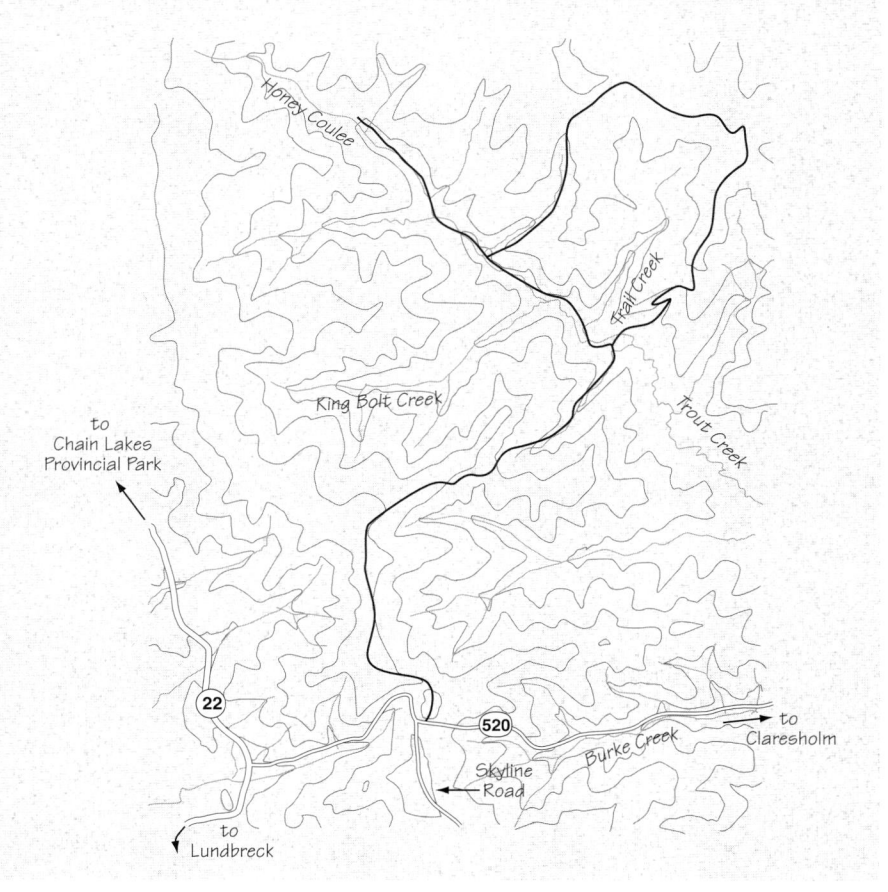

Eroded steps in the valley walls show the passage of successive Ice Age glaciers.

soil, followed by geranium in slightly dried soils, then golden bean in the moister part of the meadow and balsamroot and locoweed in the drier parts. The grassland flowers disappear at the edge of woodlands, replaced with clematis, Jacob's ladder and alpine forget-me-not.

The road leads higher until it reaches the crest of a ridge heading northwest and follows the summit to a very rough road descending a coulee toward Trout Creek. The ridge crest is cloaked in splendid forest, including some mighty Engelmann spruce and Douglas fir. Most of these ancient trees are scarred survivors of the fires that swept the hills early in the 20th century and are hundreds of years old.

The trail winds quickly down the side of the coulee through a thick fir and pine forest into a band of aspen, then connects with the road along Trout Creek. The trailhead is to the left, downhill all the way.

The low valley

From the meadow at the end of the East Trout Creek Road, another rough road heads to the northwest along the course of the creek all the way to the junction with the Trout Creek Ridge Road, about 10 km up the trail.

The first part of the valley trail crosses a lush fescue meadow covering the floodplain above Trout Creek. Groves of aspen, willow and flowering shrubs dot the meadow. The meadow is only a narrow strip on either side of the creek and the rising east and west sides of the valley are covered with shrubs and trees. East- and north-facing slopes support thick stands of aspen, spruce, fir and pine. On south- and west-facing slopes the dry grasslands lap much higher up the hills and even at higher elevations trees and shrubs are sparse.

The thinly-treed slopes expose the ribs of the Porcupine Hills. The valley walls are not in a single sweeping arc. Rather, they step downward from a series of cliffs cut into flat bedrock. The cliffs were cut by Ice Age glaciers and are buried and softened under a burden of glacial debris, giving the valley a profile like a smeared layer cake.

Here and there the trail swings through groves of aspen trees and approaches the creek. The creek is filled with clear water flowing over a bed of sandstone cobbles. In one or two hidden places the creek has carved a deeper pool, ideal for soaking trail-worn muscles.

The south-facing slopes ascend a grassland sprinkled with flowers from earliest spring until the onslaught of summer. Above lies a sparse forest of aspen and willow and above that a thicker forest of pine and fir. The ridges flanking Trout Creek are not as tall as those on the northern route, and they are completely covered with trees.

The upper parts of the hills are great for an overview of the Trout Creek valley and as a chance to see and experience the transition between grassland and woodland. The best thrills, though, are along the valley floor. The floor has water, lush grazing and browsing, good cover and protection, and escape routes. Many birds and animals appreciate the benefits of lowland life.

The road continues upward along narrowing lanes through groves of trees and shrubs until it reaches higher elevations and unbroken forests. The forested trail extends 3 km to the headwaters and the north approach to Trout Creek Ridge.

Trout Creek in winter

Trout Creek is in the throat of chinook winds and foothills dessication. From time to time the valley is covered with snow, and winter conditions are superb for skis and snowshoes until the next chinook blasts through.

Then, the snow will sublimate and collapse into granules, glaze over with an icy crust, then disappear altogether. If you want to use your winter toys, then use them as soon after a major snowfall as possible.

On the other hand, a thin, hard surface of snow is ideal for cleated snowshoes and snow hiking. The entire region is open to a few well-equipped humans and a lot of animals looking for a tranquil midwinter refuge.

White spruce prosper near the source of spring-fed Trout Creek.

Special Places

Special Places for a Quick Visit

Police Outpost Lake

Police Outpost Lake is as far west as the North-West Mounted Police penetrated. In 1891, four officers were sent to establish a post. This remote place on the border was too isolated for most of the men and too expensive to maintain. It was closed in 1899, reopened with one officer in 1902, but the buildings were in such bad shape he boarded with one of the few settlers in the region. The force had a hard time recruiting officers for this isolated posting, and it was closed again in 1909. In 1915 and 1916, two officers used the site as a camping place on their rides along the border looking for enemy aliens and deserters. There are no surviving remains of the Police Outpost.

The wetland is ideal habitat for water-loving plants and birds.

The wetland lies in a depression below the cloud-covered summit of Chief Mountain.

Special Places

The dovetailed corner of an old cabin rests on a block of argillite carried here by mountain glaciers.

Located on the transition between grassland and parkland, Police Outpost Provincial Park preserves a compact remnant of the Aspen Parkland Ecoregion. The lake is neatly bisected with grasslands to the east and parkland to the west. Most trees are aspen, but there are a few white spruce and western cottonwood.

The landscape is fairly flat, except near the southeast corner of the park. The groves of aspen fold over a thrust fault that presents a face of exposed late Cretaceous sandstone and shale. Everywhere else, the rock is covered with a thick layer of glacial debris and a thin layer of dark soil.

The lake is only 3 or 4 m deep, but fed with cold spring water making ideal conditions for rainbow trout. Over 50 species of birds have been seen in the park, from savannah sparrow on the grasslands east of the lake, pileated woodpeckers in the woods, and grebes and ducks in the bulrushes growing below the aspen on the west end. There are at least 240 species of vascular plants including several rare or unusual species. In spring blue camas, unique in southwestern Alberta, tints the fresh grass. The grass attracts deer and moose, with white-tailed deer encountered in the aspen forest.

Immediately to the west of the park is the Outpost Wetlands Natural Area, a system of ponds, wetlands and waterways near the head of Boundary Creek. There are crude trails through ideal habitat for waterbirds, including cinnamon teal, sandhill crane, great blue heron, and many ducks and shorebirds. Muskrat, mink, Columbian ground squirrel and even moose are fairly common.

The park is not designed for wheelchairs, but parts of it have fairly wide, level and firm trails.

7

Montane Ecoregion

The Montane Ecoregion is synonymous with the foothills of southernmost Alberta. Viewed from the lofty and rugged Rocky Mountains, the foothills are seductively rounded and lightly clothed. From the grasslands, the foothills are daunting and mysterious under a cloak of great trees. Foothills are transitional landscapes between prairies and mountains. They share the characteristics of both, and along with strong local elements create an entirely singular landscape.

Except for a few islands of aspen parkland, the whole of southern Alberta's foothills are parts of the Montane Ecoregion. Much of this region is part of Alberta's system of forest reserves, generally accessible to the public. The remainder is included in the province's system of lease lands.

The fate of lease lands is undecided. In late 1998, the government of Alberta completed a review of public lands and recommended that leaseholders be allowed to refuse public entry if leaseholders feel it is necessary to protect their interests in the land. By early 1999, no new regulations were in place, but it seems likely public use rights will be diminished in favour of the government's staunchest rural supporters.

The look and feel of the Montane Ecoregion: grass and conifers on rocky ridges.

Scattered landscapes

Islands of montane hills are separated by the sea of grass penetrating from the east and by mountain slopes reaching from the west. Unlike the grasslands ecoregions that exist as connected landscapes—huge areas of unbroken plains and prairies—the montane landscape is divided into bits and pieces.

The Montane Ecoregion is separated by prairie and mountain into four distinct ecodistricts. They are each different even though they share characteristics that are common throughout the entire Montane Ecoregion.

The Cypress Hills form a montane ecodistrict of their own. This landscape is something of an anomaly. The kind of landscape cloaking the Cypress Hills is usually seen against a background of mountains, but the hills are far to the east straddling the Saskatchewan boundary in the middle of the Dry Mixed Grass Ecoregion.

Similarly, the Porcupine Hills form another montane ecodistrict and also have a unique natural history. The hills are cloaked in typical montane plants, but they are not true foothills. Unlike the other foothills, the Porcupine Hills were not formed by the forces of mountain building and glaciation. Rather, the hills are the remnant of a long-past era when the floor of the Cretaceous sea stood much higher than the land does today. Mountain building first crumbled and tilted most of the soft western sandstone bedrock, then glaciers ground away many metres of rock. Neither the Porcupine Hills nor the Cypress Hills participated in this cataclysmic history.

The largest montane ecodistrict includes the hill country west of the Porcupine Hills. This is true foothills country, extending from Chain Lakes in the north to the Crowsnest Highway in the south and includes the Whaleback Ridge district, the south end of the Livingstone Range, Lundbreck Falls, and the middle parts of the Belly and St. Mary rivers, close to the Montana border.

The fourth montane ecodistrict lies south of Highway 3 and west of the Belly and St. Mary rivers, in the valleys of the Castle and Carbondale rivers, and below the northern flank of Chief Mountain in Montana.

There are Special Places described for each of the montane ecodistricts.

A family of sandstones

The montane foothills are underlain with soft freshwater sandstones created between 60 and 80 million years ago. The sandstones were laid in flat beds separated by thin layers of shale. The soft pastel bedrock is exposed in many places, especially along riverbanks and other erosion channels. Most bridges in the Montane Ecoregion were built at places where there is exposed bedrock, the ideal foundation for a bridge. Bridges are great places for a close look at the shattered foothills bedrock.

Each layer of sandstone is named after a river in southern Alberta—the oldest are the Belly River Sandstones, dating to 80 million years ago, the youngest are the Willow Creek Sandstones (66 million years ago), and the St. Mary River Sandstones are middle aged at about 70 million years. These older sandstones may be covered by thin beds of Porcupine Hills Sandstone and shale laid down much more recently in the Paleocene epoch only 55 million years ago. Sandstones, young and old, are the most common rocks walkers will experience in the montane foothills.

Between the formation of the Belly River and St. Mary River sandstones 70 million years ago, a final great surge of Cretaceous seawater flooded much of the Interior Plains, laying down a thick layer of shale and silty sandstone. This is part of the sedimentary formation found at Red Rock Coulee, only the mix of sandstone and shale are inverted.

At Red Rock Coulee, which was far out in the deeper waters of the shallow Cretaceous sea, there is much more shale than sandstone. Farther west, closer to the sea shore and the source of fresh mountain water, sandstones prevail.

Keep an eye open for scraps of limestone and dolomite. In the grasslands, erratics and gravels usually include Precambrian granite, carried from the northeast on Ice Age continental glaciers. In montane country, large blocks of limestone are scattered amongst the hills and there are no fragments of granite. The limestone debris was carried by glaciers moving out of the Rockies, and includes the stuff of the great mountains.

Steeply tilted sandstone, the hallmark of the true foothills.

Making foothills

The last, dwindling forces of mountain making in the Jurassic and Cretaceous periods managed to crush and crumple the smooth and flat sandstones lying just to the east of the rising Rocky Mountains. This left the terrain in a jumble of steeply angled, broken spines of rock thrusting onto a skyline of many ridges. The Porcupine Hills, however, avoided the violence; there, the beds of stone seem level and in the same order as they were laid down long ago. Because the forces of mountain making were finally exhausted at the base of the Porcupine Hills, the hills are not true mountain foothills.

During the Pleistocene Ice Age, glaciers flowed across the plains from the north and east and from the western mountain valleys to cover most of the region. The broken sandstone rock of the foothills was first smoothed and rounded and then buried under a thick layer of gravel, sand and silt. After the glaciers melted away, wind and rain carried much of the glacial debris off the foothills ridges, leaving their rocky spines exposed. Again, the Porcupine Hills and Cypress Hills are the exceptions. Their uppermost elevations were not touched by the Ice Age glaciers.

Thin beds of sandstone, shale and coal tipped up along the Crowsnest River.

The Montane Ecoregion

Area: 5714 sq. km or 0.9% of the province.

Topography: Very hilly.

Elevation: Mostly between 1200 m and 1800 m.

Climate: The Montane Ecoregion is one of the wettest parts of Alberta. There is considerable rain in each summer month, but like elsewhere east of the mountains, scant mid-summer moisture sets a limit on plants and animals. Snow cover is deeper than in the grassland, and lasts longer in the spring, especially on east-facing slopes where the powerful western winds pile it in deep, sculpted cliffs. On average the Montane Ecoregion is about 2°C cooler than the Fescue Ecoregion to the east, and 2°C warmer than the Subalpine Ecoregion to the west. Freezing temperatures occur in any month, but winters are fairly mild. The Montane Ecoregion occurs at high altitude, compared to the eastern grasslands, and a blanket of arctic air freezing all the Interior Plains will be thin and weak in the high Montane Ecoregion. Chinook winds regularly whip warm air across the hills, pushing the arctic air east across the grassland.

Soils: Chernozems in the grassy parts; Brunisols in the wooded parts.

Humans: Much of the area has been logged, fenced or turned into cattle grazing land. Gas facilities and access roads are everywhere.

12 Carbondale Hill

Mode: foot
Rating: easy
Time: 3 - 4 hours
Distance: 9 km
Maximum elevation 1798 m
Elevation gain: 460 m
Map: 82 G/8 Beaver Mines

Carbondale Hill, southwest of Pincher Creek, and the surrounding grassland and riverside are typical of the moist and cool Montane Ecodistrict in the south of the province, but rather atypical in the overall scheme of the montane foothills because most of the foothills are neither moist nor cool. It is the unusual local climate that sets Carbondale Hill apart in the montane landscape.

The route starts on the bedrock of the Castle River, crosses a fescue meadow, enters a fringe of aspen, and ascends a forest of white spruce, then lodgepole pine, Douglas fir, Engelmann spruce and finally limber pine. The route tops out on an exposed ridge of pinkish sandstone bedrock, dressed in montane plants.

The walk begins on the gray sandstone ridge overlooking Castle River Falls and ends at the top of one of the highest montane hills in the region.

River edge
In early spring, autumn and winter the Castle River is quite shallow, and the water is as clear as air. The bottom is paved with a mosaic of coloured cobbles and trout can be seen flashing in the deeper pools.

Carbondale Hill, at 1798 metres the highest of the southern montane foothills.

Getting there

From Pincher Creek, south of the Crowsnest Trail, head west on Highway 507 to a T-intersection north of the hamlet of Beaver Mines. Turn south and drive on Highway 774 until just before the road crosses the Castle River. A large sign points north toward the Castle Falls Campground. The trailhead is in the campground.

Camping

The Castle Falls Campground is a complete campground and comes with picnic tables, fire pits, cook shacks, fire wood, toilets, drinking water, garbage tanks and most of the amenities. The fee is about $15.00 per night. Campsites are located right beside the water, in a montane river bottom landscape.

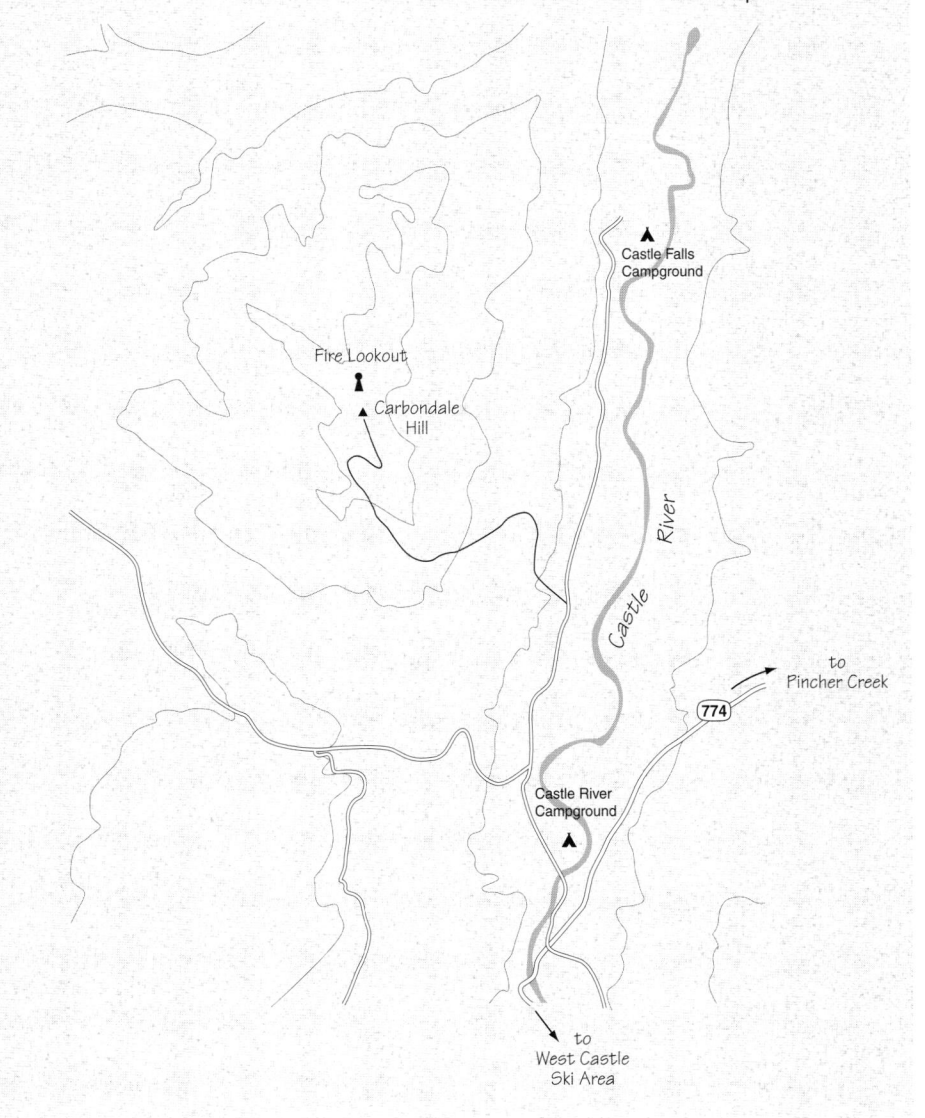

Carbondale Hill

Trout pools below the Castle Falls.

The Castle and West Castle rivers are famous Class I trout waters, especially for cutthroat trout, Rocky Mountain whitefish and bull trout. There are plenty of good places for fish to spawn and over-winter. Unlike most other streams and lakes in the region, the Castle River is very productive of fish and no artificial stocking is needed. Elsewhere, waters are planted with rainbow trout, eastern brook trout, brown trout and exotic California golden trout.

The river's tranquil pools disguise the Castle's violent potential. Like most mountain and foothill rivers in 1995, the Castle River added to the once-in-a-hundred-years flooding of southern Alberta, and the signs of deluge will remain fresh for years. Everywhere on the floodplain adjacent to the river there are new shoals of sand, pebbles, gravel, boulders and even rocks the size of small cars.

The soft alluvial riverbanks above the falls were scoured wider, leaving behind a new foreshore of water-smoothed boulders. Castle River Falls tumble over an exposed ridge of harder sandstone, and even this ridge has a freshly scoured appearance. Anywhere near the river, thin Chernozems and Luvisols were stripped away leaving fresh Regosols behind, made up of rock, sand and silt, and organic mush. Already plants are colonizing these much less fertile soils, especially aspen, thistle and fescue grasses.

Some trees were violently torn from the river's edge in 1995, but there are still healthy montane plant communities all along the Castle—white spruce, aspen and willow close to the water, and lodgepole pine, buffalo berry, saskatoon and rose farther up the bank.

Meadows

Walk north through the fringe of trees and along the river for a few hundred metres until you reach a fence marking the campground boundary. Follow the fence west through the trees and away from the river. The fringe of river trees is quite narrow, and the trail soon passes west into a broad meadow of fescue grassland, now fenced and used for grazing cattle. The tall stand of grass includes smooth brome, European timothy and crested wheat grass, all intrusive species.

The trail reaches the road and then follows it north for a little more than a kilometre. On the east side of the meadow is the fringe of white spruce trees along the Castle River and on the west rise the southern montane hills.

Up hill

The trail to the top of Carbondale Hill is on the west side of the main road, and follows a narrow but good service road all the way to the fire lookout. Vehicles are not allowed on the service trail, and a chained steel gate blocks the way. As soon as the trail starts the ascent the open fescue grass meadow is left behind.

The lower slopes of Carbondale Hill are cloaked in montane forest, with only small patches of fescue grassland scattered on exposed, south-facing slabs of sandstone. The trees along the base of the hill are small aspen, gradually encroaching on the tall grassland. In years past, occasional fires would have swept the dry grasslands clear of invading trees.

Aspen soon gives way to close-spaced lodgepole pine, and a shaded, cooler understorey. At lower elevations, there is Oregon grape with holly-like leaves and heavy chains of waxy blue fruit. At slightly higher elevations, thimbleberry forms an almost impenetrable green blanket of dinner plate-sized leaves growing to waist height. Both these plants indicate the moister nature of the southerly montane landscape, and neither are found in the drier Whaleback Ridge and Porcupine Hills montane ecodistricts.

Higher up the hill, the trees thin out, and thimbleberry gives way to raspberry, Indian paintbrush and wild rose surrounded by sparse fescue grasses. Near the summit, there is the expected flourish of montane flowers, including vetch, Agoseris, beardtongue and lupine.

Volcanic rock

About midway up the slope, the trees thin a little and a short side trail leads to a resting place on a shelf of exposed rock. The splendid view to the south may be the main attraction of this viewpoint perched high on the flank of the hill, but the dull pink and green rock tells an interesting story of its own. Carbondale Hill includes a great deal of volcanic rock while most other hills and mountains are built entirely of sedimentary rocks.

The rock on Carbondale Hill is part of the formation known as the "Crowsnest Volcanics." Some of the rock is coloured pink from inclusions of feldspar and garnet crystals, and some is coloured green from inclusions of olivine.

The volcanic rock was laid down about 93 million years ago during the Cretaceous in a series of explosions lasting thousands of years. At the time, the great continental plates were colliding and forming the Rocky Mountains. The violence of mountain building opened a breach in the earth's crust, releasing a flow of molten material. The material was blasted into the atmosphere, or it flowed like mud along the bottom of the Cretaceous sea cover-

Thimbleberry.

Carbondale Hill

Exposed volcanic rock shelf overlooking Castle River, Table Mountain and Prairie Bluff.

ing the Interior Plains; there were no rivers of glowing lava. The breaches themselves have never been found, because as plates of rock ground over each other the volcanic throats were sealed off and buried under many metres of mountain rock.

There were at least three volcanic "hotspots" in the Crowsnest Pass and together they blew out about 70 cu. km of material into the air and covered an area from the Castle River as far north as the upper Oldman River valley. Except for a few places in the nearby Crowsnest Pass where the volcanic bed reaches a maximum thickness of 500 m, the rest of the volcanic bed is completely covered with thick layers of sedimentary rock.

The rocks above and below the volcanic material are typical Cretaceous sandstones and shales, indicating that the volcanoes blasted the molten rock from underwater. The volcanic material was then sealed below a layer of sandstone and shale laid down in shallow fresh water toward the end of the Cretaceous. The underlying sandstone is best viewed at the bottom of the hill and along the Castle River. The overlying sandstone was ground away by Pleistocene glaciers, leaving the volcanic sandwich exposed on the surface. The unique volcanic rock continues all the way to the summit of the hill.

Summit

Finally, on the last slope leading to the top, Engelmann spruce and Douglas fir make their appearance. Limber pine, whitebark pine and creeping juniper cling to the upper windswept ridges of sandstone. Even at the top there are a few shrubby aspen, showing that all of Carbondale Hill lies below the subalpine zone.

The view from the top is magnificent. On the middle horizon to the north and east, the landscape is characteristic of the Montane Ecoregion—a fringe of spruce and pine trees and shrubs along streams, floodplain fescue meadows, gentle hills between drainage channels, their flanks covered with fescue grass and lodgepole pine, and crested with buff sandstone, stunted Engelmann spruce, Douglas fir and limber pine.

Far on the northeastern horizon lies the northern parts of the Montane Ecoregion. To the west and southwest, the horizon is filled with the towering summits of the Flathead Range on the Continental Divide. Northwest is Willoughby Ridge and Ironstone Lookout, just below the towering summits of Andy Good Peak and Mount Coulthard. Table Mountain is clear on the southeastern horizon, and Barnaby Ridge lies due south. Just between Table Mountain and Barnaby Ridge, Newman Peak is in sight on the east end of Avion Ridge. These are all Special Places or important landmarks described in later chapters of this book.

Carbondale Hill in winter

The southern montane hills receive much more snow than the hills farther north. By late winter, the Castle River valley is mantled with enough snow to make it southern Alberta's premier terrain for snowmobiles. Fortunately, the road north from the campground is sealed behind a sturdy iron gate and snowmobiles are not allowed along the lower part of the river.

The road is easily followed on foot to the trailhead and the route to the top of Carbondale Hill is blanketed with thick, firm snow, ideal for skis and snowshoes. The route to the top is one long, unrelenting uphill climb on skins or wax. The trail is wide with plenty of room for turning and braking, but the return trip can be accomplished on skis in a single high-speed glide.

The weather can be tricky. The high mountains along the Continental Divide deflect powerful chinook winds over the Castle River. The last flakes of snow are wrung from the winds before beginning their plunge across the foothills and grasslands to the east. The mountains to the west and the hills to the east may be gleaming in sunlight while the summit of Carbondale Hill is obliterated in snow showers. The hill is usually decorated with fresh pristine snow revealing the recent movements of many animals including moose, elk, wolf, squirrel and hare.

Deeper southern montane snow assures more moisture in the spring, and thicker fescue grasslands.

153

Spruce

Engelmann and white spruce grow together on the lower slopes of Carbondale Hill.

This is a good place to discuss spruce, the icon of the foothill and subalpine landscapes of southern Alberta. Spruce are also the main reason why there are such places as the Carbondale Fire Lookout and its splendid view in every direction.

There are two species of spruce in southern Alberta—white spruce and Engelmann spruce—and they overlap in range and appearance. Telling them apart can be difficult.

The spread of spruce

White spruce are the most common spruce in Canada and, in fact, in the entire boreal regions of the globe. During the last part of the Pleistocene Ice Age, when the vast continental glaciers were finally melting away, conifers survived in vast forests covering the American Great Plains far to the south. As the ice withdrew to the north and east, plants and animals moved into the newly uncovered land. Tundra plants were the first pioneers, but as the land drained and warmed trees quickly followed, especially white spruce. White spruce are well adapted to cold climates and harsh conditions.

Trees survive extreme cold in two ways. Some trees hold their sap within the walls of their cells, where it can supercool to -40°C before freezing and killing the cell. If enough cells are killed, the tree freezes to death. Other species shunt sap out of the cell and into the spaces between cells where it freezes without harming the tree. White spruce and other species found in the very far north today, including black spruce, aspen and paper birch, use the latter technique. Besides being well-adapted to severe cold, white spruce can grow on the poor soils left by a melting glacier.

Spruce have winged seeds spread by blowing wind. In the 11,000 years since the end of the last glaciation, spruce were spread by wind from the middle of the North American continent all the way to the Beaufort Sea in the west and Labrador and Subarctic Quebec in the east.

In the east, it took spruce 7,000 years to migrate from Pennsylvania where vast forests of white spruce survived glaciation, to the north coast of Labrador over 2500 km away. Spruce trees proceeded north and east spreading at a steady rate of about 300 m each year. In the west, an entrenched high pressure cell covered the dwindling ice dome over Hudson Bay, creating a mighty anticyclone of clockwise wind blasting up the channel of land exposed between the western edge of the glacier and the Rocky Mountains. Once the advancing spruce forest came within the domain of this wind, seeds were carried in one mighty leap of 2000 km almost instantaneously. The spruce were migrating at least 3 km each year, 10 times faster than in the east.

The winged seeds of Engelmann spruce were probably spread the same way, and the ranges of the two spruce overlapped more than they do today. Changing environmental conditions favoured white spruce for widespread distribution and restricted Engelmann spruce to a subalpine habitat.

Cause of confusion

White spruce survives in its global range by thoroughly adapting to environmental realities, and adaptation makes a general description difficult. Even in a small area such as the Montane Ecoregion of southernmost Alberta, extreme local variations in exposure, slope, soils and elevation make for very different appearing white spruce trees.

Engelmann spruce are restricted to subalpine habitat, but they too must adapt to radical differences in local environmental conditions. Like white spruce, Engelmann spruce show the effects of slight differences depending on where exactly they grow.

In the foothills and mountains of southernmost Alberta, white spruce and Engelmann spruce occupy similar and overlapping habitats. In the Montane Ecoregion, they look alike, their seasonal rhythm is the same, and they are associated with the same kinds of other plants and animals. Furthermore, the two species hybridize, resulting in considerable genetic variation wherever species overlap. This results in trees that share the characteristics and appearance of both species.

There are only two species of spruce, but there are many different kinds of spruce.

Differences

There are ways of telling the trees apart, at least if you are looking at a pure strain of spruce and not a hybrid. As both species of spruce come in many sizes and shapes, depending on local environmental conditions, it's best to look at the finer details.

First, find a freshly fallen branch with cones still in place. With a fallen branch in hand, you won't have to molest the tree.

Look closely. Engelmann twigs are gray or brown and rather hairy, but white spruce twigs are shiny smooth and may be slightly orange or purple. Run a sprig of needles gently through your hand. A branch of Engelmann spruce will feel quite bristly, since its sharp needles curve outward. The blunt needles of the white spruce curve inward, and the twig will run smoothly through your hand.

Crush a few needles between your fingers. Engelmann spruce needles are aromatic—the distilled sweet scent of mountain air. White spruce is pungent, reminiscent of turpentine.

Check where you are. If you are at lower elevations close to 1000 m, Engelmann and white spruce grow together, but if you are near the tree line at 2000 m, any spruce you do see are probably Engelmann spruce. White spruce are never found in the upper Subalpine Ecoregion.

Cones

Seed cones really tell the story. They look very similar lying there on the ground, but there are important differences. Up close, Engelmann spruce cones look rather untidy, with irregular and loose-fitting scales, and the whole cone is often split at the end. Each scale on a cone is widest at the middle, with a jagged and split tip.

White spruce cones are arranged in a neat and orderly fashion, with scales laid on in precision rows forming a short, compact cylinder. The scales are tight fitting, smooth at the tip and flexible. Even old white spruce cones can be squeezed hard by hand, hoof or wheel and spring back to shape. More likely, brittle Engelmann cones will crush and splinter.

Commerce and spruce

Both species are prime resources for a primitive forestry industry in southern Alberta. Spruce logs were worth a lot of money in the mid-1990s, and many stands were cut and exported to mills in British Columbia. The southern mountain roads and passes thundered with trucks hauling mature trees to market as farmers, ranchers, the province, municipalities and First Nations peoples sold their forests. A few small local sawmills milled a fraction of the green spruce logs into construction lumber, but most of the forest left the province as round logs. By late 1996, the price for logs had crashed, the boom was over, and another chunk of wilderness was gone.

13 Whaleback Ridge

Mode: foot, bicycle, horse, ski
Rating: moderate
Time: 3 - 8 hours
Distance: 11 km
Maximum elevation: 1760 m
Elevation gain: 400 m
Map: 82 G/16 Maycroft

Whaleback Ridge and the surrounding area is the brightest jewel of montane landscape in western Canada. Here, thick fescue grassland, lodgepole pine, Douglas fir, limber pine, sandstone, creeks and the Oldman River combine in a landscape of unparalleled beauty. The Whaleback country can be enjoyed in all seasons, using almost any mode of human-powered travel—foot, snowshoe, bicycle and even ski if you have skis you don't mind sacrificing to the grindstone bedrock.

The Montane Ecoregion flows from the summit all the way to the Livingstone Range.

Today's walkers are by no means the first people to use the Whaleback district for camping, sport and recreation. The large meadow near the Livingstone Gap was known by Indians as "The Old Man's Playing Ground." It was a favoured place for athletic events, when large camps gathered to try their skills and strength. There are at least 150 archaeological sites scattered throughout the area, some of which are 12,000 years old.

Three hundred years ago Indians learned that the best way to see the drier, northerly montane country is on horseback. Horses move fast enough to cover the district's variety, and the entire montane is no stranger to having large herbivores wandering around. It's as though horses were invented to ride montane country—wide open spaces, not-too-steep hills, some trees for protection, water here and there, and endless good things for horses to eat.

Getting there

Compared to the high mountains that form the western backdrop, the Whaleback seems rather inconsequential. However, the ridge is over 30 km from south to north, and all the ups and downs along its length amount to over 3050 m of elevation gain and loss. A major challenge no matter how the ridge is travelled.

There are several points of access to the Whaleback ecodistrict. The route described here was selected because in a day walkers can see the variety contained in this ecodistrict, from wet bottom land to rocky heights.

Access is via Highway 22, and the main landmark is the Maycroft Bridge over the Oldman River, 22.5 km north of Highway 3. Heading north and immediately after crossing the bridge there is a westward turn-off. One branch of the road at the turn-off curls down toward the Oldman River and the campground beneath the Maycroft Bridge. Pass the campground and keep driving west about 12 km. The road crosses several cattleguards and closely follows the Oldman River.

In about 10 km, the road crosses a small bridge over Bob Creek and turns to the north. The road ends about 2 km north at a fence and the last cattleguard. Keep going along an often very bad road for another half kilometre until the road ends in a small clearing beside Bob Creek. This is the trailhead.

Just before the last cattleguard on the way to the trailhead, the headquarters of the A7 Ranch lies nestled in the valley beside Bob Creek. It's about as pretty an old-time ranch homesite as any in southernmost Alberta, and an example of a careful and considerate rural lifestyle.

Camping

The nearest campground nestles just above the canyon of the Oldman River under the Maycroft Bridge. There is a cook shack, two pit toilets, a water pump but no water fit for drinking, and a patch of gravel where a vehicle can be parked or a tent pitched for about $10.00 for the night. As in most simple campgrounds, users must keep the place clean. Bring absolutely everything needed for comfort.

Near the campground, the Oldman River has worn a narrow slot into the bedrock, exposing a slice of underlying light brown Cretaceous sandstone. If you have an extra hour of daylight at the campground, walk downstream under the bridge and continue for about 1 km for a good look at the pristine Oldman River edge.

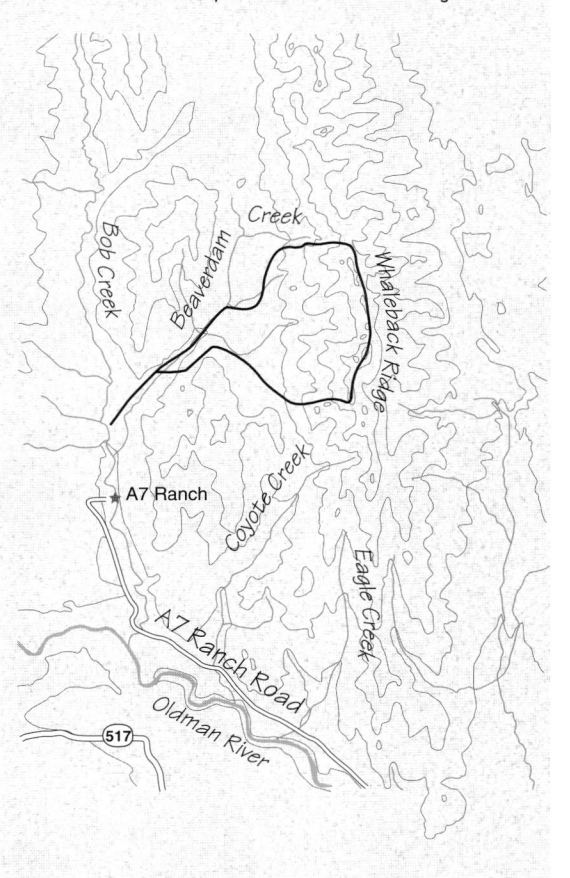

Horses in the hills

Resident Percherons.

Today, taking horses into the wilderness is controversial, but rather than arguing one way or the other, I will simply discuss how my friends and I do it.

Wherever possible, we go where there are established trails. The best horse trails follow restricted-use roads. Horses have little impact on old forestry, mining, oil and gas, and ranch roads. Horses like these roads where they have some space between themselves and unknown but apparently fearsome forest creatures. In fact, there are black bears, cougar and excitable cattle in the Whaleback, well worth the respect of horses and humans.

Next best are trails established by all-terrain vehicles and other animals. These trails can be quite narrow for a horse in the close confines of forested landscapes, but they are ideal in grasslands.

We rarely barge off a trail and into pristine places. Usually, other animals long ago figured out the easiest routes for hoofed travel in montane country. Horses usually find old animal trails to be very comfortable even carrying a human.

Highlines

When in camp, we highline our horses by stringing a rope high up between two stout trees and then tying the horses onto the rope. We pick trees far enough apart that the horses can be moved along the highline, spreading their impact over a wide area. There is plenty of room between the horses, and between them and the nearest tree roots, and the horses are tied they so can lie down or move.

The rope is about 2 m above ground, the horses are 5 m from the nearest tree, and 3 m from each other. The tree trunks holding the rope are wrapped with wide, soft, mohair saddle girths and the rope is tied into the stainless steel rings of the girth, minimizing impact on the tree bark.

We select strong trees at least 20 m apart, separated by a pool of grass. Prairie soils can take a lot of insult from hoofed animals and spring back. Soils under trees, however, are looser and softer and cannot take the abuse. Many native grasses are quite resistant to grazing and trampling, such as blue grama grass in the dry eastern grasslands and fescue grass in the west, but other grasses cannot stand horses walking around on them.

Riding horses weigh about 550 kg and delight in throwing their entire weight into a plunge against the rope for a distant fescue seed head. We use an 8.5 mm dynamic mountaineering rope and forged carabineers to absorb a lot of the horses' incessant tugging and reaching for eats. The combination of soft girth straps and dynamic rope absorbs most of the horses' restless energy. The trees barely know the horses are there.

Imported eats

The horses eat hay, usually an alfalfa-wheat grass-brome mix. The hay is dairy grade, cut at its peak of quality early in the flowering stage. There are few mature seeds that survive horse digestion and later taint the landscape.

Most places we take horses, the water is unfit for human consumption without serious treatment. The horses are picketed far from surface water anyway, and led to drink.

Souvenirs

Horses build huge appetites riding the hills, and tend to eat a lot. Horses are not particularly efficient digesters, compared to ungulates, so this means piles of manure. Horse impact includes horse droppings under the highline.

We carry a plastic manure fork designed to lift horse pellets cleanly from grass. We use the fork to break up the pellets and then throw them far and wide into the surrounding grassland and brush. This avoids submerging a small plot of grass under a large pile of horse manure, and it spreads the benefit of horse nutrients amongst plants that don't usually get much fresh, organic nourishment.

Our idea, when we leave for home, is to make it impossible for anyone to see we and the horses even visited the place. A doubtful goal, of course, but a good one nonetheless.

Camp Creek.

Whaleback Ridge

A creek flowing between parallel hills is grassy on one side and heavily treed on the other.

In the recent past, we trailered the horses to just north of the last cattleguard where the Crown lease land begins. From there, we rode high on the flanks of Whaleback Ridge to the east and all the way to the Livingstone Gap in the west.

Beaverdam Creek

The route starts in a small meadow divided by Beaverdam Creek, then follows the creek all the way to its headwaters high on the flanks of Whaleback Ridge. This route shows just about everything the drier montane landscape has to offer, from a small creek fringed with shrubs and luxurious grasses all the way to the barren rock of a montane ridge.

Start on this route by following the battered road across Bob Creek and through a grassland of thigh-high fescue, June grass and wheat grass liberally laced with fringed brome grass. Early in the season, the water may be above ankle deep, but the bottom of the creek is paved with rounded cobbles of sandstone and later in the summer when the water is low, enough well-placed rocks may allow walkers a dry crossing.

Across the creek, the road passes by a narrow ribbon of shrubs, aspen and black cottonwood and into a broad grassy meadow.

Fescue meadows

The flats along the creek are decked with river-borne silts and glacial materials, covered with a layer of black Chernozems supporting a dense fringe of aspen and willow. The creek is carved into the valley floor and an even few metres away from the water's edge the well-drained soils are considerably drier and thinner.

Whaleback Ridge

The flats just above the water and beyond the fringe of aspen and Bebb willow are blanketed with lush fescue grassland. In spring and early summer, the grasslands are filled with flowering plants—anemone or prairie crocus, three-flowered avens, lupine, golden bean, vetch and sticky geranium. Later in the season, shrubby cinquefoil, aster, yarrow, buttercup and fleabane fill the few spaces between clumps of tall fescue, northern wheat grass and Parry oat grass.

The old road wanders north and east, just below a high bank of glacial debris deeply carved when Beaverdam Creek was a more substantial glacial drainage stream. Less than a kilometre from the stream crossing, the road branches with the north branch following Bob Creek and the other heading east straight up the steep bank above Beaverdam Creek. Take the east branch of the road where bicycles will probably be carried or pushed up the steep 20 m-high bank.

The lower ridges

Along the base of the ridge lies a strip of aspen woods on a layer of thicker surface materials, mostly glacial gravels and silt. The aspen are well protected from the relentless westerly winds, and in turn shelter a profusion of even taller grass and an understorey of willow herb, Richardson's geranium, clematis and aster.

As soon as the route starts to ascend the ridge, surface waters sink into the steeper river deposits and aspen disappear. The landscape reverts to fescue grassland thick with prairie anemone, golden bean, vetch and wolf willow. Near the top of the bank, lodgepole pine make their first appearance.

The last of the trees disappear as soon as the gravel bank begins to level off, and the ground is covered with a drier and leaner fescue grassland. In spring and early summer, the meadow is dotted with tall stalks of death camas, prairie onion and nodding onion.

A wetland blanketed with sedge and shooting star, fringed with willow and saskatoon.

Lease lands

Lease lands are special places in Alberta law. They are lands leased to individuals or corporations for a particular purpose. Southernmost Alberta is sprinkled with all kinds of leases, including water, petroleum, forestry and especially ranching leases.

Until recently, most people understood the law of leases to mean that the public could enter on the land for purposes not contrary to the terms of the lease. You could not bring your own herd of cattle into a grazing lease, but you could camp there and ride your horse, bicycle or just hike.

In 1995, the courts of Alberta decided that a lease was equivalent to title, and the leaseholder could decide what was or was not a compatible activity on the lease land. Since 1995, permission must be asked at the A7 Ranch before camping at the Bob Creek crossing or even entering the southern part of the Whaleback. These days, the best approach is to camp at the Maycroft Bridge and make day trips into the Whaleback ecodistrict.

Cattle and other critters

The Whaleback Ridge is Crown land leased for purposes of cattle grazing. Domestic cattle and wild animals must live together in these large tracts of multiple-use lands. The habits and preferences of cattle and various wild ungulates make sure there is little competition and interaction between the species.

Cattle prefer to graze grasses and other herbs on lower, gentler slopes warmed by the sun. Wild ungulates prefer shrubland on higher, steeper and shaded slopes. Elk and cattle prefer grasses, but moose and deer prefer to browse on shrubs. The combination of preferred foods and feeding sites helps make sure cattle and wild ungulates have little to do with each other in well-managed grazing leases.

If the lease land is not well managed, there will be competition between species, and the rancher will make certain that if any animal suffers it will not be the cattle. In 1997, at the insistence of ranchers, the provincial government extended the season for hunting deer and allowed hunters to take larger numbers of deer. That is how conflicts between species are handled in Alberta; if there is competition between wildlife and making money, wildlife always loses.

Moving cattle into the lease lands, early spring.

The level benches are blanketed with fescue grass and tall white camas.

The top of the bank overlooking Beaverdam Creek is the first great place to stop and take in the view. From this modest elevation, the transitions below from flowing water to shrub fringe, taller aspen groves and dry ridge top can be completely followed with the eye.

Toward the top

To the east, about 3 km away, is the much higher Whaleback Ridge. The tallest point on the horizon is the objective for this route, but a sampler of a montane variety must be hiked across first.

The road to the ridge begins by following the channel of Beaverdam Creek, crossing the lower slopes of smaller montane ridges and moving across a gently declining swath of grassland. Grasses include fescue and oat grass, but also species that prefer the cool cover of the aspen—fringed brome, blue wild rye, awned wheat grass and hair grass. Grasses here are greener and much taller than grasses exposed to the blazing summer sun. This is a favourite place with deer, moose, elk and bighorn sheep.

The creek channel is clearly marked by thickets of Bebb willow, saskatoon and rose bushes. The drier margins of the creek are redolent with the sweet-pungent scent of wolf willow. The trail stays above the channel on the north side until it descends a shallow gully toward a crude crossing of the creek.

Here, the rough road again divides. The branch heading north turns away from the creek and follows the shoulder of a low ridge of montane hills. This, too, is a splendid bicycle or horse path leading to the northern limit of the public lands. The route described here takes the east-heading branch and crosses the creek toward the heights of the Whaleback.

Wetlands

The trail follows the east side of the creek, gradually climbing up toward the ridge. There is running water below on the valley floor, draining an extensive wet brushland tapering into fescue grassland. Slightly higher is a dry and windswept savanna landscape of solitary pine and fir surrounded by high grass and flowers.

Whaleback Ridge

A windswept rocky ridge overlooking the dry montane hills.

At the foot of Whaleback Ridge, the trail disappears into a low-lying area of aspen, black cottonwood and willow. The moist ground is crowded with sedge and shooting star, one of the most beautiful flowers in southern Alberta. Beaverdam Creek crosses the aspen glade and disappears into a coulee cutting through the side of the ridge. The cool and wet coulee is choked with trees and shrubs. The route to the top turns away from the creek and follows the crest of a spur ridge where foot travel is much easier.

Approach ridge

The landscape on the ridge above the wetlands changes dramatically. The edge between grassland and forest is savanna-like, with widely spaced, solitary trees. The ground cover is mostly fescue grass. In early summer, the entire slope may be covered with spears of Indian paintbrush and balsamroot, whose golden yellow flowers reflect the bright face of the sun.

Higher up, the trail leaves the fescue grassland and savannah and plunges

Prairie crocus or Pasque flower.

into a cool forest of lodgepole pine. The shaded soils are typical forest bottom Luvisols, relatively cool and moist. There is little ground cover here or higher up where Douglas fir soar to 20 m and form a dense umbrella over the trail.

164

Spruce forest

Mighty spruce clothe the north-facing slopes near the top of the ridge. The ground is littered with deadfall, but here and there are thick growths of aster, cow parsnip, wild rose and yarrow, wherever there is enough light for a small patch of grassland wildflowers to persist.

Forest birds begin to appear, including the gray jay. Gray jay lives in higher forests, and quickly becomes familiar to walkers in the southern highlands. It is a fairly large bird, about the size of a robin, that flies silently on soft, insulating feathers, appearing suddenly whenever the trail snacks are brought out.

Jays and their relatives

Farther east, Cree and Ojibwa Indians know gray jay as Wesakejak, the incarnation of the trickster hero. In their cultures, Wesakejak is a handsome fellow, persuasive and somewhat devious. He schemes well, but is rather clumsy and fumbling. He likes to test the credibility of his fellow creatures, ending, he always hopes, in him getting somebody else's meal.

Gray jay and gray jay's numerous relatives act exactly as Indians describe Wesakejak. Walkers in southern Alberta will meet crows, magpies, ravens, blue jays, Steller's jays and Clark's nutcrackers. They are handsome and entertaining, catching a walker's attention with song and dance, but always with an eye on the picnic. A slight lapse of attention and any of these slick tricksters will make off with your lunch.

In 1996, raven joined magpie and crow on the Alberta government's official hit list that authorizes the indiscriminate killing of these birds. Apparently, a rancher complained that ravens were molesting his cattle, so provincial wildlife managers changed the regulations to satisfy the ranchers.

At the top

Approaching the top of the ridge, the trail curves south toward the head of Beaverdam Creek through a grove of tall pine, fir and spruce.

The route to the top of Whaleback Ridge follows a long spur jutting out from the crest of the ridge and sweeping down to the valley floor. The dry and exposed south-facing side of the spur is almost free of trees and shrubs, making for easy foot travel. Still, the ascent involves 300 m of steep gain through a field of thin fescue grassland. Flowers abound everywhere, and on good days hawks and eagles soar on the air lifting over the ridge crest.

Suddenly near the top, groves of Douglas fir thicken, whispering and moaning in the endless wind. The ridge is marked by a spine of exposed sandstone, intricately decorated with orange, green, gray and black lichen. Cracks and crevices along the sharp backbone of the ridge are home to limber pine and wind-contoured Douglas fir. Wildflowers are sprinkled wherever they find a sheltered pocket in the sandstone and where a little additional moisture might be trapped.

Limber pine.

Whaleback Ridge

The Montane Ecoregion from the summit of the Livingstone Range.

Landscape of change

The trail goes quickly from shrub-lined creek, across the rolling, grassy valley bottom to the top of the high ridge. The swift transition is accompanied by ever-changing views.

With each metre higher up the Whaleback's flanks, the horizon expands to magnificent proportions. At the top of the ridge there are knobs of exposed sandstone clear of tall trees. Most of the drier montane landscape of Alberta can be seen from this one sweeping panoramic viewpoint.

The Livingstone Range dominates the western horizon. A little south of west, the tower of Thunder Mountain, the highest summit on the horizon at 2515 m, guards the south side of the Livingstone Gap. North of the Gap is Livingstone Fire Lookout at 2159 m; like all fire lookouts, this one provides a splendid view and can be reached from the other side of the range.

Directly below the eastern flanks of Whaleback Ridge lies Big Coulee, a vast sweep of fescue grassland broken with the merest threads of intermittent creeks and streams. The streams are sparsely fringed with sedges and taller grass, but no shrubs or trees. Beyond are the montane Porcupine Hills, and beyond them the endless grasslands of the east.

The Oldman River's path across the grasslands is traced by groves of tall cottonwood lining its shores. The green of the well-watered trees contrasts sharply with the parched grassland until both river and trees disappear into the grasslands on the eastern horizon.

14 Beaver Creek

Mode: foot, bicycle, horse, ski
Rating: moderate
Time: 3 - 6 hours
Distance: 12 km
Maximum elevation: 1780 m
Elevation gain: 370 m
Map: 82 H/13 Granum

Beaver Creek is the essence of montane country in the Porcupine Hills. The creek's headwaters are high on the southern slopes of the hills, surrounded by a dense forest of mature pine and spruce. It flows first through the Porcupine Hill's montane landscape, across a narrow band of the Fescue Grass Ecoregion, and finally joins the Oldman River in the Mixed Grass Ecoregion. Beaver Creek combines the features of these three ecoregions.

At Beaver Creek, you may explore a prime place of river and forest landscape set in a lush fescue grassland crowned with montane landscape high above.

The campground is in a forest setting near the waters of Beaver Creek. At most places and in most times, the creek is barely more than a metre wide or more than knee deep, but it flows year round. Even in winter there is a small but steady flow of water. Much of the Porcupine Hills is very dry in summer and any body of water attracts a lot of thirsty animals. In the early evening splendid young mule deer wander through the campground sampling a little of this and a little of that on their way to drink at the creek. The campground is also home to a great many rodents, including least chipmunk, deer mouse and various voles.

Chances are good quiet travellers will see lots of ungulates near the creek. In its own way, Beaver Creek is as important here as the more impressive Oldman and Castle rivers are in their parts of the Montane Ecoregion.

Beaver Creek winds out of the hills and across a valley meadow to join the Oldman River.

Getting there

The best access to Beaver Creek is Highway 785, the road leading to Head-Smashed-In Buffalo Jump. The route takes Highway 785 across the Mixed Grass Ecoregion between Fort Macleod and the Buffalo Jump, then through the Fescue Grass Ecoregion from the Buffalo Jump almost to the campground in the spruce-fir forest of the Montane Ecoregion. The distance by car is so short that the transition from one ecoregion to another is easily appreciated.

About 15 km west of the Buffalo Jump, take the gravel road heading northwest toward the Porcupine Hills. A small green sign points out the correct road.

In another 15 km the road enters Beaver Creek's shallow valley, and a few kilometres later the road passes the signed entrance for the campground. Once on the back road to Beaver Creek, you cannot get lost.

Coming from the north on Highway 2, turn west at Claresholm and follow Highway 520 until it reaches a forest services shack and a signed T-junction leading to the Skyline Road. Take the southern turn to the left and head up into the Porcupine Hills. In about 10 km, the road rises 310 m through fescue grasslands and montane foothills. Near the top of the hills there is another T-junction, a forestry services shack, and a place to enjoy a magnificent view of the Whaleback Ridge and Livingstone Range to the west. Take the turn to the south along the Skyline Road, which runs the length of the hills.

Located 2 km south of the forestry junction on the Skyline Road is a hard left turn onto the supply road for the forest fire lookout station. The steep, rough road ends at a gate, and a short walk leads to the summit of the Porcupine Hills at 820 m. The view from the helicopter pad is splendid. Looking west are sweeps of fescue grassland and the Livingstone Range in the Rocky Mountains. Between lies the Whaleback Ridge.

To the east most of the fescue grassland is in view, all the way to the margin of the Mixed Grass Ecoregion. At least 20 km of the winding Oldman River can be traced by the tall, green cottonwoods along its prairie banks.

About 5 km south of the fire lookout turn-off there is a sign pointing the way to Beaver Creek. Follow that road 8 km farther south to the campground. Settle in.

Camping

There is a basic campground just above the creek—fire pits, gravel pull-ins, a few battered wooden tables, his-and-hers outhouses, and that's about it. No garbage cans, no firewood and no camping fees. Cattle and other animals wade around in Beaver Creek, making the water unsafe for almost any human purpose. Users are expected to keep the place tidy. For self-sufficient walkers, the campground is a congenial base for roughing it.

Every tree within 10 m of a fire pit shows the sad signs of recreational tree hacking, a traditional outdoors activity in southern Alberta. Fortunately, the devastation is superficial. Most people who visit the Beaver Creek Campground do not like to get out of sight of their vehicles and 1 m away from where a wheel can roll the place is still pristine.

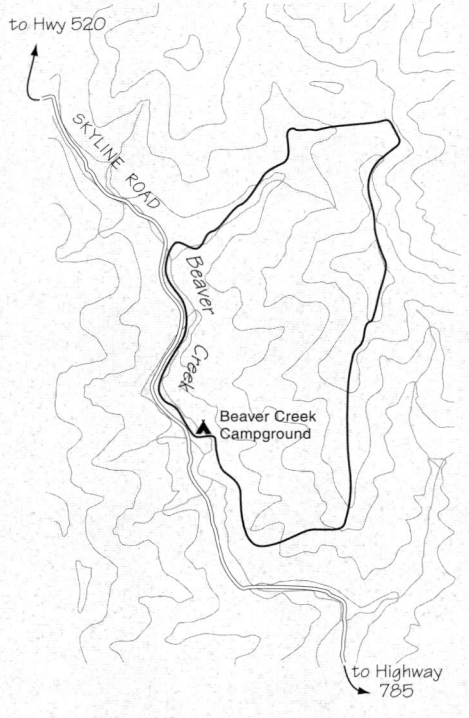

The upper valleys are cloaked with open conifer forests on the west side and aspen on the east.

Less than a kilometre down the road from the campground, spruce give way to aspen and then a ribbon of fescue grassland tied to the vast prairie beyond. Two kilometres up the road, both sides of the valley are fringed with spruce and fir to at least 150 m above the creekbed. On the southwest-facing slopes above the creek, tattered ribbons of grassland extend a kilometre north of the campground.

The higher elevations of the Porcupine Hills are heavily forested with thick, tough and unyielding spruce and fir. Penetrating the forest is almost impossible, and crossing a meadow of thick fescue grassland on bicycle is like peddling through a half kilometre of water—hard work. The whole area is a favourite with the off-road-vehicle set, especially the motorcyclists. These folks lay down single-track trails through grasslands and forests that are otherwise impenetrable to bicycles, or even on foot. The trails are good for horses, but horses may not take the sudden commotion of a racing motorcycle in good humour.

The route begins at an elevation of 1425 m, at the bottom of a cool, wet valley where the diversity and density of plant growth is a remarkable contrast to the grassy hillside a little higher up. White spruce, some of great size, are the most obvious trees along with a lush understorey of shrubs and herbs, especially flowers. There are a few large Douglas fir here and there as a reminder of the montane landscape only a hundred or so metres up the slopes where the fierce winds blow.

Chinook winds and summer rain

Chinook winds blow east of the Rockies all the way from northern British Columbia to New Mexico, but the most frequent and the strongest chinooks howl across the low foothills and grasslands of southernmost Alberta.

Chinook winds build when a mass of cold arctic air settles east of the Rockies. At about the same time, a low pressure system in the northwestern Pacific begins to spin in a counter-clockwise direction, hurling strong wind over the lower mountains of western and central British Columbia. The warm, wet wind dumps rain on the coast and snow in the interior mountain ranges.

The wind picks up speed as it approaches the Continental Divide, the high point on its journey. More snow is dumped in the western Rockies as the wind hurtles over the Divide and heads down the eastern side into the cold arctic air below. As the wind speeds down the eastern slopes and across the grasslands, it compresses and heats, arriving at ground level many degrees warmer than the arctic air in front of it.

The last moisture condenses where warm air meets cold air, forming the chinook arch, a horizon-to-horizon band of cloud. The wind is so strong it pushes the arctic air far across the Interior Plains. The wind is warm and dry, so in a day or two 30 cm of snow is melted and evaporated away, or sublimated directly into the dry air. If the chinook lasts, topsoils melt and dry out, and then loose soil begins to blow east.

During a chinook, things are far different in the mountains, where warm and cold air collide. From Lethbridge, the visible face of the mountains gleam white and blue in bright sunlight. Immediately beyond the mountaintop horizon of the Continental Divide, the sky seethes with gray snow clouds; the mountains are getting a dump of snow while the Montane Ecoregion and Fescue Grass Ecoregion bask under clear blue skies, a warm sun and a torrent of wind.

The wind may last a week, until the Pacific low is worn out, transforming the winter landscape. Following a strong chinook, there is no visible water left on the western range, but there is 30 cm of new snow up in the mountains. After the blow, there is often a day or so of colder, stormy weather, followed by a few cold and clear days while another chinook builds up.

A chinook buries the Livingstone Range in snow and bathes the Porcupine Hills in sun and wind.

Beaver Creek

The Cowley Pine, long dead and still a symbol of southernmost Alberta's chinook winds.

Effects of wind

Such a massive force of nature must leave its mark on the landscape, and indeed it does. Plants, animals, landforms and even humans are shaped by the winds.

In the case of humans, there are many devices used to adapt to wind—city requirements for fences on posts set in concrete; special interlocking roofing shingles; 4 or 5 m-high plastic wind fences surrounding the windward sides of houses; gravel sprinkled on the roads in winter rather than sand, which just gets blown away.

In the winds, humans suffer bad migraines, rhinitis and are generally upset. Nose bleeds are more common in the dry air. An unfortunate few are laid low by chinook winds, but spring back when the cold weather is better suited for skiing. Horses are jumpy and best left alone.

Long ago, the aboriginal people who first occupied these lands anchored their tents with 30 or 40 rocks weighing 10 kg each. Big rocks are not that easy to find in the grasslands and tipi rings are testimony to the power of wind.

Whether afflicted by the chinooks or not, everybody misses the warm winds when they do not blow. In the winter of 1996-97, snow first fell in November and stayed in Lethbridge until February when, finally, a chinook melted it away. Usually, snow would have come and gone at least a dozen times in those four months. People were dancing in the streets when +10°C was reached. My friend said his dour and dignified Holstein dairy cows were leaping about like young heifers. An awesome thing to see.

Summer rain

Here, in the southern montane foothills, summer rain falls in an unusual pattern, much to the benefit of local plants and animals.

There is a precipitation peak in May and June and another in August and September. In the rainy spring months, Alberta's storm track is moving north bringing rain with it. Once the track passes to the north, clear weather settles in. In late summer, the storm track moves slowly back across southern Alberta, bringing another few weeks of rainier weather in preparation for winter. The mid-summer months are pleasantly clear and dry.

North of Black Diamond, this effect is not felt, and from that point northward there is only a July peak in summer precipitation. The southern Montane Ecoregion gets about 20 per cent more rain than the montane landscape farther north, and walkers will easily see and experience the difference, especially in the forests.

Where it leaves the Porcupine Hills, Beaver Creek follows a wide valley first carved by a glacial river.

Along the creek

At the north end of the campground, a well-used track leads into the backcountry. The trail is pounded 20 cm deep into the sod and a bit wider than a motorcycle tire. Motorcycles, bicycles, horses, cattle, deer and other animals keep the track dead of life.

The trail leaves the campground and wanders through a dense closed forest of white spruce where almost nothing grows on the ground. The soil is moist and rich in tree remains. Wherever there is a gap in the dense tree cover and a little sunlight filters through to the ground below, there are stunted willow shrubs and a few struggling blossoms of startling-white Richardson's geranium.

The well-worn trail soon leads to a crossing of Beaver Creek. The verge on the crossing is a thoroughly churned mess of manure and mud. It may take some nimble bike and body tossing to get across dry and clean.

Upward

The trail upward from the creek passes over a series of broad benches marking layers of bedrock. The Porcupine Hills are not really part of the foothills. In the foothills farther west, such as Carbondale Hill and the Whaleback, the underlying Cretaceous sandstone and shale bedrock was broken and tilted when the Rocky Mountains were built. The bedrock under the Porcupine Hills, however, was just beyond the reach of mountain building and the bedrock still lies flat and level. The bedrock was not broken when the mountains were built, but the flanks were ground and smoothed by Pleistocene glaciers, then buried under a mantle of glacial gravel, sand and silt. The first bench is met only a few metres up the trail and away from the water.

The first bench is covered with about half a kilometre of tightly packed, mature aspen, spruce and fir forest. The forest is an excellent example of the habitat found along streams in the Porcupine Hills montane ecodistrict.

The forest nearest the creek is a dark and cool place where there are few plants other than mighty spruce and their seedlings. Across the creek, the trail leads directly uphill toward the rich grassland on the higher slopes.

The high grassland

The grasslands are fescue grasslands, and there is plenty of fescue to be seen, with their feathery seed heads dancing in the hot breeze. But, there is also brome and European timothy. Both these species, much-loved by wild and domestic ungulates and horses, were brought from Europe long ago to enrich grazing for cattle. They are ecological souvenirs of improved range management practices. High on the brow of one meadow, just below a magnificent spruce, is a patch of alpine timothy, the natural kind of timothy for this place.

Neither indigenous nor introduced grasses, in all their splendour, suppress the wildflowers. In summer, the meadows riot with brown-eyed Susans, bergamot, sticky asters and goldenrod. The rich, dark Chernozems of the lower meadows hold yarrow, bedstraw and Canada milk vetch.

In the shaded fringe between grassland and forest, the cooler soil is decorated with Richardson's geranium, sticky geranium, pale Agoseris and yellow salsify. Scattered here and there in the forest and grassland, larkspur is in fresh, full bloom. Larkspur is a rather scarce plant in the southern Rockies and foothills, and a good thing, as larkspur is poisonous to ungulates and horses. The grassland continues to near the top of the slope.

At the top

The trail crosses at two more benches of buried bedrock before reaching the spine of the Porcupine Hills. In places, the trail is very steep, especially where it crosses the heads of valleys feeding Beaver Creek. The trail crosses the flank of the ridge reaching the high point at 1860 m. At this elevation, the ribbon of fescue grassland reaches deep into spruce and fir forests. The

Showy fleabane.
Western wild bergamot or horsemint.
Richardson's geranium and box-elder beetle.

ribbon leads upward, where it joins with a higher montane landscape of sparse pine and fir.

The trail then crosses a last meadow of grassland pioneers and again plunges into the cool of dense forest and understorey. The transition from forest to grassland and back to forest is accompanied by changing aromas. The forest is sweet with geranium, cow parsnip and moist loam. In the meadows, the air is rich with the scent of bergamot and the flinty smell of dry, sun-drenched soil.

Fire

An old spruce, killed by fire a century ago and now colonized by lichen.

Fire has always been part of the landscape of southernmost Alberta. Ever since there were dry plants to burn, there have been forest and grassland fires. In nature, most fires are started by lightning. With humans came "controlled" uses of fire and, unfortunately, a great deal of uncontrolled uses.

Domesticated fire

The aboriginal people of Alberta depended on large ungulates for their livelihood, and deer, elk, bison and pronghorn in turn depended on rich grasslands. Later, hungry horses joined the people and the ungulates, and prime grassland was at an even higher premium. The people purposefully set grasslands ablaze to reduce encroachment by shrubs and trees, expose the soil and new growth to light and air, and to enrich the prairie soil with mineral ash. Burning the prairie is still practised by aboriginal peoples today, and by peoples throughout much of the world.

Aboriginal peoples also set prairie fires to drive off or kill off their enemies, but only as an act of desperation because, unlike planned burns, these fires could not be controlled. Aboriginal people also may have set fires in forests to rejuvenate the grassy, sheltered understorey preferred by ungulates in winter. Whether they did or not, nature and especially lightning achieved the same effect by creating wild forest fires.

Undomesticated fire

Forest fires are most often caused by lightning, if there are no humans around, and it has always been that way. That being so, the plants and animals living with lightning have evolved ways of coping with fire.

Lodgepole pine cones are usually clamped tightly shut when they are new on the branch. The small seeds reside under the cone scales, and won't be released until the air temperature is high enough. Then, the scale will open and release the seeds. In places where generations of lodgepole pine have grown up with little threat from fire, the cones open up in a few hot summer days. In other places, where lodgepole pine is exposed to a lot of fire over the generations, cones are sealed with resin that will not melt and release the seeds until the temperature reaches at least 40°C.

Indeed, there are many species that depend on fire to propagate, to reduce competition from other species, and to gain new nutrients. Fire was just another mighty feature of nature accommodated by plants and animals living in a hot, dry environment.

Fire suppression

Later, civilization penetrated every mountain valley and pass, and forests were exposed to uncontrolled fires—human carelessness—and then, the market. In the first decades of the 20th century, the human population in the foothills and low elevation Rockies of southern Alberta increased. They set fires, and the fires got out of control.

People and nature together caused serious and near devastating fires throughout the region. Finally, in 1912, the federal government established the Rocky Mountains Forest Reserve for the purposes of forest management and fire control. These lands were transferred to the province in 1930 and since then most forested lands in Alberta have been under provincial control.

The goal of fire suppression is to maintain the market value of the forest, an important part of Alberta's economy. Preserving forests from fire also preserves wildlife and places to walk.

Results of fire suppression

No doubt, fire suppression kept good trees available for sale and for decades several logging and milling outfits operated in the foothills and subalpine regions. It is definitely in the market's interest to fight forest fires. Fire suppression has also interrupted the order of forest succession and, perhaps, harmed the fabric of the forest.

In the past several thousand years, forests have sprouted, grown to seedlings, survived to vigorous immaturity, then maturity, and may have lived about 75 years before they were hit by natural fire. If the fire was low and cool, it burned off the understorey without harming the bigger trees. If the fire was high and hot, the entire forest might burn off, right to the mineral layers of the soil. Such a fire is a fire of devastation. By suppressing fire for the past near century, a great deal of forest litter—that is, forest fire fuel—has piled up, and once a fire gets going these days, it is often a very devastating fire.

Carbondale Lookout, alert for lightning strikes during a summer thunderstorm.

Beaver Creek

Beaver Creek is open all winter where it riffles over a bed of exposed sandstone.

Back to camp

Once across the trickle of the creek's headwaters, the trail leads to a good double track, then to the main road heading back to base. Turn south, and the campground is about 3 km downhill all the way.

Alternative trails

Other motorcycle trails lead in every direction from the campground and from the main road north and south. The motor trails lead to interesting viewing points or a place to see some other intriguing feature of the landscape.

Motorcycles are rarely encountered on the trails, leaving them free for alternative users including hikers, bicyclists and horse riders. And wild animals. Most motorcycle trails are well used by deer, moose, elk, coyotes, rabbits and smaller scurrying creatures. They are good company for walkers wanting to see wild things in the Porcupine Hills.

Where the access road crosses the cattleguard at the south end of the public lands in the Porcupine Hills is located a steep trail onto a ridge overlooking the lower stretch of Beaver Creek and the exact place where the eastern grasslands meets the western forests. The view to the south takes in Chief Mountain, the Waterton and Oldman River valleys, and the southern Livingstone Range. To the east, the fescue grasslands ripple across the landscape, reaching the horizon and fading into the distant haze.

Beaver Creek in winter

In winter, the road to Beaver Creek is covered with impassable snow. The closest approach is from the south. Snow clearing stops at the last ranch house on the road, 5 km from the campground. In places the road is covered with a metre of snow, but snowmobilers have packed a good winter trail for foot travel, especially using skis and snowshoes. In winter, skiers must find their own trails.

15 Cypress Hills

Mode: foot
Rating: easy
Time: 4-5 hours
Distance: 10 km
Maximum elevation: 1455 m
Elevation gain: 245 m
Map: 72 E/9 Elkwater Lake

For hundreds and thousands of years, the Cypress Hills have been an oasis of green in southeastern Alberta's characteristic pale brown landscape, a place to enjoy trees, water and lakes. The hills still offer a welcome respite from the blazing sun and relentless wind, along with some truly unique features including rocks, landforms, plants and animals not found anywhere else in southern Alberta or, in fact, Canada. The Cypress Hills loom high above the surrounding horizon of treeless, undulating grassland offering "a perfect oasis in the desert we have travelled" according to Captain John Palliser in 1859. Such an unusual and attractive place is unique in southernmost Alberta's natural history.

There are several popular, well-built trails throughout the park and there are plenty of opportunities for off-trail exploration. The most interesting trails and routes will carry you from a grassland near the bottom of a hill system, through a wetland and upward into the different kinds of woodlands on the ascending slopes, and finally reaching the high grassy viewpoints on the plateau above.

The route described here is almost perfect: it begins at the mouth of a small creek in the townsite, ascends the sun-washed south slope of a grassy hill, passes beneath the spreading branches of tall white spruce and lodgepole pine, crosses a long tongue of fescue grassland fringed with aspen, and finally emerges onto the high plateau and some of the best viewpoints in the park. The return route follows a different stream through a thick cool forest of spruce, cottonwood and aspen and emerges back at the trailhead.

Horseshoe Canyon—Beaver Creek

The first part of the route follows the Horseshoe Canyon trail, which has its trailhead just to the west of the entrance to the Beaver Creek Campground in the townsite. There is plenty of public parking near the trailhead and the trail is equipped with signs and maps.

The green Cypress Hills rise abruptly above the arid grassland.

Getting there

The Cypress Hills is a major provincial park appearing on road maps as a large block of mottled green straddling the boundary with Saskatchewan. Drive 22 km east of Medicine Hat on Highway 1, the Trans-Canada Highway, to the junction with Highway 41. The Saskatchewan border is 25 km east of the junction with Highway 41. The turnoff is thoroughly signed with huge glowing billboards. Turn south on Highway 41 for 72 km. Once at the park boundary, there are signs to all the roads, campsites, services and amenities the park has to offer.

The most popular road to the park is Highway 41 south from the Trans-Canada. Nearing the park, the highway crosses a rolling tumult of hills, narrow drainage channels, rather taller and thicker grasses than near Highway 1, and even a few small wetlands. The landscape is shaped by massive deposits left behind at the demise of the great Ice Age glaciers. Every variety of moraine feature occurs near the Cypress Hills.

For something really different try approaching the park from the south where Highway 501 in Alberta joins Highway 13 in Saskatchewan. In 1885, geologist R. G. McConnell described the southern approach to the Cypress Hills as "desolate and repulsive," but he was travelling on the back of a thirsty and hungry horse accompanied by a train of ox carts. Today, we can admire the dessication in an air-conditioned vehicle on good Alberta highways.

The southern approach to the hills heads arrow-straight up a long and gentle incline to the plateau above. The great glacier that made the hummocky landscape along the northern approach flowed around the hills and only grazed the southern flank. Instead, the southern flank was inundated with water draining off the glacier and toward the south and Missouri River. As a result, the entire vista from the southern brow of the hills takes the eye downward and to the south, where the land is tilted to better catch the blaze of summer sun.

This is the place to find burrowing owls, cactus, rattlesnakes, scorpions, biting spiders, yucca, sage, greasewood and many other stern reminders of a harsh dry landscape. Another reminder is a large official sign announcing "No Services or Residences—Next 85 km."

Camping

There are 14 campgrounds and 548 campsites in the park ranging from backpackers' tent pads to full service for the most elaborate RV units. The town of Elkwater is located in the park and offers a small general store, an eatery, a fuel station, motels and a few other convenient services. Some of the campgrounds are open year-round with good access to the park's 24 km of groomed cross-country ski trails and a modest set of downhill ski runs.

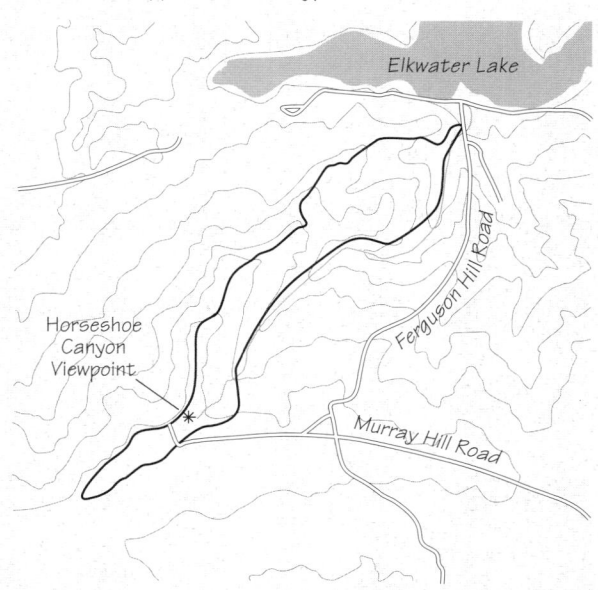

The trail begins just above the mouth of Beaver Creek where it flows into Elkwater Lake. Much of the landscape at the trailhead is heavily modified by the town and campground, but the low-lying patch of willow and water-loving grasses near the lake is a favourite winter stopping place for moose and mule deer. In summer, the tall boggy growth is filled with bulrush, cattail, red-winged blackbirds and yellow-headed blackbirds.

The creek flows in a shallow cut etched along the bottom of a much larger drainage channel first carved by flows of glacial meltwater. The entire margin of the lower part of the creek is thickly lined with willow and small aspen, but even a few metres away from the water's edge the trees disappear, then the shrubs until grassland takes over entirely.

Horseshoe Canyon trail

The trail moves away from Beaver Creek and up the flank of a now-dry coulee extending all the way to the top of the plateau. The trail is on the south-facing side of the coulee, and the lower part of the trail crosses a broad dome of fescue grass and prairie flowers. Here and there are patches of exposed sandstone and shale, lying quite flat and level.

The hill is made of undisturbed bedrock rather than glacial debris covered with a metre and more of powdery loess and, finally, a thin layer of Chernozemic soils, the prime soil of grasslands. The drab beige loess is spotted with jewel-like iron concretions about the size and shape of a baseball.

The opposite north-facing side of the coulee has a skirt of small aspen trimmed with dense willow and rose bushes and a cloak of white spruce and lodgepole pine. The soils are much the same as on the south-facing side, but the dark organic layer is thicker and rarely as desiccated as the other, exposed side of the coulee. The contrast between the two sides tells the story of crucial environmental variables at play, especially exposure to wind and sun.

The few metres of transition between grassland and forest are marked with a fringe of shrubs, including buckbrush, wild rose, bearberry, ground cedar, buffalo berry, wolf willow and black currant. In the taller grasses beneath the shrubs there are heart-leaf arnica, false Solomon's seal, clematis and showy aster.

A profile of the Cypress Hills—wetland, grassy meadow, aspen grove, spruce and pine forest.

An island in a sea of grass

The Cypress Hills are very irregular in shape, but generally lie east-west about 70 km north of the U.S. border and straddling the Saskatchewan boundary. The hills are up to 145 km in length and 40 km in width. Because the entire Interior Plains are tilted very slightly downward to the north and east, the east end of the Cypress Hills in Saskatchewan stands at 1060 m elevation and the western end in Alberta at 1460 m. The eastern end of the hills stands about 450 m above the surrounding prairie and the western end rises 760 m above the dry grassland.

The western summit of the Cypress Hills at 1457 m is the highest point in Canada between the mountains near the coast of Labrador and the foothills of the Rocky Mountains. That fact alone sets the Cypress Hills apart from any other place in much of Canada.

Geology

The Cypress Hills are like a stack of pieces from a jigsaw puzzle, where each piece is curiously shaped and slightly smaller than the piece below. Each piece represents a layer in the geological history of the hills and surrounding landscape.

Like the rest of the Interior Plains, the Cypress Hills are underlain with thick beds of sedimentary sandstone and shale created during the Cretaceous and early Tertiary periods, between 120 and 45 million years ago. The top surface of the hills is capped with the Cypress Hills Formation, a conglomerate composed of cobbles and pebbles embedded in a calcium-rich sand cement. The raw materials in the conglomerate were carried eastward and downward 45 million years ago by rivers flowing out of the ancient Rocky Mountains. This is the youngest bedrock in the region.

In the distant past, vast parts of the western Interior Plains were plated with a similar shell of conglomerate, the inevitable result of mountain wasting. The great Ice Age glaciers obliterated most of the conglomerate bedrock and pushed the debris even farther east and south toward the Missouri River and beyond.

Ice

During the Pleistocene epoch, the great glaciers of the Ice Age flowed toward and around the hills at least five times. The ice mounted the northern side of the hills, but not the southern side. As a result, almost 120 sq. km of

A boulder of Cypress Hills Formation conglomerate.

Wild turkeys stroll Elkwater's main street.

the Cypress Hills were untouched by the force of ice. The hills are still covered with relatively recent conglomerate, while all the surrounding plain was ground down layer after layer to eventually reveal a surface of sandstone and shale laid down over 100 million years ago.

The Cypress Hills probably formed a divide between the ancestral South Saskatchewan River and Missouri River systems, and as the great ice sheets retreated at the end of the Pleistocene, meltwater rushed past the northern and western sides of the hills, gouging out steep escarpments. The retreating glaciers deposited huge volumes of debris, conspicuous today in the chaotic hills lying north of the park. The work of ice and water carved the north side of the hills into steep and vertical cliffs dropping abruptly in the grassland, but the sheltered southern side gradually tapers into the near-desert far plains.

Toward the end of the Ice Age, when the environment was cold, dry and blasted with powerful winds, and when the summit of the Cypress Hills rose above the horizon of glacial ice, a mantle of fine-grained windblown material called "loess" accumulated on the top of the hills. Since the end of the Ice Age, the hills have experienced relatively little additional erosion. The scant rainfall of southeastern Alberta quickly sinks into the fine-grained loess without accomplishing much erosion.

The result of this exceptional geological history is a pleasant plateau emerging from a level sea of grassland. The tall hills enjoy lower temperatures and more precipitation than the arid and hot Dry Mixed Grass Ecoregion, resulting in a very different and agreeable landscape. In his book on *The Landscapes of South-ern Alberta*, Chester Beaty dedicated part of a chapter to the Cypress Hills and their advantages in a sea of arid grassland. He wrote "there is nothing 'unusual' or 'mysterious' about the Cypress Hills—after all, given sufficient elevation even parts of Hell would presumably become tolerable."

Life

With their green fields and forests and plentiful streams and wetlands, the Cypress Hills are ideal habitat for many species of plants and animals not found in the surrounding grasslands, including some species not found elsewhere in Alberta or Canada or North America. The Cypress Hills display remarkable transitions from grassland to wetland, and parkland to forest. Steep gradients, shallow coulees, low passes, rocky headlands, and hills interlocked with flatland offer plentiful opportunities for an astounding variety of plants and animals. Like the hills themselves, plants and animals are a rather chaotic blend of grassland, montane and mountain species.

Grassland

Considering the location of the Cypress Hills, grassland species should come as no surprise. Where the flat plain rises to meet the steep slopes of the hills, the grassland is typical of the Mixed Grass Ecoregion west of Lethbridge. Even lower on the hillside, moisture and protection run out and the Dry Mixed Grass Ecoregion dominates the landscape. The lands directly south of the Cypress Hills are the driest lands in Canada.

The high plateau summit of the hills is mostly covered with the kind of fescue grass-

Cypress Hills

The west end of the plateau is distinctly montane in appearance.

lands found far to the west below the Rocky Mountains. However, the Cypress Hills are located on the northern margin of the Great Plains and include many species common in the United States, but rare in Canada. Included within the mix are species usually associated with landscapes closer to the Missouri River, including red-sided garter snake, western painted turtle and bull snake.

Montane

The higher elevations are covered with aspen, black cottonwood, lodgepole pine and white spruce broken with pools of open grassland, resulting in a characteristic montane landscape. But, there are important differences between the Cypress Hills and western Montane Ecoregion. There are no Douglas fir in the Cypress Hills, the hallmark of the western montane foothills. On the other hand, there are pronghorn, sage grouse and scorpions in the lower parts of the Cypress Hills and these species are unknown in the west. Because the heights of the Cypress Hills were not affected by mountain building, there are no exposed, sharp-edged ridges of bedrock and no limber pine or whitebark pine rooted on the ridge.

Mountain

The Cypress Hills are home to numerous species usually found only in the Rocky Mountains, including species of land snails, butterflies, birds and flowering plants. In 1990, Margaret Walker, an experienced naturalist, reported her surprise at finding a clump of glacier lily hidden in a cool, shaded glen deep in the Cypress Hills. Glacier lily is usually thought of as a herald of spring in the Rocky Mountains. It is still a mystery how these mountain species made it all the way east to the Cypress Hills. A. L. Russell, an early ecologist working in the area, commented that seeds and spores might be blown on the strong western winds, birds can fly and many animals can walk. But Russell, a specialist in snails, could not see how four species of land snails made it all the way to the Cypress Hills overland from the nearest mountain 300 km west.

There are two favoured theories accounting for how mountain species are found so far from the mountains. As the great continental glaciers melted at the end of the Pleistocene, a succession of plant and animal communities moved into the freshly exposed land. As the ice receded to the north and east over several thousand years, tundra and then forest followed. At one point, perhaps 7,000 years ago, a thick coniferous forest covered most of the land between the mountains and Manitoba. As the environment continued warming, all the forest was replaced by grasslands except at the cooler and moister heights of the Cypress Hills. Where the forest survived, so too did a variety of mountain species.

Or perhaps plants and animals survived the Ice Age on the unglaciated summit of the hills, surrounded by hundreds of kilometres of thick ice. The summit would have been severely cold, dry and wind-blasted, but there were lots of other ice-free places where species survived the millennia of the last glacial age and then spread widely as the ice retreated. It's still an open question.

Species come and gone

Elk, bison, swift fox, cougar, plains wolf and grizzly bears were hunted out near the turn of the 20th century, but elk were reintroduced in 1938, moose and red squirrels in the 1950s, wild turkey in 1962, ruffed grouse in 1920, and ring-necked pheasant and gray partridge in the early decades of the century. Streams were stocked with brown trout in 1924, brook trout in 1933, and with rainbow and cutthroat trout at various times over the years. These reestablished and introduced species now flourish along with many other species of grasses and flowering plants that leaked into the area from the surrounding zone of civilization.

The indigenous survivors of extinction and alien competition number over 200 species of birds, 400 plant species including 47 species that occur only in the Cypress Hills, four species of trees, 30 species of shrubs, 58 species of mammals, at least 100 species of butterflies, 13 species of reptiles and amphibians, and an unknown number of insects.

Humans

There are 59 species of mammals in the Cypress Hills, including humans—over 650,000 people in 175,000 vehicles visit the park each year. The Cypress Hills—on both sides of the provincial boundary—are amongst the best-loved and most-used parks in Saskatchewan and Alberta and for very good reason. The things that attract people to the park today are the same as have attracted people for the past several thousands of years—water, shade, trees, animals and plants, and an opportunity for adventure.

The Cypress Hills have probably been a landmark for the past 15 to 20 million years. For millions of those years, the hills were surrounded by water, ice or cold desert, but they have been green and lush for the past 10 to 12,000 years. At least 90 archaeological sites suggest that aboriginal people occupied the hills over most of that time, even in severe centuries when the desiccated grassland below was all but abandoned by humans and other animals.

The historic record confirms that many aboriginal populations used the hills—Assiniboine, Cree, Peigan, Blood, Blackfoot, Arapaho, Shoshoni, Gros Ventre, Kalispel, Crow, Dakota and Métis. In lean years, tribes fought for control of the hills and settled into uneasy truces along boundaries following easily recognized landmarks—drainage channels, lakes, summits and passes. In fat years, the hills were a regional centre for trade, diplomacy, idea exchange and marriage. Apparently aboriginal people took good care of the Cypress Hills, even in the harshest years. In late July of 1859, when Captain John Palliser arrived in the Cypress Hills, the grassland region was at the height of a protracted drought. Palliser was eloquent on the landscape attractions of the Cypress Hills, including pure water, abundant game, towering forests and tall grass.

In 1859, the tribes near the Cypress Hills were feeling the claws of eastern civilization as American, Canadian and European trappers and traders crept into the heart of the west. These traditional pioneers in Canadian history naturally followed the travel routes and trade protocols established over centuries of international contact between aboriginal peoples.

By the turn of the century, Indians had been confined on their reserves, the Métis had migrated northward, and the hills were taken over by settlers, ranchers, loggers and sawyers, and even miners digging for clay, silica sand and coal. This was the end for many species of plants and animals as humans modified the environment to better suit their economic ends. Trumpeter swans once nested on the Twin Lakes near the headwaters of Battle Creek, one of the park's major streams. The outlet of the lower lake was dammed in the 1930s and the impounded water backed up to create Reesor Lake. The habitat needed by nesting swans disappeared and so too did the swans.

Cypress Hills

The ridges leading to the plateau are forested with aspen on the south and spruce and pine on the north.

The trail gradually climbs the coulee and nears the top of the ridge above the coulee. Several adjacent ridges meet here to form a large patch of flat land covered with dense forests of small aspen, large pine and huge spruce. The aspen, spruce and pine are so dense that few plants grow in the cool muted light filtering through the trees.

Grasslands are reduced to large meadows tightly hemmed in by trees and shrubs. Much of the crest is covered with forest, but where grasslands cover the crest of the ridge a few metres above the trail there is a spectacular open view of Elkwater Lake, the lower part of Beaver Creek, and the townsite with the vast mixed grassland beyond.

The trail carries on, following the ridge through a succession of thick forest and grassy meadows until the route opens onto the flat and level plateau topping the Cypress Hills. The trail curves slightly to the west along the steep escarpment marking the working edge of Pleistocene glacial ice. The first part of the escarpment is hidden behind a screen of pine and aspen, but the trail soon comes to the steepest part of the escarpment where few trees can endure, and a view opens up to the north and west.

At this higher elevation, the meadows are typically covered with fescue grasses, oat grass and wheatgrass, the same kinds of grasses found in the Montane Ecoregion far to the west. The tall, luxuriant grasses keep company with other plants also found near Carbondale Hill, Whaleback Ridge and Beaver Creek—white camas, shrubby cinquefoil, Indian paintbrush, yarrow, bluebell, golden bean, brown-eyed Susan and with iridescent shooting star glowing amongst tufts of dry grass.

The steepest part of the escarpment—Horseshoe Canyon—forms a great arc over a kilometre in length. This is the place to see the conglomerates of the Cypress Hills Formation. The formation shows as an exposed band of what looks like decorative but poor quality concrete. It lies about 3 m directly below the very edge of the escarpment. The slope lying below the conglomerate is littered with cobbles and pebbles of quartzite washed out of the eroding rock. The grassy edge of the escarpment can be followed west until the rim is again overgrown with pine and spruce.

The trail ends at a well-built viewpoint and vehicle turning loop. With binoculars and a map, the details of the northern flanks of the Cypress Hills can be enjoyed at leisure. But, the return route is waiting.

Nichol Springs Campground

The trail turns away from the escarpment and heads east across a meadow and into the forest peeking over the north-facing side of a coulee system and onto the grassy plateau to the south. The trail stays just inside the edge of the forest, forming a tunnel through the straight trunks of young and vigorous pine and spruce. The cool and shaded forest, so welcome to walkers on hot windy days or cold windy days, allows only a subdued understorey of anemic grasses and flowers.

A few white spruce, survivors of earlier fires, overlook a coulee filled with aspen.

Just beyond the edge of the spruce and pine forest where it grows out of the coulees and onto the flat plateau lies a broad fringe of aspen groves. On the plateau, enough sunlight filters through the quivering aspen leaves to encourage tall growths of gooseberry, saskatoon, chokecherry and pincherry.

The aspen groves support more birds and animals than either the grassland or the coniferous forests. The luxuriant undergrowth and protection from wind and burning sun attract the largest numbers of nesting and resting birds, including mourning dove, house wren, yellow warbler and mountain bluebird. In winter, great horned owls sit motionless on higher aspen branches, waiting for dusk.

About midway, the trail passes the Tom Trott Memorial Forestry Museum. Tom Trott was the park's forest officer from 1980 until his death in 1996, and is credited with the idea of creating a forestry museum at the site of a dismantled fire lookout tower. The outdoor museum exhibits the tools and technology used in fire suppression since earlier in the century.

What's in a name?

Lodgepole pine in the Cypress Hills style.

First, the Cypress Hills are not hills at all, at least in the familiar sense of a height built up on the surface by deposition—water, wind, volcano or ice—or mountain building. The Cypress Hills are a bas relief where the surface of all the surrounding landscape has been ground away, but they have not. They are a remnant of the landscape just before the Ice Age, now a vital part of southernmost Alberta.

There are no cypress trees in the Cypress Hills. Early Métis visitors identified the hills with the graceful pines covering the upper elevations. However, the Métis used their French name for the jackpine, "cyprès" or *Pinus banksiana*, which they knew from their homes in central Saskatchewan and Alberta, and called them "Montagne de Cyprès" or "jackpine mountains." Finally, the English misheard the French word "cyprès" and promptly made it into a familiar sound—cypress. Perhaps the correct English name should be the "Lodgepole Pine Plateau," because the only pine in the hills is *Pinus contorta*, usually found in the western mountains and foothills.

In fairness, the lodgepole pine on the high plateau do not look like typical lodgepole pine, which usually are tall and slender with a compact cylinder of branches. On the plateau they grow short thick trunks adorned with a globe of foliage. They look very much like jackpine growing near the North Saskatchewan River. Connoisseurs of pine trees might see that the trees in the Cypress Hills have their cones turning inward toward their growth stem, a diagnostic trait of the lodgepole pine. Jackpines hold their cones pointed away from the stem. To further add to the confusion, some trees have thick divided trunks, elongated limbs and look like limber pine.

The Cree decided the hills were notorious for summer thunderstorms and plentiful water in the midst of a near-desert and named them "the thunder breeding hills." The Stoney named them "the grizzly bear hills" after the plains grizzly bear, the highest animal on the food chain and a potent indicator of the rich and plentiful landscape found at the hill's higher, cooler, moister elevation. The Peigan name—"the divided mountains"—has two meanings, recognizing the distance the Cypress Hills are from similar hills much farther west, and the distinctive west and east parts of the hills themselves.

The Blackfoot name says it all—"the mountains that shouldn't be"—especially for walkers seeking a respite from dry hot, or dry cold grasslands.

The Graburn Ranger Patrol Cabin is an especially fine example of a traditional, Canadian log cabin. The cabin was used by patrolling forestry officers as recently as the 1970s, and is now an exhibit of handcrafted dovetailed joints and pole chinking.

In a kilometre the well-signed trail reaches the Nichol Springs walk-in tent campground, where there are toilets, a kitchen shelter, tables, fire pits, a water pump and fencing to keep out the cattle. From here, the route passes through a stile in the fence and toward the headwaters of Beaver Creek.

Beaver Creek trail

The trail closely follows the banks of Beaver Creek through a towering forest strewn with small marshes and bogs. This leg of the route is completely different than the sun-baked and wind-blasted hike up the Horseshoe Canyon trail. Except for the last hundred metres, the Beaver Creek trail is entirely beneath the shelter of trees.

Fire swept the Cypress Hills in 1886, leaving the forest completely charred. Some cottonwood trees survived nearest the wetlands. In the burnt woods, aspen recovered first and the oldest aspen trees are about 100 years old. Next came the lodgepole pine, their seeds melted out of their resin-sealed cones, and the oldest pine is about 90 years of age. Most white spruce are even younger. Today, spruce is much less common than it was 100 years ago or than it will be 100 years from now. This is the usual sequence of forest growth after a fire. However, groves of old-growth spruce and cottonwood near the creek bottom survived the fire and are now giants of their kind. Every ancient white spruce, festooned with gray and green tendrils of tree lichen, seems to have its resident red squirrel chattering a warning of human presence, and the base of every spruce is buried under a blanket of freshly shelled cones, the squirrel's favourite food.

The cool and shaded mixed forest along Beaver Creek.

Cypress Hills

Here and there down the length of the creek valley the sun reaches the ground with a pool of warmth and light. If it falls on well-drained ground, there is a lush growth of tall grasses and flowers. If the sunlight falls on wet ground, there is an equally lush growth of sedges and reeds. In most places near the water, the creek's edge is occupied by a tangle of spruce, aspen, deadfall and cottonwood trunks felled by beaver long ago.

Beaver Creek flows year round in most years because it is fed by springs as well as meltwater. Most streams originating in the Cypress Hills flow into small, highly alkaline ponds that the summer sun eventually dries out and bakes into a shimmering pan of salt. Wetlands are unusual places in the dry grasslands, and wherever there is standing water there are also a great many species of plants and animals that could not exist elsewhere, including orchids.

There are 14 species of orchids growing in the Cypress Hills, and all of them prefer the undisturbed wooded margins of streams and creeks. A pure yellow variety of the striped coral-root orchid grows only in the Cypress Hills and Quebec. The striped form of the round-leaf orchid has been found in two places in the Cypress Hills, and nowhere else on the continent. If you go looking for orchids near the water's edge in June and July, be careful where you step because most orchids are small, delicate and few in number.

The creek flows in steps down a series of steep sections spaced with level sections. In the steeper sections the stream is very narrow and trees press to the very margin of the water. In the level sections, water pools enough to form wetlands. By winter, Beaver Creek is at its lowest rate of flow and the slow seep of spring water spreads out and freezes in strangely hilly layers and sheets of hard blue ice. These thick beds of ice fill the bottom of the valley

Kittentails, usually an alpine tundra plant.

Moss phlox on a bed of conglomerate pebbles.

in some places and make very treacherous footing.

Gradually, the gradient decreases, the wetlands get larger, and the forest thins enough to give glimpses of the grassy hillside climbed on the upward trip along Horseshoe Canyon trail. Finally, there is a last grove of aspen and willow and the trail ends in the Beaver Creek Campground.

Alternatives

The Cypress Hills are full of surprises and many pleasant days and seasons could be spent exploring every nook and cranny on foot, ski, snowshoe and bicycle. The Saskatchewan side of the park is every bit as interesting as the Alberta side. The Fort Walsh National Historic Park is in Saskatchewan, the fabled lower Battle Creek and the Gap, a glacial floodwater channel carved between the east and west blocks of the Cypress Hills. The Gap is dotted with potholes, ponds and a few larger lakes, and has been an important travel route for several thousands of years. This is a great place to see wetland birds.

The Murray Hill Road reaches from the Tom Trott Museum along the length of the plateau grassland and leaves the park at its western end. The grassland extends westerly for a little over 4 km before reaching a steep downhill trail through a dense forest of lodgepole and aspen woodland. The trail ends in the thickets at the bottom of Medicine Lodge Coulee.

The forest of graceful, slender lodgepole pine on the western flanks of the hills is open and airy. Travel through the pine forest is easy, with a few sidesteps to avoid clumps of willow and bearberry, or a carpet of twinflower and bunchberry. Where spruce trees take over from the shrubs and pine, very little undergrowth flourishes in the perpetual forest shade. Beneath the trees in the deep forest there are only a few species of moss and lichen.

Lower down the slope where there is more north-facing shade, tall groves of white spruce, decorated with streamers of beard lichen, mark the places with moister soil.

The old road takes a few last turns through the trees and then emerges abruptly from coniferous forest, passes through a narrow fringe of aspen and enters the lower, drier mixed grassland prairie. The grass species are typically dryland species—blue grama grass, needle-and-thread grass, and wheat grass—dotted with the colours of cactus, moss phlox, cushion vetch, yellow umbrella plant, prairie onion and pussytoes. Sage and a few clumps of creeping and common juniper stand slightly higher than the grasses.

Horseshoe Canyon and a bed of conglomerate covered with loess and fescue grassland.

The Cypress Hills in winter

There are good winter services in the park, including RV camping, eateries, lodging and fuel. The park has 27 km of groomed cross country ski trails, graded from "easy" to "difficult." There is also a downhill rig boasting a vertical drop of 167 m!

If your aim is to ski, either downhill or cross country, watch the weather carefully and try to time your visit with a recent snowfall and before a chinook wind. Snow is thin at any time in the season, and wherever it is exposed to sun and wind it quickly disappears. The Horseshoe Canyon-Beaver Creek route described in this chapter is just as interesting in winter as in summer. Most visitors arrive in the summer months, making the hills rolic with voices, motors and electronics, but in winter the Cypress Hills are quiet with birdsong and wind.

The town of Elkwater and the nearby winter campgrounds have a resident population of 50 mule deer, four moose, uncountable squirrels and fewer than 50 humans, all going about their business on the public streets. Waterton Lakes National Park has mule deer and bighorn sheep in the townsite, and lots of other backcountry towns have urban white-tailed deer, mule deer, moose, elk and pronghorn, but no other town has a flock of nine wild turkeys strolling about gobbling loudly. In early spring, the majestic tom turkey guides his hens down the back streets and through the cottage yards, his feathers all on display. The tom drags the tips of his extended wings on the pavement creating a loud rasping sound while the hens gobble and dart at edibles lying under roadside trees. These loud and showy birds don't seem concerned about attracting predators with all their gaudy noise.

At least six months of the year is winter, and the Cypress Hills, like all the Special Places, has a winter story to tell.

Freezing spring water keeps the surface of Beaver Creek slick with ice.

Special Places for a Quick Visit

Lundbreck Falls.

Lundbreck Falls

Lundbreck Falls Campground manages to capture the look and feel of the drier Montane Ecoregion in a tiny patch of land along the side of the Crowsnest Highway. The falls themselves are the main attraction, dropping 8 m over a sheer wall of sandstone. There are two firm and flat pads, one on each side of the falls, where wheelchairs can roll almost to the lip of the canyon.

The campground lies a few kilometres off Highway 3, near the middle of a paved loop of access road. The access road and the joining section of the main highway make an excellent bicycle or foot route about 8 km long.

The section of the Crowsnest River just below the falls is exactly where the freshwater flowing out of the growing Rocky Mountains merged with the marine waters of ancient Cretaceous seas. As the Rockies rose just west of Lundbreck, huge burdens of erosion debris were carried to the east, gradually raising the floor of the sea and pushing the saltwater to the east until there was only freshwater flowing across the flat shoreland. The force of mountain building then broke the bedrock and tilted the shards on edge, forming the nearby foothills. A close examination of the water-polished river canyon reveals the intricate layering of sandstone, siltstone and shale.

There are also trails leading along the edge of the river below the falls where the fabric of the Crowsnest River can be explored close-up. In the right season, the trails are lined with fly fishermen after the river's famous trout. The river-edge trail through the campground has been reinforced with a fine collection of rocks dredged from the bottom of the

Special Places

At the sandstone lip of Lundbreck Falls.

Special Places

river. Continental glaciers left no exotic granites here; instead, the shoreline includes round boulders of limestone, dolomite and volcanic material ground out of the western highlands by mountain glaciers.

Even a casual stroll along the river and then up one of the trails leading above the canyon and floodplain is an excellent introduction to the essence of the Montane Ecoregion. Between the shrub-lined water and the arid grassland are groves of fir, aspen and thickets of wolf willow, splashed with patches of grassland and flowers. The exposed ridges of bedrock on the near horizon are home to classic examples of sculpted limber pine growing in one of the windiest places in Canada.

Oldman River Campgrounds

There are two campgrounds on the middle part of the Oldman River, just west of the Livingstone Gap at the mouth of Dutch Creek and on the Oldman just upstream of the confluence of the Livingstone River. The campgrounds are in the eastern, sandstone part of the Oldman's valley and the surrounding hills are softly rounded with a rocky ridge covered in limber pine and Douglas fir. This is classic montane landscape.

However, the campgrounds are on the western side of the Front Ranges and not too far from the Continental Divide. This means the hills share a montane aspect and a subalpine aspect. Only the south-facing sides of the hills are cloaked in montane grassland and savannah, where there is maximum exposure to sun and wind.

The north-facing sides of the hills are cloaked in thick subalpine forests of white spruce, lodgepole pine and thin groves of aspen. Looking north from the campground, the view is similar to the Whaleback. Looking south, the view is like the flanks of Thunder Mountain.

The campground roads and trails are only fair for wheelchairs, depending on whether or not it has rained recently.

Windswept limber pine overlooking a rock garden of limestone boulders in Crowsnest Creek.

8

Subalpine Ecoregion

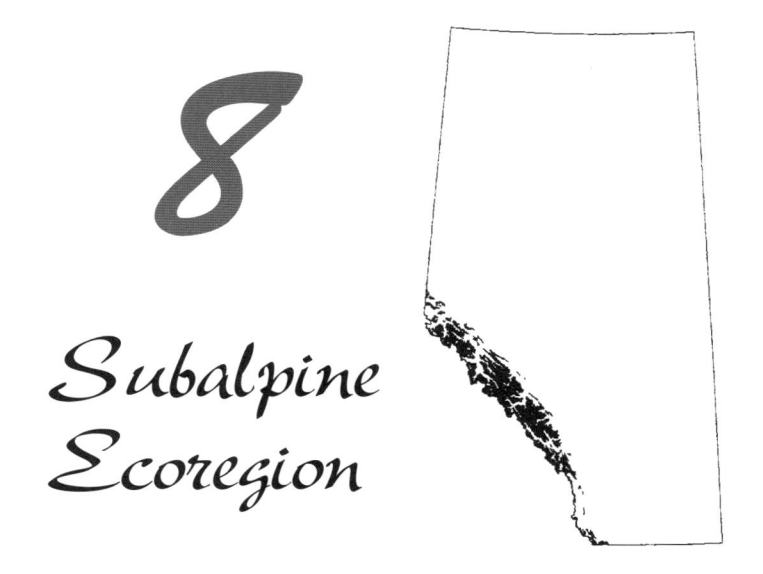

The Subalpine Ecoregion is where grasslands, hills, coulees and flat prairie rivers are left behind. Crowded into a ribbon between the grasslands and foothills to the east and the Continental Divide to the west, the Alpine Ecoregion soars 2000 m above the prairie of southernmost Alberta.

The various grasslands can be compared easily to each other and even the foothills and grasslands can be compared, but neither of these compare to the Subalpine Ecoregion. Subalpine country is deep forests, small swift streams, lush understorey, rock and steepness. There may be patches of fescue or other grass on south-facing slopes if soils are rich enough, but the great grasslands are far below to the east. Travelling in subalpine country usually means gaining and losing many metres of elevation. It is not at all like smooth prairie and hill travelling. The subalpine landscape is the landscape of mountains and forests.

Subalpine forests

The Subalpine Ecoregion is a thickly forested landscape. Technically, the Subalpine Ecoregion begins just above the highest growing aspen and extends to the tree line.

The eastern face of the subalpine landscape can be seen from far out on the level grasslands. The blue-black of forests lapping up the steep mountain slopes are in subalpine country. Where the dark band of trees ends, so cleanly and sharply when seen from 100 or more kilometres away, rockland and the high Alpine Ecoregion begins.

Lower elevations

The lower parts of subalpine valleys are dominated by lodgepole pine and large groves of white spruce. Forests are especially tall and close-packed at lower elevations and near creeks and rivers. Mountain streams run over steep and rugged bedrock. They are swift, white and cold. Tall forests crowd right to the edge of the racing water. Where they can get a rooted grip, willow and alder grow on muddy soils between the river and the forest of white spruce and pine.

Middle elevations

At higher elevations, Engelmann spruce and subalpine fir appear. Even higher up, pine disappears, white spruce reach their limit, and Engelmann spruce and fir grow together in densely packed clumps and islands of trees surrounded by subalpine meadows. Soils under the forests thinly cover the bedrock of ancient limestone, dolomite, sandstone and shale.

High elevation

Near the tree line, trees are often no taller than shrubs, bent and twisted, lying close to the ground where they are buried under deep winter snow and protected from brutal, high-elevation winter storms. Trees growing highest in the Subalpine Ecoregion are little more than ancient twigs, similar in size to seedlings of the same species found in the lower subalpine. At the highest subalpine elevations, soils are likely immature Regosols and Brunisols—rocky debris with just enough organic material to nourish the tiny trees and a few other hardy plants.

The subalpine landscape is extremely varied. Slight differences of elevation, exposure, aspect, slope or position relative to prevailing winds create entirely new expressions of subalpine characteristics. The endless variety and the challenge of mountain travel are what attract walkers to the mountains.

In lower and middle parts of the Subalpine Ecoregion, the upper Oldman River is heavily forested.

Subalpine

Near the tree line, Avion Ridge supports a mere fringe of wind-stunted fir.

The Subalpine Ecoregion

Area: 26,060 sq. km or 3.9% of the province.
Topography: Extremely rugged, mountainous.
Elevation: In a 600 m band between 1500 and 2100 m.

Climate: Annual precipitation amounts to about half a metre a year, with great variation from place to place. The subalpine landscape receives only slightly more moisture than the montane landscape, but there is only a single summer precipitation peak in July rather than an early and late peak as in the southern Montane Ecoregion.

The Subalpine Ecoregion receives more snow than any other part of Alberta. It is also one of the coldest parts of Alberta. Freezing temperatures are frequent in all months, with a frost-free season of only 30 days or less in late July and early August. Winters are cold, and the plentiful snow lingers on the ground well into July. The snowpack is the source of southern Alberta's magnificent rivers.

In mountain country, temperatures drop about .7°C for every 100 m of altitude gain. In summer, valley bottoms are warmer than upper slopes in the day, but often colder at night as mountain air drains into the valleys. In winter, upper slopes are often warmer because an arctic air mass overlying the foothills and grasslands below thins out in the subalpine valleys and does not reach the upper slopes at all. Mid-day in January can be -15°C in Lethbridge at 1100 m and +5°C on mountain slopes above 2000 m.

The subalpine experiences few chinooks; the chinook winds pass in a great wave far above, then plunge into the eastern foothills and grassland.

Soils: Almost all the soil families are represented in the Subalpine Ecoregion, from rich Chernozems to barren Rockland. At higher elevations, soils of any kind are often contained in very small pockets, divided by rock, scree, water, snow or ice and pounded by the forces of erosion.

Humans: Much of the Subalpine Ecoregion is protected in parks and ecological reserves, or located in remote areas not yet penetrated by industrial technology. There are places throughout southwestern Alberta where the subalpine can be travelled in all its pristine splendour.

16 Goat Lake–Avion Ridge Trail

Mode: foot
Rating: moderate to difficult
Time: 8 - 10 hours
Distance: 15 km
Maximum elevation: 2500 m
Elevation gain: 940 m
Map: 82 G/1 Sage Creek

Goat Lake and Avion Ridge join in one of the most spectacular subalpine routes in Waterton Lakes National Park and even in southernmost Alberta. The trail begins in the paved parking lot at the western end of the Red Rock Canyon Parkway at 1500 m and ends after 8 km of fairly strenuous hiking on the crest of Avion Ridge at 2300 m. On the way, hikers are treated to huge scenery, and wildflowers and wildlife not seen elsewhere in the southern Rocky Mountains.

There are 950 species of vascular plants in Waterton Lakes National Park. Of these, 175 are rare by provincial standards and 53 by national standards. There are more plants and more rare plants in Waterton than in either Banff or Jasper national parks. Banff and Jasper have a combined area of 17,472 sq. km, and Waterton has an area of only 512 sq. km. And that's just the vascular plants.

A singular bed of brick red argillite dominates the landscape from Mount Galwey in the east, looming over the sweep of grassland far below, and west to the crest of Avion Ridge. This is one of the few places in the Canadian Rockies where hikers can see and touch some of the most ancient sedimentary rocks in North America. Red Rock Canyon, the trailhead for this route, is the best place to see the red mountains, laced with green siltstone and bands of pale gray dolomite. The trail begins immediately to the east of the bridge at Red Rock Canyon.

The trail begins by crossing a footbridge over Red Rock Creek, the best place to see the famous argillite. The trail soon connects with a seldom-used truck track. The trails are marked with signposts.

Goat Lake, at the base of the sheer cirque cliff, hangs over the u-shaped valley of Bauerman Creek.

Getting there

Waterton Lakes National Park is a United Nations World Heritage Site, so there will be no difficulty finding it. There are three approaches.

The first is straight west on Highway 5 from Lethbridge through Cardston. Highway 5 approaches over mixed grasslands, fescue grasslands and montane foothills until running abruptly into the steep face of the Rocky Mountains.

Highway 6 heads south and toward the park from the Crowsnest Trail at Pincher Creek. Highway 6 begins east of the montane foothills lining the Crowsnest Pass. Following the swath of aspen-fescue foothills and montane foothills that parallel the line of the mountains, the Eastern Slopes of the Rockies are rarely more than 3 km away from the highway.

Highway 17 heads north from Montana to become Highway 6 when it crosses into Alberta at the Chief Mountain border crossing. The route from Montana passes first through fescue grassland, then through magnificent montane foothills landscape, following the Belly River. Near the turn-off toward the park, the road passes through an isolated remnant of the Aspen Parkland Ecoregion where the Wishbone Trail is located.

Each route shows off prime southwestern Alberta scenery. These roads are best travelled before noon on a clear day when morning light floods the grasslands, foothills and mountains illuminating the vastness of the landscape.

Camping

There is camping for all tastes, from primitive backcountry to RV heaven. The campgrounds in the park are both excellent. If you like mountain resort towns or want full RV hook-ups, showers and all the amenities then the townsite campground is the one for you. The Crandell Campground is midway up the Red Rock Canyon Parkway, offering fewer comforts in a superb setting along Blakiston Creek with the rugged red tower of Mount Galwey as a backdrop.

If you want to avoid the high cost of overnighting in the national park, there are first rate campgrounds a few kilometres away along any of the access highways.

Backcountry camping requires a permit and you can only overnight in approved places. The backcountry campgrounds have prepared tent sites, pit toilets and bearproof food caches. Walkers must carry everything in and everything out. There are no services of any kind in the backcountry.

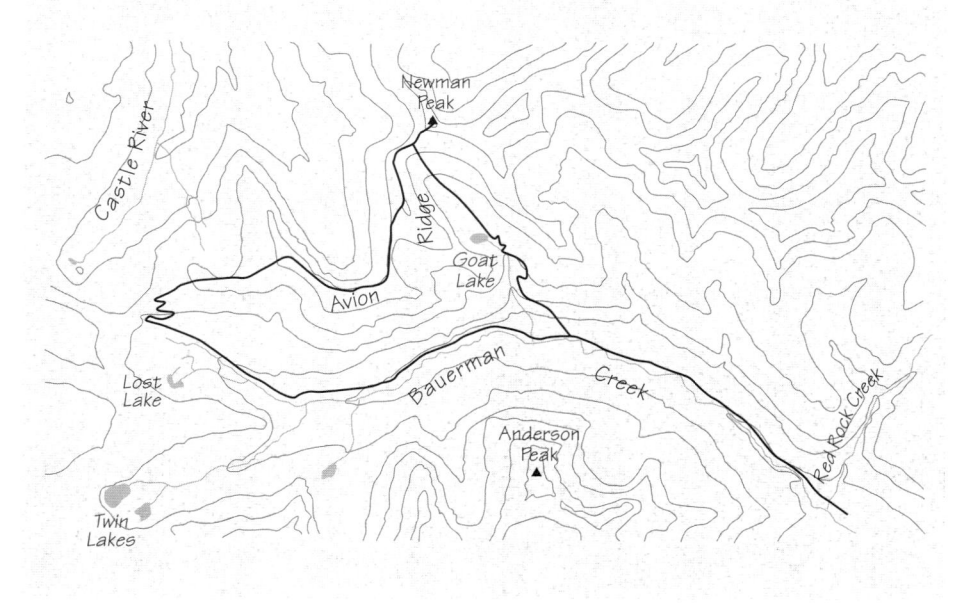

Goat Lake

The lower trail follows Bauerman Creek through a thick subalpine forest of spruce and pine.

Riverside valley

In the first 3.9 km and 60 m height gain, the trail gradually climbs along Bauerman Creek through a forest of spruce and pine, laced with aspen, fescue meadows and wetlands. At lower elevations, still close to water and rich soils, trees are dominant, but there are plenty of luxuriant flowers—yarrow, fireweed, northern bedstraw, fleabane, cow parsnip, pearly everlasting and strawberry.

Every season brings in a new regiment of flowers, and Waterton Lakes National Park contains more species of wildflowers than any other place in southernmost Alberta.

Glacial valleys

The Goat Lake trail turns off the valley trail toward the north, and immediately begins a stiff ascent of 400 m in 2.5 km. The trail meets the excellence of national park standards.

Beargrass, south of the Avion Ridge trail.

199

Red and green rock

Red Rock Creek is very appropriately named with its blazing red canyon walls and floor. There is nothing else quite like it in the Rockies.

Beginning of life

The red and green rocks belong to the Grinnell Formation in the Purcell Supergroup, laid down about 1.5 billion years ago in the Proterozoic era, but the history of the rocks begins even much earlier.

Over two billion years ago, masses of land drifted together on the fluid mantle underlying the earth's crust. This huge mass of land lay across the equator surrounded by vast, shallow tropical sea teaming with microscopic life, mostly bacteria and algae. About 1.7 million years ago, the super-continent began to break up and pull apart. There have been four similar continental collisions and breakups in the past 2.5 billion years of world history, so this was nothing new.

Tropical seawater poured into the newly formed rifts between the continents. In the seawater soup of life, the early bacteria consumed raw minerals like sulphides and calcium compounds, while the early algae consumed carbon dioxide and excreted oxygen. As usual, the lands rising above sea level were tormented by the forces of erosion, especially wind and water erosion.

The silt and mud draining into the sea after wind and water had done their work were rich in iron. Where the seas were clear and shallow, microbes produced oxygen, and the iron was precipitated as oxidized rust-red mud. When waters were too deep or silty or fresh to support microbes, oxygen production fell off and iron settled as thinner layers of unoxidized green mud.

Mountains from mud

The coloured mud built to great depths, and compressed into thick layers of red argillite, scored with bands of green shale. Because these sediments were laid down in water, the beds of rock were flat and level, following the grand contours of the depths. Ripple marks and drying cracks, the signs of a shallow seabed, are preserved in the floor of Red Rock Canyon.

During the Proterozoic era, the site of Lethbridge was only 250 km from the sea. The eastern shore of the sea ran parallel and close to the north-south track of the Rockies, but there were no Rocky Mountains yet. The land above water was loose material, carved by large rivers and blown by wind, without much life. The land was eroded by wind and water and the erosion debris was ejected into the sea, just to the west of southernmost Alberta.

The Proterozoic era lasted almost 600 million years. Over that time, a combination of seawater deposits, freshwater deposits and an active surface crust resulted in several different kinds of rock built up in layers 9 km thick, including limestone, sandstone, mudstone, shale and volcanic rock. This ancient rock is exposed in only one other place in Canada, over 1000 km away in the northwestern part of the Rockies. Waterton's red and green rocks are a record of timeless processes—evolution, life's energy, irresistible forces of nature, vast time.

Today, the level seabeds are twisted and shattered, bent at crazy angles making them even more beautiful. But, that is part of the much more recent process of mountain making, a subject discussed in the chapter on the Alpine Ecoregion.

Goat Lake lies in a classic cirque valley. About 13,000 years ago, the valley and all the others seen from Avion Ridge were filled with glaciers. Even the mountains were mostly covered with ice. The thick ice was seeded with broken rock, and as it slowly crept down the mountains the glaciers ground the underlying rock as surely as a file cuts metal. Masses of rock were ground off the towering mountains and carried downward and to the east.

A thicker, heavier glacier occupied the valley of Bauerman Creek, and the Goat Lake glacier was a tributary, just as Goat Creek is now a tributary of Bauerman Creek. The larger glacier carved a deeper valley, and when the ice melted away the Goat Lake valley was left hanging far above the floor of the main valley.

The trail heads up from the bottom of the main glacial valley and follows Goat Creek into the hanging valley.

Goat Creek

As soon as the ascent alongside Goat Creek begins, the landscape changes. The relatively thick and rich soils along Bauerman Creek quickly thin out giving way to exposed bedrock and coarse mountain debris. The low-lying fescue and aspen meadows between the spruce and pine forests are replaced with subalpine spruce and fir, exposed rock and sparse ground cover.

The trail switchbacks up the headwall close to the creek. Willow and birch crowd the very margin of the creek, wherever there is a roothold and enough good soil.

At the lip of the headwall, the trail passes through clumps of Engelmann spruce and subalpine fir, underlaid with fescue grasses, bearberry, smooth gooseberry and cow parsnip. Early in the season, the trail is lined with glacier lily, the banner of subalpine spring.

Just beyond this magnificent display of mountain splendour lies the bowl of the cirque and the backcountry campground.

Goat Creek plunges over the lip of its hanging valley.

201

Goat Lake cirque

Spruce and fir forest fills most of the cirque and surrounds three sides of Goat Lake. A cliff of ancient Purcell dolomite towers above the west side of the lake.

The entire cirque is occupied by the creatures characterizing the Canadian Rockies—mountain goat, bighorn sheep, mule deer, gray jay, golden eagle, Columbian ground squirrel and occasionally grizzly bear. The sheer cliff is where the goats live, easily watched from the lakeside campground.

The well-trod trail ends at the lake, because for most walkers Goat Lake is their destination, but the high point of this route is the ridge lying far above the lake.

The Avion Ridge trail

The ridge is gained by hiking to the cirque wall 1.6 km to the northwest of the lake. A steep ascent of 320 m leads from the foot of the cirque wall and into the col at 2320 m elevation. The col lies between Newman Peak, to the northeast at 2500 m, and an unnamed summit to the southwest at 2350 m. Both are only a short distance from the low col at the head of the cirque.

Seen from the north side of the lake, the route to Avion Ridge is obvious—across the cirque valley to the col or low point between the two summits on the northern horizon. The route stays on the east side of the creek. Take any of the animal or human trails heading toward the col. The first kilometre passes through a splendid subalpine wood of spruce and fir, laced with grassy meadows. Then, the trail heads up 30 m of near-sheer dolomite rockwall: This is the first difficult section of the route—keep alert.

Above the rockwall, the final approach to the col is across a slope of broken shale dotted with islands of krummholz, or wind-shaped trees. The trail from the col to Newman Peak at the east end is above the tree line, in alpine country. To the west, the longer part of Avion Ridge, the route gains and loses the tree line several times as the trail follows the steep, rocky spine.

At the col

Once at the col, you must decide how far you want to go. Newman Peak, a short hike up a scree slope, is less than 1 km away at 2500 m of elevation, 500 m above Goat Lake, but only 180 m above the access col on Avion Ridge. The ridge runs a little over 6 km from Newman Peak to just below the Continental Divide in the west. With all its ups and downs, the route following the steep ridge to the west gains 245 m and loses 345 m before descending below the Continental Divide.

Up the rockwall from Goat Lake cirque to Avion Ridge.

Goat Lake

Flowers are thick on the north slopes of the ridge out of the wind.

Heading west

The second crux lies at the west end of the col. A faint trail winds below the western summit, saving about 125 m of elevation gain, but with serious exposure if there is a strong wind whistling around the cliff. Instead, head straight up the crest of the ridge toward the summit. With some modest scrambling, the exposure is avoided. This puts you at one of the high points on the route, with a tremendous view.

The view to the north and west takes in the upper Castle River valley. From the summit of Newman Peak, the mechanics of mountain glaciation are easily imagined. The view to the south and east is a mirror image of the Bauerman Creek valley, hedged by mountain sculptures. From here on, the overall travel plan will decide whether you are going to turn back at this point, or press on along the ridge.

The long traverse above the tree line.

203

Goat Lake

Headwaters of the Castle River.

One night expedition
The round trip to Avion Ridge can be done in a day, but it is far better to camp for at least one night at Goat Lake. The cirque is a subalpine gem with all the key ingredients of mountain paradise—a well-shaped spruce and fir forest, profuse flowers, sheer cliffs, a crystal brook, abundant wildlife and a small exquisite lake. A clear summer night can be spent watching the stars' stately track around the rim of the cirque, with the North Star fixed overhead.

Two nights expedition
A longer route follows the entire length of Avion Ridge west into the shadow of the Continental Divide. At its western end, the trail leads down to Bauerman Creek and Snowshoe Cabin, a modest Parks Canada services outpost. There is a campground beside the creek with an easy trail leading back to the Red Rock Canyon parking lot.

If you really want to see it all, take two nights. Hike in to Goat Lake for the first night. The next morning, hike to the col, drop your pack and ascend Newman Peak. Pick up your pack and head west to the end of the ridge. Descend to the backcountry campground at Snowshoe Cabin on Bauerman Creek for the second night, and head back to the Red Rock Canyon parking lot the morning of the third day.

Waterton in winter
Goat Lake and Avion Ridge are inaccessible in winter. The Red Rock road is chained off and not maintained. In late winter, expect to see herds of 100 and more elk grazing the windblown grassland covering the glacial moraines just east of the mountains.

Waterton Lakes National Park has a lot to offer for winter travellers, from trackset skinny skiing through backcountry touring, ski mountaineering and ice climbing. Because the park is off the beaten track compared to Banff and Jasper, backcountry ski routes are seldom travelled. Beyond the park's boundaries is pristine backcountry extending far into Montana and British Columbia, rarely visited in winter except by hard-core outdoor enthusiasts.

17 Upper Oldman River Cabin Ridge

Mode: foot
Rating: moderate
Time: 4 - 6 hours
Distance: 8 km
Maximum elevation: 2513 m
Elevation gain: 990 m
Map: 82 G/16 Maycroft

The upper Oldman River valley is one of the largest relatively undisturbed places in the Rocky Mountains of southernmost Alberta. It is a superb place to study and experience relations between three of Alberta's ecoregions—the Montane Ecoregion, the Subalpine Ecoregion and the Alpine Ecoregion.

There are two trails of interest. The first leads to the top of Cabin Ridge, a splendid sandstone and shale hill blanketed with prime montane and lower subalpine landscape. The second trail leads high above the source of the Oldman River, nestled in a cirque carved out of the limestone along the Continental Divide.

The upper valley

The upper valley extends from the southeast at the joining of the Oldman and Livingstone rivers to the Continental Divide in the northwest. The valley is about 46 km in length and up to 19 km in width taking in about 50 sq. km of subalpine and alpine landscape. At the start of the valley, the Oldman River is at 1480 m elevation, and at the small cirque pond where the Oldman River begins the elevation is 2075 m.

The lower valley floor contains high hills that look very much like montane foothills. As the land climbs west toward the mountains, the montane look and feel gives way to characteristic subalpine country and finally, high up the valley's walls, reaches the rugged alpine High Rock Range along the Continental Divide. The upper Oldman River valley is compact, so there is plenty of interaction between the valley's various parts.

The trail to Cabin Ridge begins almost directly opposite the entrance to the campground. The destination for this route is the top of the southern end of the ridge, but energetic hikers can keep on going along the entire length of Cabin Ridge, a total of 15 km one way.

Rounded sandstone hills in the eastern valley.

Getting there

There are three road approaches to the upper valley, and all are scenic. The first is from the north, following the Highwood Trail to Highwood Junction, where there is a service station and small food store. Turn south on Forestry Trunk Road 940 for 48 km to the Oldman River Road. Two kilometres west is the campground.

The other route leaves Highway 22 and follows Highway 517 across the last of the montane foothills and through the Livingstone Gap. Highway 517 ends where it joins Forestry Trunk Road 940. The Oldman River Road is 10.5 km north of the junction.

The last route leaves Highway 3 at Coleman and takes Forestry Trunk Road 940 due north for 36 km to the Oldman River Road. The Forestry Trunk Road is gravel, usually in dusty but good condition and the scenery is superb.

Camping

There are abundant camping options in the Oldman River valley. There is a fine campground a little more than 2 km west off Forestry Trunk Road 940, on the Oldman River Road into the valley. It is a full-featured campground in a splendid setting of pine and spruce forest winding along the edge of the Oldman River. There are pit toilets, firewood, water, garbage tanks and fencing to keep the summer-resident cattle out. The fee is about $15.00 per night.

Anywhere west of the campground there are plenty of random camping sites. They are free for the taking, but include no services. Anyone using a random site is expected to leave the place clear and clean for the next user. Many of these sites are right beside the river, under a tall pine or spruce, with a fescue meadow just a few steps away. This is ideal country for horses and riders.

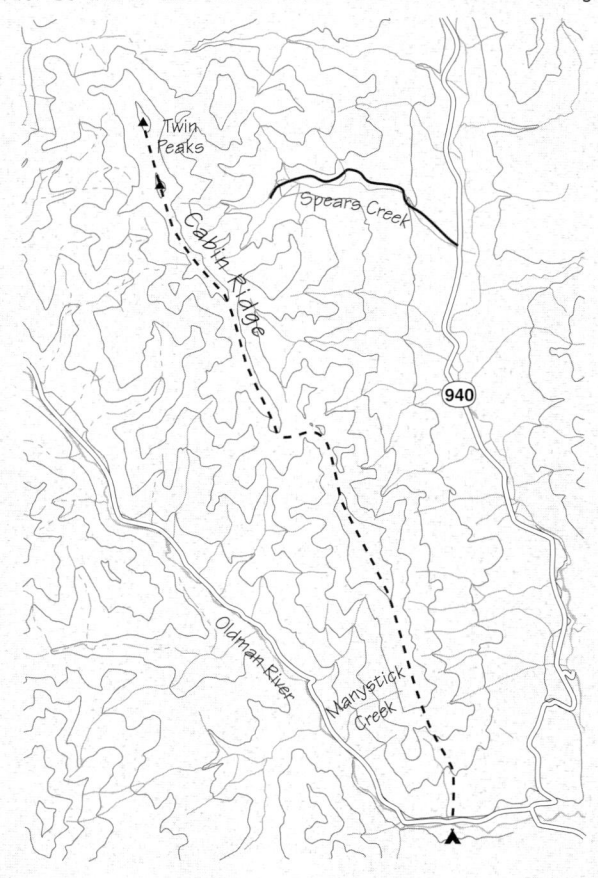

Head straight up the steep southern toe of Cabin Ridge. Motorcycles and cattle have carved trails part of the way up the slope, but these intrusions will be left behind when the slope gets too steep for wheel or hoof. Pick a suitable track, or simply head up the hill, making a few switchbacks to rest your Achilles tendons.

Southern slope

In a few metres, the rich river edge stands of lodgepole pine and white spruce are left behind. The route then crosses a narrow band of aspen and begins the main ascent up a slope of fescue grasslands. The south-facing slope feels the full force of summer sun and winter winds, so the grasses are rather sparse with many patches of thin soils exposed on the surface. A closer look at the exposed patches will show that most of the rubble in the soil consists of pieces of shattered and worn sandstone or shale.

Patches of low-lying juniper and bearberry sprawl close to the surface. The profuse flowers growing here are mostly species that don't mind a dry, exposed place to live, including prairie groundsel, lupine, golden bean, shrubby cinquefoil and yarrow. Early in the spring, the flank of the hill may be covered with three-flowered avens, prairie anemone and vetch. The lower slopes are pocked with ground squirrel dens and tracked over with the distinctive earthworks of the northern pocket gopher.

Pocket gophers

Pocket gophers are unusual animals. They are called pocket gophers for the fur-lined bags suspended behind their cheeks, which they use for transporting food. They feed by tunnelling below succulent roots and stems and pulling them down into their burrow.

They live almost their entire lives underground in a network of burrows and tunnels. They have a blunt head, small eyes and ears, powerful shoulders, large clawed feet and sturdy incisor teeth. The teeth show all the time because the pocket gopher's lips close behind the teeth, leaving them exposed for work while sealing the mouth against soil.

In its eastern upper valley, the Oldman River fills a steep-walled slot cut through a sandstone bed.

Hard rock and soft rock

The upper Oldman River valley is a study in the very different effects geology has on landforms, soils, vegetation and even human activities.

The west wall of the valley is composed of marine limestone and dolomite laid down over 300 million years ago in the Devonian and early Carboniferous eras. The east side of the valley is Jurassic and Cretaceous marine shale and sandstone about 100 million years old. During the last great period of mountain building in the late Cretaceous and early Tertiary eras from 120 to 50 million years ago, the ancient limestones and dolomites were bent, broken and thrust onto the much younger sandstones and shales to the east.

The cliffs of the Continental Divide at the western end of the valley are at the leading edge of mountain building. Being so close to the action, the younger sandstones and shales farther east were also broken and tilted, but were not covered by the massive limestone beds moving in from the west. The western end of the valley ends against the wall of limestone and dolomite, and the eastern part of the valley is carved through sandstone.

The ancient limestone mountains on the Continental Divide are very tough and resistant even to the brute force of glaciers. The results are the stark cirque walls and cliffs looming high on the western horizon. The Cretaceous sandstones in the eastern part of the valley are soft, and were easily ground into rounded and steeply rolling ridges, rather than summits and peaks.

Since the end of the Ice Age, about 11,000 years ago, the usual forces of erosion have taken over, including gravity, water, wind and frost. More or less the same forces of erosion have acted uniformly throughout the valley, but the resulting sides of the landscape are quite different.

Erosion

During the Ice Age, between two million and 11,000 years ago, the valley and surrounding mountains were sculpted by glaciers into the landforms of today—cirques, U-shaped valleys, sculpted cliffs, sleek ridges and a curving river course.

The nearby forces of mountain building upended the level beds of sandstone and shale.

Glaciers grew in the cirques and flowed to the southeast, grinding the rock beneath it and pushing a mound of debris before it. The late glaciers were powerful, but short, extending only 5 km down the valley. As a result, glacial debris is mostly found in the upper valley. Since the glaciers originated in the limestone mountains, the glacial debris is rich in carbonates.

Water and frost have taken their toll on both sides of the valley. The western cirques and cliffs are all surrounded by high and steep scree and talus slopes, which pass precipitation like water through a sieve. Water hits the chunky rock, washes downward, and settles far beneath the surface, emerging in small springs here and there as the ultimate source of the Oldman River. Signs of water erosion are rare and slight on the higher mountain slopes.

The sandstone and shale ridges on the eastern side of the valley are much less permeable and the effects of water and frost show up as deeply etched streambeds and the wavering hillside lines of soil creep. Ridges are exposed to strong western winds, and west-facing slopes are blown free of anything smaller than pebbles. The wind and water debris below these hills contains only sandstone and no carbonates.

The importance of carbonates

Carbonates react with acids, the products of organic decomposition, releasing a water soluble salt. Precipitation carries the salts deeper into the soil. Most plants do not like an acidic environment, and limestone and dolomite in the soil act to neutralize acids. Alder, for example, can colonize impoverished mineral soils because they are nitrogen fixers, but they shed acidic leaves. Alder can tolerate acidic soils, but many other plants cannot. When alder grow on mineral soils high in carbonates, the acids of decomposition are neutralized, and the fresh soil is quickly invaded by less tolerant plants.

On the other hand, carbonates are tough rocks and do not erode easily into soils or hold water for plants. Limestone rock is often free of vegetation.

The sandstone at the eastern end of the valley is very low in carbonates, and tends to sustain acid soils, especially under coniferous forests. Acids build up in the soil, repelling some plants and severely limiting others. Sandstone erodes easily into soft landforms with better ability to keep water near the surface within the reach of plants. Usually, wherever a slope of sandstone hillside escapes the brute force of winter wind and summer sun, soils are thinly grown over with plants.

The Upper Oldman River valley contains a mix of carbonates and sandstones, a good balance of minerals in the soil. These conditions are mostly found adjacent to the river on the valley floor where blended soils, sufficient water and protection from winds combine to support a rich mountain river landscape.

Plant potential

The two kinds of mineral soils in the valley—rich and lean in terms of carbonate content—support different kinds of organic soils with different implications for the plants that live there.

In areas very low in carbonate, the soil is quite thin, chemically acidic, low in water retention capacity and subject to erosion. As a result, vegetation is sparse, usually failing to cover the surface of the soil. These soils are easily disturbed and once disturbed, they are prey for erosion by water and wind. Once the surface erodes, the nutrients needed for plant growth disappear and vegetation takes a very long time to re-establish.

Soils on carbonate-rich parent material are less acidic or neutral in reaction, thicker, retain water better and are more resistant to erosion. In most places, there is sufficient vegetation to cover and protect the soil from wind and water erosion.

Walkers moving through the valley of the Upper Oldman River can see the different vegetation patterns on the western limestone side of the valley and the eastern sandstone side. In practical terms, hikers will find it much easier to move across the sparsely vegetated, soft-sculptured eastern side of the valley than they will the densely forested, rugged western side of the valley.

Glaciers left the eastern sandstone hills rounded and the western limestone mountains a mass of cliffs.

Over the winter, the pocket gopher digs tunnels at the base of the snowpack, lining the snow tunnels with soil excavated from their underground workings. In spring, the lining looks like lengths of thick black rope thrown on the new grass.

Pocket gophers keep their tunnels tightly sealed against entry by carnivores. As a result, the air in the tunnels is very high in carbon dioxide, often high enough to incapacitate or kill most other mammals.

Ridge top
At an elevation of about 1850 m, or about 330 m above the trailhead, the route levels a little, and spruce and an occasional fir begin to dot the hillside, creating an open savannah-like setting. This is now true montane landscape very similar to the landscape of Whaleback Ridge and the southern Porcupine Hills. Trails all but disappear at this elevation, but the route to the top is obvious.

The top of the ridge is reached gradually as the slope levels off and the trees fill the grassy areas. Near the top, sharply tilted beds of sandstone break through the surface to form ridges along the spine of the hill. The ridge top is crowded with Engelmann spruce, Douglas fir, whitebark pine and limber pine. Clark's nutcracker and gray jay populate the heavily treed ridge, closely watching what the humans are doing and commenting on every strange move. Golden eagles cruise overhead on air currents rising up the flanks of the ridge.

From any high point along the ridge, the panorama of the entire upper valley is spread out below. To the east, the horizon is filled with the Livingstone Range. Thunder Mountain dominates the southeastern skyline. To the south are high subalpine hills, cloaked to their tops with spruce and fir. On the distant western horizon is the High Rock Range on the Continental Divide.

18 The Oldman's headwaters Double Track Trail

Mode: foot, bicycle
Rating: moderate
Time: 4 - 8 hours
Distance: 25 km
Maximum elevation: 1725 m
Elevation gain: 605 m
Maps: 82 G/16 Maycroft, 82 G/15 Tornado Mountain, 82 J/2 Fording River

---

To see the other half of the valley, a much longer expedition is needed, first by vehicle, then on foot, horse or bicycle.

Right from the trailhead the landscape appears much different than on Cabin Ridge in the eastern part of the valley. Without many of the numerous tributary streams that drain the valley, the Oldman River is much smaller and meanders, rather than races through the broad glacier-carved upper valley.

Leave the campground and drive 26.5 km west. Park your vehicle where the Oldman River Road is blocked by a gate.

The trail follows an abandoned mining road through the river floodplain. There are creek crossings and boggy areas, so be prepared to get your feet wet.

There are people who can ride a bicycle all the way to Memory Lake, but the fun part may be over about 3.5 km from the trailhead. There, a series of very steep, rubble-covered hills with bogs between them is reason to stash the bike and walk the rest of the way.

The motorized four-wheelers never give up. They run out the power winch from the front of their vehicles, lash it around a stout pine, and pull their way upward and onward. The winch cable quickly lacerates the pine's bark, girdling the tree and killing it. Nobody

In the upper valley, the shallow Oldman wanders through a wide subalpine meadow.

211

trusts a dead tree, so each year a new live tree is selected as the anchor. Many fording-places crossed by ATVs are ringed with dead trees to the limit of a 30-m winch cable.

The valley floor

Near its headwaters, the Oldman River is a crystal ribbon running over a bed of dull-coloured limestone and sandstone cobbles. In places it widens a little and riffles over a bar of larger cobbles, and in other places it narrows and submerges a deep hole. The shallow bars are fringed with a few metres of rocky beach, but most of the riverbank is overhung with thick shrubs, grasses, sedge and flowers. The very point where land meets water is swaddled with emerald green moss.

Dipper birds use the moss to build large and damp-looking nests. Dipper birds flash along the river at high speed only a few inches above the water. They alight on a protruding rock, call loudly for a few seconds and then jump into the rapids where they walk along on the bottom, picking at small insects and crustaceans. The sight of birds strolling on the bottom of the clear, fast water is quite amazing. Just as suddenly, they jump back onto a rock, give themselves a brief shake, and once again appear totally dry. Their feathers are covered with a particularly effective oil that sheds water better than off a duck's back.

The bed of the upper river appears stable and established, but in many past seasons, the Oldman wandered in its bed and carved into a floodplain that is only a few centimetres above the river water. The flat floodplain is home to water-loving species including sandbar willow, bog birch, smooth willow, a few shrubby cinquefoil for colour and thickets of tall sedge. Beneath the shrubs the boggy soil is covered with horsetail rush.

The floodplain is a few metres wide and ends at a low bank carved into the overburden of glacial debris pushed down the valley from the west and erosion debris coming down the hills to the north and south. Immediately above the floodplain, the thin soil is much drier, and willow and sedge are

Yellow stonecrop on sandstone soil.

Roseroot and moss campion growing on limestone soil.

Oyster Creek drains the montane hills north of the Oldman River.

replaced by shrubby cinquefoil, bearberry, juniper and buffalo berry. Where there are few shrubs, fescue grasses abound along with flowers also found in the Montane and Fescue Grass ecoregions—three-flowered avens, mouse-ear chickweed, northern bedstraw and yarrow. But, there are also subalpine species—stonecrop, ranunculus and hawkweed.

A few metres away from the edge of the bank the forest begins, a closed canopy of lodgepole pine mixed with groves of fir, white spruce and a few aspen. Beneath the trees there are few plants except the bright yellow flowers of heart-leaf arnica gleaming in cool forest shade.

The upper valley

The floor of the upper valley is almost flat and level, built up with a mix of white and gray pebbles of glacial and river debris brought down from the limestone and dolomite mountains to the west. The thicker, muddier soils along the valley bottom support lush growths of grasses, sedges and wildflowers. Closer to the creeks, a dense layer of willow, birch and shrubby cinquefoil imperfectly covers gardens of strawberry, shooting star and tall rushes. This is prime grizzly and black bear habitat.

Just west of crossing Oyster Creek, the trail ascends a small ridge, a lateral moraine of the glacier that once filled a cirque in the mountains along the Divide. The moraine is built of rapidly draining carbonate rock, covered with a mere skim of soil and supporting a forest of sparse pine. Once the moraine joins with the flank of Mount Gass, pine gives way to subalpine spruce, and as the trail goes on upward the trees begin to thin and get shorter.

Oldman River Headwaters

Memory Lake fills a shallow depression scooped out by glaciers flowing from the Continental Divide.

Memory Lake

Right at the foot of the mountain wall the trail divides with one branch curving to the north and leading to Memory Lake. The other branch follows a surveyors' cutline up the side of the mountain. If you are heading for the high country, drop your pack at the junction and visit the lake.

The north branch of the trail ends at Memory Lake, a small tarn carved into the underlying rock by glaciers and fed with precipitation flowing through and under the loose mountain debris. Beyond a thin fringe of sedges and grass, white spruce crowd the lake's margin. A few water birds may be found on the lake, but they are rare. Away from the water, and at higher elevations, white spruce yield to Engelmann spruce, alpine fir, alpine larch and whitebark pine.

Fires ripped through the valley in 1910 and 1936, so many of the trees are only a few decades old and seldom more than 10 m high near the lake and much smaller at higher elevations. Here and there, however, stands of Engelmann spruce and whitebark pine were spared, and some of these are over 400 years old, placing them amongst the biggest trees of their species in the province.

High cirque

The west branch of the trail takes a straight line up a jumble of glacial moraines and scree and levels out high above Memory Lake in a small cirque.

The subalpine landscape runs out in the cirque. Here, the last trees are represented by stunted krummholz in a mat of glacier lily, grass-of-parnassus, arnica, bearberry, groundsel, alpine forget-me-not and mountain heather. The floor and wall of the cirque are riddled with tunnels dug by Columbian ground squirrels, and even higher up rabbit-like pika warn the world of human presence.

Habitat diversity

The great variety of habitats in the upper valley of the Oldman River and proximity to the Continental Divide has allowed diverse plant and animal life to flourish. The extensive wetlands adjacent to mature forests is a prime breeding habitat for songbirds, including species of warbler and thrush.

Moose and mule deer browse amongst the wetland shrubs and sedges. Elk spend their summers and their autumn mating season here before moving slowly down the valley just ahead of hard winter weather. They will spend the cold months below the Whaleback Ridge. Bighorn sheep also summer in the valley before moving across the passes along the Continental Divide and into British Columbia for the winter. The roughest and highest places are occupied year-round by mountain goats.

Alternatives

The upper Oldman River valley is exceptional for the diverse habitat, plants and animals contained in its relatively compact expanses. A few days spent exploring the valley is a solid introduction to the mountainous landscape of southernmost Alberta.

The hills of limestone glacial debris below the mountains overlooks clearcuts on the flanks of Pasque Ridge.

There are plenty of places to go in the upper valley, and access is generally good thanks to generations of exploration for minerals and natural gas, mining and logging. Most of the little creeks flowing into the Oldman River are followed with some kind of a trail, but all too often they lead to clearcuts and old burns.

Conservationists have been working for well over a generation to have the upper valley set aside as a protected area, so far without success. Each summer, the welts of new seismic cutlines, access roads, cut blocks and recreation vehicle trails appear on the hillsides and along the streams.

In winter, the valley is truly remote wilderness. The roads are poorly maintained over the winter, if at all, and it may not be possible to drive far beyond the Forestry Trunk Road. In just the right conditions, before the warm chinook winds melt and glaze a fall of fresh snow, the valley is ideal for exploration on skis and snowshoes. Winter recreationists must remember they are a long way from other people and they must be prepared for any and all unexpected events.

19 South Twin Creek

Mode: foot
Rating: moderate
Time: 4 - 6 hours
Distance: 11 km
Elevation change: 180 m
Map: 82 J/1 Langford Creek

South Twin Creek conceals a tremendous surprise and delight for the walker looking for something really different in the foothills—a small lake of clear, blue, cold water. The pond, really, is perched on the jutting pulpit of a rocky ridge overlooking the soft contours of the aspen foothills surrounding Chain Lakes. Thanks to a quirk in geological history, there is no other place like this in the rest of the ecoregion. The result is a splendid destination for a day trip or overnight.

Right from the highway, the trail ascends the valley wall above South Twin Creek. The creek will not be seen again for the next 1.5 km. The creek is 50 m below the trail in places, and the trail is carved through a dense forest of large white spruce and Engelmann spruce, with a tincture of lodgepole pine and aspen.

There are few openings in the subalpine forest with a view, but near the head of the meadow there is a good

The spring-fed ponds rest on the prow of a sandstone ridge high above the foothills.

Getting there

Head for the junction of Highway 532 and Highway 940. Highway 532 leaves Highway 22 and winds its way west up a long valley between low, rounded hills until it begins its final assault on the pass connecting the foothills to the east and the mountains to the west. In the winter, the last few steep kilometres of driving can be treacherous. From the pass, follow the road downward to the Shell gas plant at the junction with Highway 940, and turn south. In about 1 km, the southern road crosses North Twin Creek and then South Twin Creek.

The creeks are small and easy to miss in a dry year, but there are small hard-to-read signs marking both creeks. There is a well-signed cattleguard on the south side of South Twin Creek. If you drive over a cattleguard, you just went past the trailhead. The trailhead is immediately north of the cattleguard and looks like what it is—a narrow exploration road sliced through a tall stand of white and Engelmann spruce. Park as far off the road as possible, but expect your vehicle to be covered with road dust when you get back.

Camping

There is excellent camping in all directions from the trailhead, including campgrounds at Indian Graves on Highway 532, Cataract Creek north on Highway 940, and Livingstone Falls south on Highway 940. If you need everything to keep your RV alive, go to Chain Lakes Provincial Park and its better amenities. South of Kananaskis Country there is plentiful random camping.

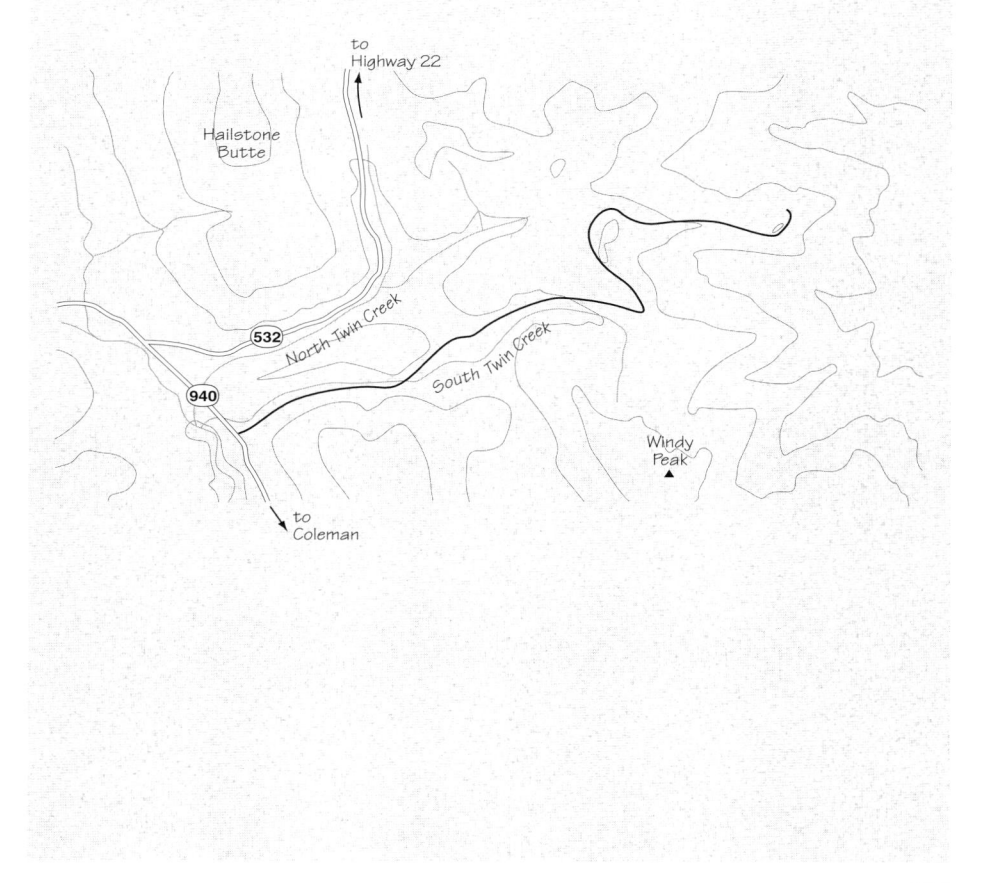

Narrow escape

As it happens, the beds of Cretaceous sandstone that piled up to make the ridge containing the lake are relatively flat and horizontal. This is in spite of the forces of mountain building happening only a few metres away to the west. Sandstone beds much farther east of the mountains are bent, folded, twisted and even flipped upside down. At Kimball Park, for example, over 40 km from the nearest mountain, the sandstone beds are gently curved and tilted completely on end. Here, the ridge of horizontal sandstone above the Twin creeks is tightly connected to the limestone mountains of Hailstone Butte to the north and the Livingstone Range to the south. A narrow sandstone finger reaches east amongst looming mountain neighbours.

Glacial tumult

Then there were glaciers. The area around Plateau Mountain and the Porcupine Hills must have been a tumultuous place during the Pleistocene Ice Age. Neither Plateau Mountain nor the Porcupine Hills were covered with glacial ice, and the perched lake is right between them. As the ice flowed around these places, the main glaciers were joined by smaller tributary glaciers flowing out of higher country to the west. The Livingstone Range, like other ranges in the Eastern Front, was a divide where glacial icefields at the crest of the range divided into lobes flowing east and west.

The pass or col midway on the South Twin Creek route marks the divide. One part of the Ice Age glacier moved east to join the much larger glacier filling the valley between the Porcupine Hills and the Front Ranges. The lobe flowing west met the system of glaciers that carved the valley of the Livingstone River. Both sides below the pass, east and west, have a similar bowl-shaped upper end leading into a U-shaped valley, the hallmarks of glacial erosion.

For some reason, the ridge containing the lake was not ground into the round-top shape of all the foothills in sight. Instead, it was left just flat enough to hold a small lake. Perhaps because in the process of mountain building the ridge's sandstone beds were left flat, glaciers had a hard time gnawing on the end grain of the rock, and the rock lasted longer than the ice.

Glaciers carved both sides of the ridge into steep cliffs, but not the flat top holding the lake.

A low hill separates the streams of North and South Twin Creek.

view of the rounded hill separating the North and South Twin creeks. The hill is limestone and marks the leading edge of mountain building. From this point on, all the way to the lake, the bedrock will be sandstone.

The soil is a Brunisol, fairly thick by foothill and mountain standards, over a mix of limestone and sandstone debris, sand, silt and clay. Near the trailhead, the soil contains more limestone fragments and the soil near the pass contains more sandstone. The thick forests barely allow much understorey, but flowers include geranium, arnica and bedstraw wherever there is enough light. In winter there is not much evidence of animal traffic in the deep, cold forest. The trail to the pass, however, was tracked over by the many animals who like a good trail as much as anybody. The pass connects two quite different environments, and animals take advantage of both by moving between them.

Subalpine meadows

The trail leaves the subalpine forest where the creek joins a meadow of wetlands, grasslands and shrublands. The meadow is sheltered in the lee of the tall limestone hill, and protected by the fringe of tough subalpine trees. The wetland is at the bottom of a drainage system that collects all the water flowing down South Twin Creek. The entire drainage system is contained in less than 2 sq. km, but it is enough to support plants and animals that are unusual elsewhere.

Compared to the few animal tracks in the towering subalpine forest, in winter the meadow is crossed and recrossed by runways for hare, squirrels, small rodents, coyotes and deer. The snow is thoroughly drilled with mouse peepholes. Chickadees and crows call from their concealment in the trees. The presence of these animals was not so unusual, but they all seemed to be packed into and around the meadow. As well, there may be the well-defined tracks of at least two wolves. Animal

South Twin Creek

The trail wanders up the windswept slope toward the crest of the ridge.

tracks are especially dense and various near the meadow and in the close fringe of shrubs, aspen clumps and spruce. The meadow, with its wetland, is a prize place even in winter.

The exploration road crosses a bit of bog where the creek begins to take shape, then follows the edge of a clearcut extending to the north and west. It is a sad thing to see in such splendid country, but there it is. Stop and have a look.

Clearcut

A clearcut is exactly what the name implies—a piece of forest cut clear of every tree. The longtime argument from the forestry industry is that clearcutting a forest is the best way to harvest fibre and the best way to manage commercial forest resources. Of course, there are a great many people inside and especially outside the forest industry that disagree completely and Canadian history includes a lengthy record of violent conflict between forest users and forest preservationists.

This is not the place to settle the argument, but clearcuts are very gruesome when set amongst the splendours of Alberta's natural landscape. Walkers will simply have to hope and pray the clearcutters are right, because it is unlikely either governments or foresters will give up the practice. In Alberta, the political preference is to make resources into money and if some resource cannot be made into money, it is ignored, or worse, persecuted.

The valley above the meadow and on the east flank of the last limestone hill was logged about 20 years ago, and no trees survived the devastation. The clearcut is distinguished from a natural clearing by its clean, straight edges and by the scattered debris of saw-cut stumps and slash. From a distance up the trail toward the pass, the herringbone pattern of skid roads is still visible, but the clearcut is gradually growing over with young lodgepole pine, white spruce and shrubs.

First, a grassland

In the first 10 years after the plot was logged, grasses, sedges and herbs increased dramatically compared to the growth of these plants under the standing forest. New plant species also moved into the area and at its peak, smaller plants may have produced four times as much biomass as they did before logging. Many of these plant species are the preferred food of deer and elk, and the small clearcut was a popular place for these animals in the summer. Ground nesting birds probably increased in the clearcut, but tree nesting birds disappeared. Furbearers fled the area after it was logged, but once mice and hares began to inhabit the taller and more luxuriant grasses and herbs, weasels, coyotes and lynx may also have returned.

Until taller shrubs were established, few large animals ventured into the clearcut during winter—the garden of delights is very exposed to the eyes of watching predators. The trees are too small to offer shelter from the wind and black winter sky, or shade from the summer sun.

Then, a shrubland

The clearcut is now at the shrub and small tree stage of regrowth. The grasses and herbs are thick on the ground between tight clumps of willow, rose, buckbrush, gooseberry and aspen. Slightly taller is a liberal sprinkle of head-high spruce and pine. This is favoured summer habitat for small tree-nesting birds such as sparrows, thrushes and flycatchers, and for rodents. These small animals attract hawks and coyotes. Deer, moose and elk move into the clearcut where there are good summer eats and a clear line of sight. Few of these animals stay for the winter and winter outdoor enthusiasts visiting South Twin Creek will quickly see there are few animal tracks anywhere in the clearcut.

Other animals have departed completely, including bear, red squirrel, marten, grouse, eagles, owls and many other species that need old-growth trees and hollow trees to survive. In a few more years, the shrubs may be tall enough to give animals the food, shel-

Flowers and grass crowd the space between the lake and the rim of the ridge.

ter and cover they need to survive, but until then few animals will move into the area for a winter.

It will be at least 10 more years before trees are tall enough—more than 2 m in height—to provide winter food and cover for deer, moose and elk. Bears will also come back about 25 years after the plot was logged. By then, waste logs and stumps will be riddled with tasty insects, and the bushes and aspen will be tall enough to hide a bear and mature enough to provide an autumn feed of berries. Hares will also return in greater numbers, attracted by the tender bark of young pine trees. Hares might girdle and kill up to half of the growing conifers. In turn, hares attract even more coyotes and lynx.

An immature forest

In another 20 to 25 years, or about 50 years after the site was logged, there should be good stands of immature lodgepole pine growing amongst the shrubs and aspen covering the site. It will take much longer for spruce to become established, perhaps 60 years after it was logged. As the trees grow, grasses and herbs will gradually decline in abundance and numbers of species, but the combination of good grass growth and tall slender trees is ideal habitat for moose, deer and elk. Grouse, hares and furbearers will increase. More animals will return to the area, including squirrel and hawks.

And finally a mature forest

Eventually, perhaps in 100 years, lodgepole pine will take over from aspen and shrubs and then spruce will dominate pine, returning the clearcut to its natural state. But maybe not. The mechanics of clearcutting may have interfered with natural succession by disrupting the processes of soil formation, drainage, water quality and exposure. We may have to wait another century to see what becomes of this insult to the valley's quiet splendour.

Onward and upward

The road curves away from the clearcut and back toward the east, then climbs slightly above the headwaters of the creek and directly toward the pass. Here, on the far east side of the meadow, the look is rather montane, with open fescue grasslands, sparse spruce trees and exposed ridges of red, black and brown sandstone. The pass comes as a sudden surprise, looking over the eastern horizon far out to the Interior Plains. Splendid.

From the pass, the view east takes in the Chain Lakes, Highway 22, the north end of the Porcupine Hills, and the mixed grassland beyond. The east view is the ultimate reward of an Alberta sunset. The west view is best in the morning where sunlit waves of subalpine green merge with the distant blue summits on the Continental Divide.

From the pass, the trail climbs directly onto the shoulder of the north-leading ridge. About half a kilometre north of the pass and 80 m of elevation gain, there is a split in the trail. The east or right trail passes around the ridge summit on the flank facing the bowl below the lake. The west or left branch passes on the other side of the summit with a close view of crumbled limestone flanks of Hailstone Butte. Either way, the faint trails around the summit cross exposed, steep slopes of sandstone rubble worn from the crest and flanks of the ridge. The few trees scattered along the brow of the ridge—mostly Engelmann spruce and limber pine—are fiercely wind shaped. Wind is a feature of the valley, and the eastern inside route may be best on chinook days.

Both trails join in the final great arc of the ridge walk, heading first northwest, then north and finally due east to reach the lake. Most of the ridge is cloaked with a fine forest of spruce and pine, dappled with exposed bedrock, shrubs and patches of grass and flowers. The grasses are typical of a fescue

Powerful winds regularly blow scarce soil off the crest of the ridge.

meadow, but the flowers are a meld of grassland, parkland and subalpine species. This is a fine example of foothills landscape in the middle part of southern Alberta.

Lakeside destination

The trail descends gently along the avenue topping the ridge beyond the summit, passing through a cloak of tall spruce and pine to reach the lake. The jewel of water is girded with a narrow fringe of glowing green rush, sedge and water grasses, constrained by the wall of willows and spruce competing for the water's edge.

To the north, the rim of the lake swells in a hummock of rock to a high point overlooking the lake and the eastern foothills and grasslands. The hill is dressed with wind-blasted spruce and juniper. The view on an evening of desiccated chinook wind is spectacular. The last light illuminates the far eastern landscape in every detail. With darkness, there are stars and the moon. At night, owls call, nighthawks trill and boom, and many night visitors splash around in the lake.

The rampart above South Twin Creek is poised where important elements of southern Alberta's natural history meet—Cretaceous seas, ancient limestone, mountain building, glaciation and watershed ecology, overlaid with a delicate fabric of plants and animals and the ever-heavy hand of humans. A seismic line has been cut straight across the south side of the tiny lake, with ancient limber pine hacked off and tossed in the shrubs. Just a last reminder that nothing is sacred in Alberta except the chance of getting money.

Special Places

*Meadows at the head of Salter Creek.
Photo: Gillean Daffern.*

Opposite: Salter Creek's newly scrubbed bed and foreshore.

Special Places for a Quick Visit

Salter Creek

The trailhead for Salter Creek is in the Cataract Creek Campground, making it very accessible for anyone with a vehicle. The trail is fairly long—a little less than 7 km one way—but there is only 250 m of elevation gain. Even a few kilometres of walking will take you along a fine mountain creek and deep into the subalpine forest.

Salter Creek was named by George Dawson in 1884 after his horse packer. Dawson was the first geologist to explore this region. Salter complained mightily about the rough and rocky trail that crossed and recrossed the creek on its way over the low pass between Plateau Mountain and Mount Burke. If Salter found reason to complain in 1884, he would have had much more reason after 1995. In that year, the year of the Great Flood, Salter Creek was transformed from a little dribbling stream into a raging torrent that completely destroyed the lower part of the trail.

Now, rather than a well-used walking and horse riding trail, hikers must negotiate a jumble of loose boulders and gravel banks. The torrent of floodwater followed the narrow foot trail that over the years had been pounded into the thin turf along the valley floor. Now the trail is a raw gash almost a metre deep and several metres across, an excellent lesson in mountain hydraulics.

The upper part of the trail was not so thoroughly churned as the lower part. Nearing the pass, the thick spruce forest gives way to a wetter meadow fringed with dense willow and alder shrubs. The meadow is closely flanked by Mount Burke on the north and Plateau Mountain on the south. Stronger hikers can scramble up the scree slope below Mount Burke to reach a flat limestone shelf overlooking the entire pass and offering an excellent view of the surrounding mountains and the prairie beyond.

The lower part of the creek below the trailhead flows through a delightful grove of willow, birch and a few aspen. Dipper birds flit along just above the tumbling water and mule deer quietly browse new growth on the shrubs.

None of the Salter Creek route is suited for wheelchairs, but the roads and trails in and around the campground are wide and firm.

9 Alpine Ecoregion

The Alpine Ecoregion inspires an indelible and lasting awareness of the power of nature. The mountains are massive and mighty, created as floating continents crushed into each other over many millions of years. Many more millions of years of rain, frost and wind eroded, softened and smoothed the rubble of continental collisions. Then, great glaciers ground repeatedly across the entire landscape, transforming the softness of long ago into the starkly carved mountains we have today.

As walkers will soon discover, there is plenty of variety in the mountains of southernmost Alberta, but because the mountains only run 130 km north to south, they share many general features. Most important for mountain walkers, who are usually found sweating and toiling as well as extolling the beauties around them, they share a geological history. It is the nature and quality of the rocky landscape underfoot that sets the feel and experience of travel in the Alpine Ecoregion apart from travel in grasslands, foothills and forests.

The post-glacial landscape

One unifying force in the history of the southern Rocky Mountains was the force of the glaciers that changed quite different rocklands into very similar landscapes. The post-glacial landscape is the one that counts for walkers.

The tallest mountains rise 1500 m above the valley floor, built of stacked cliffs and shelves filled with scree and topped with snow most of the year. Seen from below, on a highway or on the trail at the bottom of a valley, the tall mountains are stupendously huge, rather chaotic, and unconquerable in body or spirit.

The same icy hand carved all the mountains, even though there are no glaciers in the mountains of southernmost Alberta. The evidence of glaciers and glaciation is everywhere.

Alpine

Ancient mountains

Before the last glaciation of North America, the Rocky Mountains would have appeared from a distance very much as they do today. Viewed from Lethbridge two million years ago, the low western horizon was filled with a line of mountaintops. From a closer viewpoint, the clear tree line separated dark subalpine forests from snowy mountain summits. All the modern rivers and smaller streams occupied the same valleys they occupy today, including the Livingstone, Oldman, Crowsnest, Carbondale, Castle rivers, and the mountain tributaries of the Waterton, Belly and St. Mary rivers.

From inside the mountain landscape, however, the mountains and valleys would have looked quite different. Before the glaciers were born, the forces of erosion had been at work on the ancestral Rocky Mountains for millions of years. The mountains were rounded and smoothed, displaying a softer face than the towering cliffs of today. Thick, rich soils supported a forest that more completely covered the valleys and slopes. Valleys were steeper and narrower and more of a V-shape. As rivers wound their way around the interfingered ridges that fell from the mountain summits, the main valleys were carved into smoothly sinuous shapes.

Then, two million years of glaciation in the Pleistocene epoch profoundly reshaped the mountain landscape.

At the tree line and the beginning of the Alpine Ecoregion on Mount Galwey.

Alpine

The summit of Thunder Mountain, a barren ridge of frost shattered rock.

The birth of glaciers

Glaciation probably began very modestly. A few exceptionally snowy winters and slightly cooler summers allowed snow to accumulate. There came a time when more snow fell in the high mountains than could melt off in the summer. The snow piled up, especially on the cold, dark north and east-facing slopes of the higher mountains. Eventually, the mass of snow and ice began to create its own local climate, favouring more rapid build up of glacial ice.

In a very short geological time—perhaps only a few decades—the snow reached depths of 20 to 25 m. At that thickness, the weight of snow is great enough to cause the formation of ice at the base of the pack.

If the ice is resting on even a slightly inclined surface, it will begin to slowly flow downward under the relentless force of gravity. The isolated glaciers grew to fill their home valleys and crept downward into the bigger valleys. The separate flows met at lower elevations and then coalesced into a single sheet. The biggest mountain glaciers spilled out of the mountains and reached far into the foothills and plains to the east.

Relentless grinding

The glaciers moving down the valleys were loaded with rocky debris, and the great mass of moving ice acted like a giant rasp. The gently curving valleys were ground much deeper and wider, and the slender overlapping spur ridges were trimmed off. The winding river valleys were transformed into the long, straight, U-shaped glacial valleys we see today.

In ancient times, main streams and their tributaries had formed their valleys together, so side streams flowed smoothly into the main stream. The glaciers in the main valleys, however, were much thicker and heavier than glaciers in the side valleys, so the main valleys were ground deeper. When the ice sheets retreated, the side valleys were left hanging far up the walls of the main valley. Today, side streams often spill great heights over the rocky lip of a hanging valley, rather than following a continuous bed to join with the main stream on the bottom of the valley.

The heads of valleys and the slopes where each small glacier was born were intensely weathered by cold and ice into broad, cliff-walled cirques. Often, glacial debris or the lip of a hanging valley trapped a small lake or tarn high up amongst the mountain walls and peaks. Cirques and tarns are only found in glaciated landscapes. As each glacier receded, the walls of the ice-carved upper valleys shed their covering of shattered rock into the valley below forming great slopes of scree or talus.

The moving glaciers carried and pushed a vast load of rock and debris into the lower valleys and eventually into the foothills and plains to the east. Moraines are the heaps of rubble left behind as the glaciers dwindled.

Lateral moraines formed as the moving ice pushed debris off to the sides. Terminal moraines were pushed in front of an advancing glacier and left in place when the glacier gradually melted back. Recessional moraines formed when a glacier stopped growing and moving downward, and as the toe of the glacier melted the great burden of debris was dropped in an arc along the leading edge of ice. Ground moraine is deposited beneath a glacier, leaving a hummocky and irregular surface of gravel and rock. Moraines are clear evidence of glaciation.

Mountains rebuilt

Compared to the great continental ice sheets that covered most of what is now Canada, the mountain glaciers were quite modest. Nevertheless, the ice filled the major valleys in the southern Rockies, burying all but a few very high peaks. Because the Rockies have only recently been free of ice and because there has been relatively little time for post-glacial erosion, the mountains appear today very much as they did when the glaciers finally melted away. The evidence of glaciers is still fresh.

All the features of a glaciated landscape—long, straight, U-shaped valleys, hanging valleys, cirques, tarns and moraines—can be seen throughout the Rockies of southernmost Alberta.

The Alpine Ecoregion

Area: 14,656 sq. km or 7% of the province.

Topography: Mountainous.

Elevation: 2100 m to the top of the highest peak.

Climate: No alpine weather stations operate in the winter months, so there is little reliable and accurate information detailing the climate in the Alpine Ecoregion, but this region is probably where some of Alberta's most extreme weather may be found. The Alpine Ecoregion will receive at least as much precipitation as the Subalpine Ecoregion, making it the wettest part of Alberta. Most summer precipitation falls in June and August. It is also the coldest part of Alberta, with summer temperatures averaging several degrees colder than in subalpine country. Freezing temperatures occur in any month, and even July experiences up to six freezing events in most years. The frost-free period is probably less than 28 days in the year. There are no chinooks in the Alpine Ecoregion, so the mountains do not enjoy spells of warm mid-winter days. The deep cold and unbroken months of winter preserve snow in this region much longer than elsewhere. Especially deep snow packs can take years to finally melt away. Strong winter winds redistribute the fallen snow, sweeping the rock bare in some places and piling metres of snow in others. Summer winds quickly dessicate the places where there is little snow cover.

Humans: Some of the lower elevations of the Alpine Ecoregion have been penetrated by mineral exploration roads and logging roads, but most of the alpine country is unapproachable with vehicles. The high mountain country is still the most pristine land in southernmost Alberta.

20 Mount Galwey

Mode: foot
Rating: scramble
Time: 4 - 6 hours
Distance: 4 km
Maximum elevation: 2335 m
Elevation gain: 940 m
Map: 82 H/4 Waterton Lakes

Mount Galwey is poised near the leading edge of the Lewis Thrust, the main geological structure that gives much of the Eastern Front Ranges of the Rockies their distinctive character and appearance. The thrust is so obvious because at Waterton there is a direct connection between mountains and grasslands, without much of the transitional foothills found to the north. From the top of Mount Galwey, just to the west of the Waterton Lakes, the sharp change from grassland to rockland is especially evident.

If you are camped in the Crandell Campground, leave your rig there and start out for the trailhead on foot, following the road. At the campground gate, the road leaves the forest and enters a narrow strip of grassland on the south side of the creek, then crosses the bridge over Blakiston Creek.

In most seasons, the Blakiston is a modest but extremely picturesque mountain stream. In spring, however, the Blakiston can be a raging torrent powerful enough to carry huge boulders downstream and out of the mountains. The evidence of the great flood of '95 can be seen everywhere along the Blakiston's banks and beds.

Across the meadow

The road crosses the bridge into a much broader belt of grasslands where the valley bottom is better exposed to the

Mount Galwey towers above the Blakiston Creek valley and the eastern fescue grassland.

Coppermine Creek crosses the flood-stripped shore of Blakiston Creek.

sun. The closest trees are almost a kilometre away on the northwest flank of Mount Galwey. The grassland between the bridge and trees higher up the slope is a splendid example of fescue grassland, extending beyond the trees all the way to the alpine part of the route.

On the south side of Blakiston Creek, the soils are mostly new Regosols formed by the continuous flooding of the creek. The floods that occur every year or so are not violent enough to scour all the fine material away, so the surface floodplain is largely covered with lush vegetation, including white spruce and aspen with an understorey of shrubs, grasses and wildflowers.

The north side of the creek includes a much broader floodplain entirely covered with fescue grassland. The soils here are dark brown Chernozems thinly covering stony parent materials. The grassland is subject to less flooding, and the surface soils are more stable and developed. The soil drains very rapidly, favouring plants that can survive in a dry setting. The grasses are a typical mix of fescues and Parry oat grass along with bearberry, prickly rose and shrubby cinquefoil. In spring and summer, lupine, fleabane, bergamot and goldenrod haze the flat grassland with colour.

The saunter across the bridge and along the parkway is a great opportunity to preview the challenge that lies ahead. From the bridge, the entire route is in sight from the Coppermine Creek picnic area to the summit. A fine line, little more than a surface disturbance, can be seen scrawled across the steep scree slope beneath the summit cliffs. That is the trail, the hard work part of the route leading almost straight up the loose mountain debris.

Mount Galwey

Getting there

The trailhead is in Waterton Lakes National Park at the Coppermine Creek picnic area, 7.8 km west on the Red Rock Canyon Parkway. The picnic area is set in a delightful glade of upper montane trees and meadows. There is a pit toilet, an open cooking shelter with tables, and small parking area. Very nice.

The usual trailhead is at the picnic area, but this route starts along the banks of Blakiston Creek, a little to the south and east.

Camping

The best and most accessible camping is less than a kilometre away, at the Crandell Mountain Campground, about 10 km from the townsite. Set in a forest of lodgepole pine, spotted with spruce and fescue meadows, the campground is in every way up to Parks Canada standards for camping comfort. And priced accordingly at about $15.00 per night.

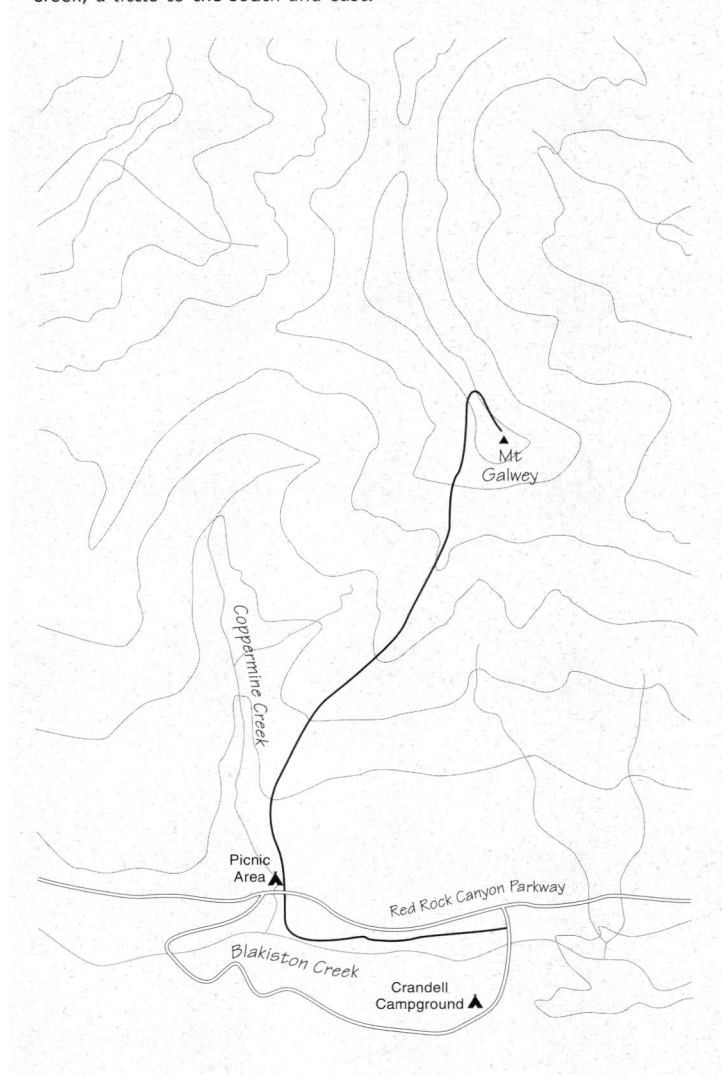

Mount Galwey

Sculpted juniper clings to the cracks in a shattered shelf of limestone.

Upward

Follow the campground road out to the Red Rock Canyon Parkway and turn to the west. In about 1 km, the parkway reaches Coppermine Creek picnic area. Near the Coppermine Creek picnic site there are a few fir, pine and aspen, where snow trapped on the lee side of the hill provides just enough moisture to give trees an early summer advantage. The creek is hidden in its narrow slot and screened by a fringe of black cottonwood, fir and willow. The creekbed is littered with the characteristic rocks of Waterton Lakes National Park.

At the picnic area, get your gear adjusted and then begin the stiff ascent by heading up the well-beaten trail immediately behind the cook shack. As soon as the trail begins to ascend away from the creek, the soils become much leaner and thinner Chernozems. The well-drained soil is a thorough mix of red and green argillites that have flaked from the flanks of Mount Galwey.

The trail leads to a bench about 30 m above the parking area with a good view up and down the Blakiston Valley, and apparently most people stop their journey there. The rest of the trail leading to the high summit is much fainter, but the route along the ridge is fairly obvious.

Mid-heights

In most places on the middle heights below Mount Galwey, naked bedrock is encountered about 50 m above the trailhead. Between the trailhead and the first band of bedrock, fescue grassland species predominate. Once bedrock is met, more usual subalpine species are encountered, including saxifrage, groundsel, blue beardtongue and draba. These mountain species are liberally mixed with the grassland species.

At 300 m above the trailhead most of the grassland species of flowers disappear, but fescue grasses, juniper and bearberry persist to the highest sub-

Mountain building and lakes

The Waterton Lakes

The Waterton Lakes are amongst the largest lakes in the Canadian Rockies, and Upper Waterton Lake, at 150 m, is the deepest in the Rockies. The size, depth and shape of the Waterton Lakes is the result of a unique combination of geological and glacial history.

By the beginning of the Cenozoic era about 67 million years ago, the landscape of western Canada was that of a sprawling upland. Hills, low mountains and broad river valleys interrupted an otherwise level plain. Then, the great forces of mountain building first crushed and broke the ancient, flat beds of Proterozoic limestone and dolomite, and thrust them high onto the much younger Cretaceous sandstones and shales that underlie the grassland regions. It was the Lewis Thrust, Livingstone Thrust, and smaller thrusts and faults that created the Front Ranges of southernmost Alberta between 50 and 100 million years ago.

Two such huge plates of displaced rock came to rest where the Waterton Lakes were eventually formed, the western slab leaning to the east and resting on the eastern slab. Where they met, there was a long valley, tightly bound on the east and west, and relatively open to the north and south. Over the next 100 million years, the slabs were exposed to all the forces of erosion—wind, water, frost, chemical action, plant action and gravity.

A river filled the valley bottom, perhaps widening into a few small lakes. The river was fed by tributaries flowing from the highlands on both sides, and together the water carried a great deal of erosion debris east and eventually onto the lowlands.

The position and orientation of the valley has profound consequences today. The Waterton Lakes are notorious for the frequency and ferocity of the chinook winds that rip along their length. The lakes lies parallel to the mountains, while all the glacial valleys flowing into them are perpendicular both to the lakes and to the line of the mountains. Chinook winds, pressing over the mountains from the west, find easy passage down the deep side valleys and when several of them dump a load of wind onto the lakes, the famous "Waterton Wind Tunnel" comes to life. On an average day, winds blow at a constant 32 km per hour, and gales to 160 km per hour are common.

The glacier-carved Blakiston Valley, filled with aspen and fescue meadows.

Glacial growth

Then, two million years ago, the great Ice Age began. By the end of the age of glaciers in southernmost Alberta about 6,000 years ago, the Waterton region was scoured by ice at least three times. Wherever people travel in the region, the finishing touches on the natural portrait were applied by glaciers.

The ebbs and flows of mountain and continental glaciers met and overlapped in the region around the park, thoroughly remaking the entire landscape. The first glaciers, born about 400,000 years ago and lasting about 100,000 years, were the mightiest. First a huge system of glaciers developed in the western mountains with an ice cap covering all but the tallest mountains in the southern Rockies. When the main glacier occupied the Waterton Valley, the floor was probably 240 m above the present floor, and the ice above the valley floor was over 1350 m thick. The glacier consumed 4000 cu. km of water.

Side glaciers flowed thickly down every available slope to the east, over the foothills and out onto the flatland beyond. At Kipp, about 20 km west of Lethbridge and 80 km from Waterton Valley, the first mountain glaciers slowed, stalled and then began to recede. The glacial debris was left behind.

At the same time, the vast continental glacier was creeping into the region from the north and northeast. Here and there, the two glaciers briefly met, blending and mixing each others' earlier destruction. Southernmost Alberta is near the margin of continental glaciers, and by the time they penetrated the higher elevations of the western foothills and grasslands, the great glacier was quite thin and exhausted.

The ice slowly pushed into the foothills and the lower flanks of the mountains, across the work of the mountain glacier. Wherever the continental glacier reached it left behind a load of exotic rock carried all the way from the Canadian Shield far to the north and east. Soon, the greatest glacier dwindled and disappeared, only to be replaced with another onslaught of ice.

This pattern of ebbing and flowing of mountain and continental glaciers was repeated over the years. Each following glacial event was smaller and weaker than the one before. Later glaciers followed in the track of earlier glaciers, scoring and underscoring the importance of ice in Waterton's landscape.

Shaping Waterton Valley

The valley holding the Waterton Lakes tells the story. There are several splendid viewpoints, including the Bear's Hump on the flank of Mount Crandell (excellent trail, 2.4 km return, 160 m gain) and the lounge in the Prince of Wales Hotel (paved parking lot, 20 m return, 1 m gain). The length of Upper Waterton Lake is in clear view due south all the way to Montana. Both sides of the entire valley can be studied at leisure and in varying degrees of comfort.

The slopes of the valley mountains do not fall cleanly in a straight line from top to bottom. Rather, the mountain profiles are gently scalloped forming a series of great concave slopes from bottom to top. Each dished slope marks the track of a passing glacier. The oldest and mightiest glacier covered the mountains entirely and opened the track for the later glaciers that filled the scallops below.

After the first great glacier, the summits and flanks of the higher mountains stood above the main glacier and supported even smaller glaciers of their own. The high elevation glaciers flowed down to join the main glacier moving along the bottom of Waterton Valley. The main glacier was still mighty enough to scour the bottom of the valley and cut into the tilted slabs of bedrock. The glacier's progress was stalled by a bed of very hard rock spanning the Bosporus strait between Upper and Middle Waterton lakes and joining Bear's Hump on Crandell Mountain on the west side of the lakes and Vimy Ridge on the east.

The glacier was almost immobilized until it grew enough to drive over and through the resistant rock and finish gouging out the rest of the lake system. Because it sat unmoving in the upper lake, while collecting the added mass of the tributary glaciers, the glacier was much larger than it would have been had it not encountered the bed of hard rock. In its efforts to climb the obstacle, the glacier ground a very large bed for itself—now the deepest lake in the Canadian Rockies.

Once breached, the Waterton glaciers ground north of the Bosporus, and joined a large glacier flowing east along the present Blakiston Creek valley. The combined glaciers bent toward the northeast, pushing beyond the mountains and onto the lower, drier and warmer eastern flatlands.

A glimpse of the Waterton Lakes from the summit.

Glacial recession

The last glacier stopped growing, and as the climate warmed over the next several thousands of years, the ice receded and began shedding its hoard of ground rock onto the eastern plain.

By 15,000 years ago, the glacier had receded all the way up the valley to the Bosporus. There, a large tablet of ice was separated from the body of the glacier, slightly protected by the cool shade of the hard rock ledge. The main glacier eventually disappeared, but the tongue of ice below the Bosporus lasted long enough to press and pack the shattered rock beneath it. When this last glacier disappeared, it left behind the shallow impressions containing the Middle and Lower Waterton lakes.

At one time, the Middle and Lower lakes may have formed a single lake, but 10,000 years of flow by Blakiston Creek from the west and Sofa Creek from the east created great fans of glacial and erosion debris filling the lower valley. The creeks are adding to the valley fan and may eventually fill the lower lake with debris. The Waterton townsite sits on a delta created by Cameron Creek and this delta, too, is still active. In enough time, all the lakes will be filled completely with erosion debris washed down the mountains.

Very different lakes

All the Waterton Lakes support interesting aquatic life. The cold upper lake supports the least life of all four lakes, including Maskinonge Lake. The water of the upper lake is cold and deep, but not very productive of fish food. Nevertheless, 17 species of fish live in these waters. They depend on sparse but reliable availability of food, so while the numbers of fish are low in the upper lake, the number of species is large.

The middle lake is shallower, with fewer species of fish because several species of deep water cold-loving fish cannot survive in the shallower waters. The middle lake is warmer, more productive of fish food, and supports greater numbers of fish, but fewer species.

The lower lake, perched on the transition between mountains and plains, is even shallower, warmer and more productive of fish food and fish. Shorebirds, waterfowl and water-loving animals of all kinds occupy the moist foreshore of the lower lake, feeding on the lake's abundant food resources.

Maskinonge Lake is the shallowest, warmest and most productive of all Waterton's lakes. The water is only a metre deep, exposed to the full heat of Alberta's summer sun. The lake is full of water plants, insects and fish, especially the northern pike after which the lake was named from the original Algonkian language.

Only the middle section of the lakes is visible from the summit of Mount Galwey, but there are few other places that give a comparable view of the transition between grassland and rockland. From almost a kilometre above the lake water, the signs of Waterton's mountain building and glacial history can be read like a map.

Beardtongue and gooseberry on argillite scree.

alpine margin. At mid-elevations, at about 1200 m, subalpine species of flowers dominate.

The steep, loose slopes are dotted with single trees and clumps of subalpine fir. The rockiest and windiest places are occupied by whitebark pine. Wherever there are a few trees to offer shaded shelter, the grasses and flowers are taller and more luxuriant.

The route follows the obvious ridge leading to a main buttress of Mount Galwey. On the way to the top, the route crosses steep grassy slopes and climbs minor bedrock cliffs. The bedrock cliffs are ribbons of colour, shading from translucent white to glossy black, with brick red and sea green between.

The middle trail levels out to cross a section of flat-lying rock beds, home to a grove of fir and pine, a few gray jays, and the white scattered remains of a bighorn sheep that died over the past winter. This ends the easier part of the route, 500 m above the trailhead.

The upper heights

The level respite ends at the base of a very steep scree slope, made up of roundish and flat discs of limestone, dolomite, shale and argillite. There is a trail leading almost straight up the scree slope toward the cliffs high above. The ascent is slow and plodding with plenty of opportunity to look at flowers and the ever-expanding view.

Finally, the trail up the scree slope curves beneath the last grove of wind-tormented fir and leads to a gap in the first cliff band and onto a broad plat-

The final approach traverses the steep, loose scree below the summit.

Mount Galwey

From the summit the Rockies roll away deep into Montana.

form of firm rock. The approach to the summit follows the crest of the platform by climbing over and through breaches in the limestone cliffs. The route leads directly toward the formidable prow of the last high cliff just below the summit. Curve to the west, staying on a shelf of firm rock covered with loose debris until it reaches a col to the north and west of the summit at 2270 m. The south scoop of the col leads to the summit at 2335 m.

The summit

The last few metres are gained by walking the exposed crest above the col. The drops to either side of the crest are not too threatening, but the element of danger is greatly amplified by the incessant winds sweeping up the cirques surrounding the summit. Make no mistake: the powerful wind would have little difficulty nudging walkers off their feet.

The view from the top is nothing short of spectacular. The summits on the Continental Divide and surrounding the boundaries of the park fill the horizon to the south, west and north. To the east, the Middle and Lower Waterton lakes are in sight, flanked farther east by the Aspen Parkland and the Wishbone Trail. Beyond the aspen groves and forests lies the endless grassland.

The summit is a chaos of broken and fractured rock showing the evidence of millennia of harsh exposure to the elements. Except for yellow lichen cowering in a few sheltered cracks, nothing grows at the summit. Welcome to rockland.

21 Table Mountain

Mode: foot
Rating: moderate
Time: 4 - 6 hours
Distance: 8 km
Maximum elevation: 2225 m
Elevation gain: 765 m
Map: 82 G/8 Beaver Mines

Table Mountain is a landmark for walkers entering the valley of the Castle River. Its distinctive cliffs and flat-topped summit loom high on the southern skyline, protecting the treasures within. Table Mountain is a special place because the route to the top crosses a landscape combining elements of four separate ecoregions—the Montane and Aspen Parkland ecoregions to the north and east, and the Subalpine and Alpine ecoregions approaching the summit. There are few other places where this particular landscape can be found, especially combined with such a fine lake as Beaver Mines Lake.

Beaver Mines Lake

The lake sits in a low pass between the Clark Range to the south and the Blairmore Range to the north. Low passes between ranges, where there is neither up nor down, are ideal places for water to collect. Beaver Mines Lake marks the low place where a lobe of glacier ground its way out of the mountains and toward low-lying land to the east. In its passage, the glacier left a small gouge in the underlying rock, now filled with water and swimming children.

Table Mountain drops steeply into a subalpine forest and then grassland. The summit is on the far left.

Getting there

Any kind of vehicle can reach the trailhead. The road follows a fine paved highway, then a broken paved highway, and finally a stretch of gravel road. You can park a metre from the trailhead if you want.

From Pincher Creek, take Highway 507 west and south until it ends at a T-junction with Highway 774. Drive south on 774 from the junction for 18 km to a well-signed road heading for Beaver Mines Lake. The highway route crosses fescue grasslands immediately west of Pincher Creek, followed by domesticated but splendid montane and aspen landscape. In the campground at the end of the road, a large sign points out the trailhead.

If you are coming from Highway 3, in the vicinity of Crowsnest Pass, turn south at Burmis on Highway 507 and keep heading south until you meet the official signs for Beaver Mines Lake. This route goes entirely through splendid montane landscape with the Rockies on the west and the grassland on the east. It is excellent for any kind of road travel, including bicycle.

Camping

The campground at Beaver Mines Lake is about as good as it gets for affordable, accessible services. All the usual amenities expected of a basic campground are there—toilets, level parking, drinking water, firewood, garbage tanks and a $15.00 fee. Every parking spot is within a few metres of Beaver Mines Lake. If you have a canoe, explore the lake, where mallard ducks crowd the shores along with melodious blackbirds amongst bulrush and sedge.

There are few other similar landscapes in southernmost Alberta. In a hard day of hiking away from their campground comforts, visitors can visit landscape delights starting at the lake's crystal shore, through a wetland, along a mountain stream, across grasslands and forests, and finally high into rockland.

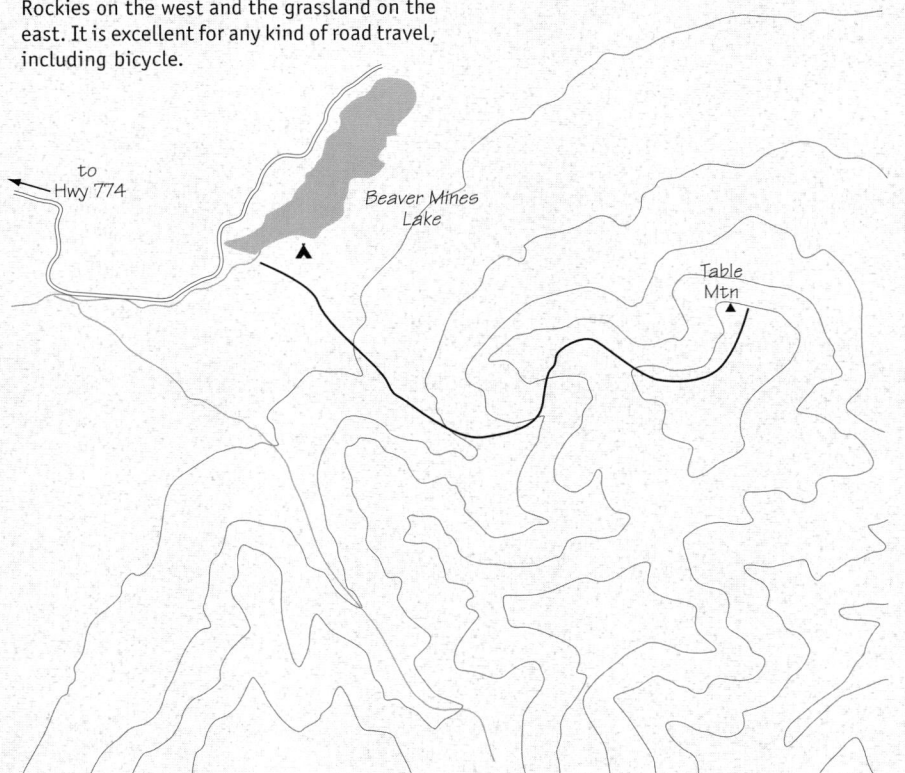

Beaver Mines Lake fills a shallow bed ground out by a long-gone Ice Age mountain glacier.

Beaver Mines Lake at the foot of Table Mountain, and Beauvais Lake to the northeast, are on a line where the montane and aspen parkland features merge. Groves and forests of aspen gradually give way to spruce and pine, but aspen dominate the northeast edge of the lake. In a more northerly direction, the montane surroundings are very similar to those explored close up on the Carbondale Hill route.

The southeast side of the lake is impounded by Table Mountain's steeply-rising foot, leading to a towering cliff wall. The lowest slope is cloaked with montane grasses, flowers and shrubs. Slightly higher up the slope, a band of subalpine lodgepole pine, white spruce and Engelmann spruce reaches the base of the cliff.

High above a prodigious scree fan and a near-vertical cliff lies alpine country and the destination for this route.

The trail begins in the southwest corner of the campground. For the most part, there is an obvious single track plunging into an aspen grove growing along the bed of a minuscule stream draining the northwest side of Table Mountain. In a few short metres, the good trail reaches the little creek, an awe-inspiring reminder of the Great Flood of 1995.

In late summer of 1995, the stream was barely wide enough to step over, and not far upstream it even disappeared under the creekbed of boulders and gravel. However, the 30 m on either side of the stream bear clear evidence of the stream's occasional might.

Table Mountain

A cliff of brick-red argillite exposed by a passing glacier.

Cliff makers

The landmark cliff of Table Mountain rises almost straight up and out of the surrounding hills and forest. Immediately to the west, Barnaby Ridge is steep, but smooth and rounded, not at all like Table Mountain's sheer north wall. The difference has to do with composition and disposition of the rock and the size and course of the glaciers that ground the rock down.

To the south, Avion Ridge is pocked with small cirques. The cirques were carved by glaciers growing on each mountain, or they were carved by lobes of a much larger glacier that covered the entire region. Either way, the glacial ice flowed downhill and into the lower valleys. The glaciers growing on the north face of Avion Ridge flowed toward the valley of the Castle River where they joined a larger glacier. The larger glacier was flowing more or less north and east along the pre-glacial valley of the Castle River.

Many smaller glaciers grew in the immediate area to carve the valleys of Mill Creek to the east and West Castle River to the west. All these glaciers from east, south and west flowed into an even larger glacier moving east from the high elevations of the Continental Divide and into the foothills and prairie below.

For most of their journey, the smaller glaciers coming north from Avion Ridge ground with ease against the long grain of the rock. Where the smaller glacier bent into the powerful stream of the much bigger, east-flowing glacier, it was turned against the end grain of the ancient rock of Table Mountain. The long grain walls were easily cut by the combination of ice and rock, but the end grain proved tough and durable. Woodworkers will understand: even with sharp tools it is easier to shape the long grain of hard wood than the end grain.

Glaciers were a dull tool when it came to end grain. Glaciers had no problem peeling the top of Table Mountain, leaving it quite flat and level, but they could only gnaw at the blunt north face. Barnaby Ridge, just 8 km to the southwest, is oriented with the flow of the glaciers, so the ice had relatively little difficulty grinding the sides of the ridge into the smooth shape it has today.

Bighorn sheep grazing near the cliff rim.

The tiny stream became a torrent and carved a deeper, wider bed through the lower forest.

Near the stream

Where it follows the stream, the trail disappears under a burden of freshly transported boulders and gravel, along with the broken and crushed debris of the dense groves of willow and spruce that filled the tributary's valley for many years before April of 1995. Some new boulders are the size of small cars.

In places, everything was obliterated under a metre and more of debris. The stream carved a new bed, zigging where it had once zagged, undercutting the mature spruce forests along the line of old bank, bringing the trees down and tossing them into the torrent of debris-laden water.

New trenches were cut several metres deep into the gravels and sands carried off the mountain over the past several thousand years. It's hard to believe a stream so small could have such power, but this was actually a very ordinary event in the history of mountains.

In small part, this is how the surface of the Interior Plains was built. Eventually, in one way or another, the rock newly loosened in 1995 will be found far below on the eastern grasslands, if it exists as rock at all. Meanwhile, the entire Table Mountain route from bottom to top is a great opportunity to see the principles of ferocious mountain erosion in action.

Bottom slopes

At the bottom of the narrow valley, close to the trailhead, the ground surface is fairly flat and level, and the fresh boulders are deposited in a broad but thin fan of rock mixed with broken trees and shrubs.

The trail quickly moves away from the stream and rises into a narrow pine forest, where a thick growth of vegetation protects the surface from extensive erosion. The trail comes out of the pine forest to again join the stream. Here, the rebuilding of the landscape in 1995 is more dramatic.

Even in the mature and protected aspen and pine forest growing on the slopes above the creek there are signs of devastation. The old trail passed immediately above the tops of shallow coulees. The coulees were gentle-sided and overgrown with aspen and shrubs. After the flood, these drainage channels were much deeper and extended 20 m and more farther up the side of the mountain. The trail was obliterated and now short, steep scrambles are needed to get above the sheer, rubble-filled and dangerous coulees.

The steeper upper part of the tributary valley is thickly littered with big rocks. The walls of the V-shaped valley are obviously freshly scoured free of the thin soils that once clung to the loose scree and glacial debris. The trail is buried under boulders, and since the boulders are not yet nicely settled in their new homes, footing is tricky. Until the boulders settle and a new trail is established, walkers must watch their footing on the middle section of the trail.

Above the destruction

The trail veers away from the stream valley and begins a series of steep upward traverses pounded into exposed bedrock. Walkers will be leaning into the trail as they toil upward, with plenty of opportunity to study the substance of Table Mountain.

Viewed from the campground in an evening light, Table Mountain is dusty-rose in colour; very nice against a pure blue sky. On the way up, the trail passes several small cliffs where the structure, grain and glowing colour of Table Mountain are laid bare.

The rock is an ancient sandstone, coloured by debris eroded from the argillite mountains in Waterton Lakes National Park. Closer up, the mountain is made of thin beds of sand and silt, each with clear joining surfaces.

Freshly-battered rock carried from the heights by a torrent that now seeps between boulders.

Table Mountain

The summit with a complete view of the southern montane hills and the Continental Divide.

The alpine top
The trail follows the steep valley until the aspen and pine trees thin out and give way to spruce and fir in the narrow subalpine part of the route. Near the top of the route, the trail passes patches of krummholz, or wind-tortured spruce and fir, and finally tops out on a wide, table-flat expanse of alpine splendour including saxifrage, mountain heather and other plants that don't demand too much to keep alive.

Above the tree line, you will feel the power of the sun beating down on a south-facing and south-tilting pan of rock. The landscape is desiccated subalpine from tree line to summit. Little water collects up here.

The summit
From the abrupt base of the mountain, montane and aspen parkland landscapes roll north and east for over 100 km across ridges cloaked with fescue grassland, aspen groves, lodgepole pine, spruce and fir. The summit of Table Mountain, at 2216 m, presides over the wide-open fescue grasslands clearly visible a few kilometres away to the northeast. Just visible on the northern horizon is the Livingstone Range, Whaleback Ridge and the southern Porcupine Hills. To the northwest, Carbondale Hill is only 8 km away. To the west is Barnaby Ridge and Southfork Mountain, and beyond that are the ranges on the Continental Divide. To the south is the Lewis Range, leading to Avion Ridge. The summit has a huge view overlooking four of southernmost Alberta's ecoregions.

22 Thunder Mountain North Ridge

Mode: foot
Rating: scramble
Time: 5 - 7 hours
Distance: 9 km
Maximum elevation: 2335 m
Elevation gain: 940 m
Map: 82 G/16 Maycroft

Thunder Mountain is the summit guarding the south side of the Oldman River where it passes through the Livingstone Range. At 2330 m, its towering height is clearly seen from other routes described in this book, including Beaver Creek, Whaleback Ridge, Table Mountain, Cabin Ridge, the upper Oldman River valley and others on a good, clear day. Thunder Mountain is the best opportunity to explore the Livingstone Range, an important part of the Front Ranges in the southern Rockies. The route involves a high-gain hike and scramble above the Livingstone Gap, a unique part of Alberta's geological history.

The Livingstone Gap

The Livingstone Gap is a spectacular canyon, ripping through the towering limestone wall of the Livingstone Range. The Oldman River and Forestry Trunk Road 940 pierce the Gap. The Livingstone Gap is the only pass through the range's entire 60 km length from just north of the Crowsnest Trail to just west of Chain Lakes.

The Gap is rather unusual. There are streams in the Canadian Rockies that make their way through the mountains by flowing around the ends of ranges and ridges or by carving a bed along faults and cracks, but the Oldman River and the Livingstone Gap breaches the mighty rock itself. The Livingstone Gap is known as a "water gap," that is a pass through a range created by flowing water.

Water gaps are created in two ways. In the first way, called "antecedence," an ancient river cuts through the rock rising from below during the very slow process of mountain making. The second way is "superposition." An ancient river erodes the surface until the hard bedrock is reached, then cuts through the bedrock as it is exposed over millions of years of mountain building. The Livingstone Gap is a superposed water gap.

There is no trail as such, so some routefinding is necessary. If you park in or near the Gap, take some time to stroll down to the edge of the Oldman River. This is one of the most beautiful rivers in southernmost Alberta and deserves respect and admiration. By hiking a route from the edge of the water to the heights of Thunder Mountain, you can revel in the tight integration of grassland and rockland.

Waterside

The Oldman River runs over a bed of limestone as it continues to cut its valley into the flesh of the Rockies. The water is clear bottle-green, running over a broad bottom littered with cobbles, boulders and huge rocks that create a rush of white water.

The river tumbles over several diagonal shelves of limestone and harder dolomite. The shelves are the leading edges of the ancient Paleozoic Rocky Mountains, wearing away under the relentless power of the Oldman River. The upper and middle Oldman River is paradise for fly fishers after bullhead and cutthroat trout.

Thunder Mountain

Getting there

Getting to the trailhead is easy. Simply drive Highway 517 until the road is pressed between the Oldman River on the north and the very base of the Livingstone Range on the south. This is about 3.5 km east of the junction with Forestry Trunk Road 940.

Highway 517 is approached from the north or south on either the Forestry Trunk Road 940 at the west end of Highway 517, or from Highway 22 at the east end. There is an adequate parking place about 200 m west of the narrowing in the highway where a truck or car can be tucked away.

Fescue grasslands and montane foothills reach almost to the exact centre of the Gap. To the east of the gap are the mellow hills of the Whaleback Ridge, and to the west are the rugged summits along the Continental Divide. Montane and mountain landscapes merge in the Livingstone Gap.

Camping

There are abundant camping sites a few kilometres from the trailhead. Coming from the east is the Maycroft Campground where Highway 517 turns west off Highway 22. The small and basic campground is located just under the bridge over the Oldman River, and comes with pit toilets, a hand water pump, a cook shack and a few picnic tables.

There are better campgrounds near Forestry Trunk Road 940 north and south of the west end of Highway 517. To the south is Racehorse Creek Campground, and the Dutch Creek Campground is to the north. Both are superb facilities, nestled in groves of spruce trees adjacent to their respective streams. They include toilets, water pumps, firewood, garbage tanks, cook shacks and fairly private drive-in sites.

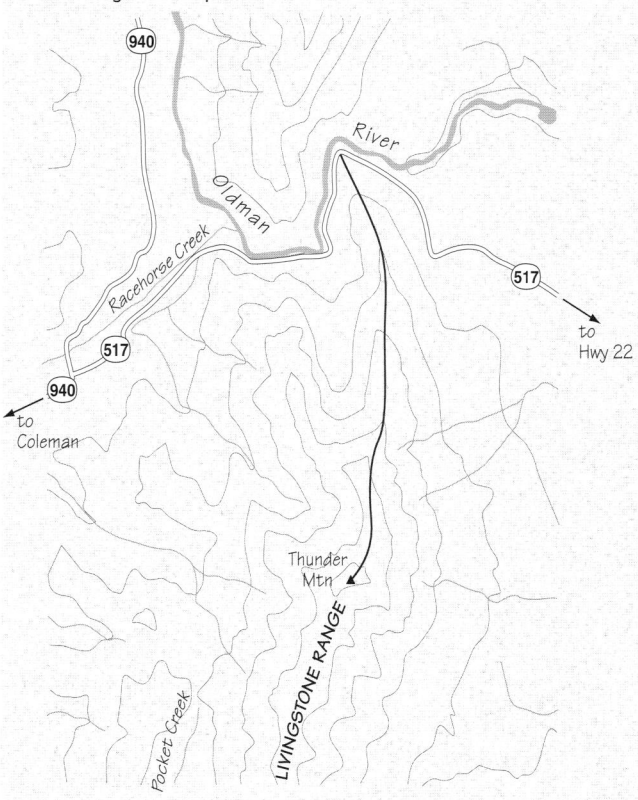

Thunder Mountain, left, above the montane foothills and the Livingstone Gap.

Canoeists and kayakers expert in Class IV and V waters will also appreciate the Oldman. But keep in mind the words of Hans Buhrmann and David Young, the masters of southern Alberta's rivers:

"The canoeist will encounter some of the finest white water to be found anywhere. Quick maneuvring, accurate assessment, and a good portion of 'canoe gumption' are necessary to run it successfully. There is not a quarter mile of river that does not contain white water. The river will not permit you to take it easy.

If you do not possess these skills, stay off this section. It could turn out to be a death trap." (Buhrmann and Young 1980)

Racing through the Gap, the river is rimmed with steeply-tilted blocks of limestone bedrock, crusted with lichen and supporting a few spruce trees, some common and creeping juniper, saskatoon and rose, and small pockets of flowers and grasses. In a few places, the water meets a shore of glacial debris, water polished gravel and sand, and a film of muddy soil. Sandbar and Bebb willow flourish along with red-osier dogwood, and rose bushes.

Slightly higher up the bank is wolf willow, filling the air with its pungent perfume, and buffalo berry, smooth gooseberry, raspberry, bearberry and shrubby cinquefoil. Between the shrubs, and covering a compact higher bank of grassland are strawberry, false Solomon's seal, fireweed, mouse-ear chickweed, golden aster, three-flowered avens, cut-leaved anemone, pussytoes, fleabane and vetch.

Every few paces reveals a new spectrum of flower colours, and wherever there are no shrubs or flowers, there is thick fescue grass. It is a splendid blend of grassland, montane and mountain plants.

Lower slopes

The route leads inexorably upward from the splendours of the Oldman River. Walk along the highway until you find the precise place where the north and south walls of the Gap are

Water gap

Well before the Rocky Mountains were created, much of the interior of the continent was covered by warm Cretaceous seas. These seas were responsible for the thick bedrock of sandstone and shale that characterize the Interior Plains. Then, mountain building began.

Mountain building was accompanied by a general uprising of lands in western North America. The rising beds of ancient limestones pressed upward and onto the flat-lying sandstones and shales laid down in the Cretaceous era and eventually forced the sea entirely out of the interior of the continent.

By the end of the Cretaceous until a few million years before the Pleistocene Ice Age, the landscape of southern Alberta was soft, rounded and not very high in profile. Rivers were well established throughout the ancient landscape, including the Oldman and Livingstone rivers.

As mountains continued to build, the surface of the Interior Plains rose and tilted more to the east and north. The major rivers picked up speed and erosive power, cutting deeply into the overlying young Cretaceous deposits, some of which were barely firm enough to call rock. As the surface was cut away, the river encountered the uprising beds of ancient, hard limestone. In this way, the Oldman River was let down on, or superposed on the emerging Livingstone Range of the Rocky Mountains.

Ancient river, new valley

No doubt, subtle landforms and shapes determined the exact course of the ancient Oldman River, but it would have been found about where it is today. The Gap happens to be located exactly where the Oldman River first took a bite out of the emerging Rockies. Once the river had established a small channel through the ancient limestone, there was no apparent reason for it to change course later.

One million years ago, the Gap was probably a clean-sided "surgical" cut through the mountains, polished by sand-laden water. Then, a million years followed when glaciers ground their way through the Gap at least three times to join bigger glaciers flowing from the north. The small glaciers were working mostly on the hard and resistant end grain of the rock exposed by ancient river action in the Gap. The Gap was gouged, then smoothed and polished by the glaciers, but the original pre-glacial "superposed water gap" through the Livingstone Range is well preserved.

Arguably, the Oldman River is the most ancient river in all of southern Alberta, since it predates the birth of the Rocky Mountains.

The Oldman River, cutting its passageway through the Livingstone Range.

closest together. The road is squeezed to its narrowest width here between the rock on the south and the steep riverbank on the north. This is the base of the ridge leading onto the Livingstone Range. If you are at the right place, you will begin the ascent directly off the shoulder of the road. Tackle the route head-on and start up the mountainside. Follow the crest of the ridge all the way to the barren summit.

The route starts in the last shreds of montane country extending west along the Oldman River. After the first few metres of ascent, the montane landscape is left behind and the trail enters a subalpine landscape of thick spruce forest. The first 40 m of gain are very steep in places, so take a comfortable route leading onto the crest of the ridge. The trees begin to thin out on the lower slopes, and picking a line of travel is easier higher up the mountain.

The Gap divides montane and subalpine landscapes.

Middle slopes
Follow the crest of the ridge along a series of steep inclines connected to short benches and relatively level walking. The crest itself and the west side of the ridge are exposed to the brutal western winds and are almost stripped of soils and plants. The surface is covered with a thin layer of rock fragments broken from the main mass of rock by the relentless forces of erosion, especially frost.

Just off the crest of the ridge and on the eastern face of the range is a dense forest of subalpine white spruce, Engelmann spruce and Douglas fir. Aspen and the grassland and montane species of flowers are left behind after the first few hundred metres of ascent. From here to the summit, the landscape is entirely subalpine and alpine.

The Subalpine Ecoregion is well known for packing variations of environments and micro-environments into compact spaces, and the Thunder Mountain route is a good example of packing. The steep sections of the trail are usually bare of trees, but the surface may be covered with patches of moss and lichen. Wherever even a little bit of soil has formed and survived the winds, there may be a few tufts of fescue grass and a flower or two, especially moss campion, draba, saxifrage, buttercup, Dryas and wild strawberry. In places with a little more soil, a mat of juniper and bearberry may be found clinging to the rock.

Where the route levels out on the benches, and where there is more protection from the relentless winds, there are groves of stunted Engelmann spruce protecting an understorey of dwarf birch, grouseberry, taller grasses and a surprising array of flowers including arnica and Indian paintbrush. The trees disappear as soon as the next section of steep ground is reached.

251

Thunder Mountain

The final approach above the tree line and far above the Whaleback Ridge.

Upper slopes

As the ridge ascends, plants of any kind thin out. At the tree line and the threshold of true alpine country, the spruce and fir are very stunted and blown almost flat on the ground. The last few trees are met at about 2000 m of elevation. From there on, the ridge narrows dramatically and the last 300 m of gain is done by walking and scrambling along a jagged line of broken blocks and boulders.

Wherever possible, keep on the eastern side of the crest because in places there is a steep drop off the western side into the cirque far below. As well, the eastern lee side of the crest is protected from the powerful western wind. Follow the faint animal trails laid down by generations of small populations of bighorn sheep and mountain goat. Animals survive here by making the best use of their energy, and typically know the way around a difficult outcrop or rockwall.

The summit

The approach to the summit is along a ridge of shattered limestone cobbles. The route is broad and secure except in extremely windy, foggy or snowy conditions.

The summit of Thunder Mountain is a tumult of thin limestone scales and sharp-edged cobbles split from the bedrock by endless millennia of water and frost action and lightning strikes. Only the fewest, hardiest plants—mostly lichens—cower in the sparse contours of the summit and somehow survive.

If you are nervous, or if it is windy, the tree line may be as far as you want to go. You will miss the summit view to the south, but the spectacle in the other three directions will be more than satisfying. From this high elevation, the nap and lay of the land can be observed in all its marvellous detail, but be sure to bring a map and compass to help identify all the features of the landscape.

Summit spectacle

Directly to the north of the summit lies the northern length of the Livingstone Range. Mount Burke lies on the far northern horizon to the east side of the range, marking the start of Kananaskis Country. On the west side of the range are the entire middle reaches of the Oldman and Livingstone rivers.

To the northeast and east of the Livingstone Range, and as far as the eye can see is the Whaleback region, the southern Porcupine Hills, and beyond them the western fescue grasslands. The grasslands sweep off to the eastern horizon, patterned with trees along the lower Oldman River valley. The Sweetgrass Hills, 220 km to the southeast, are barely in sight.

To the south is the gently sweeping arc of the entire Front Ranges, merging with the Interior Plains deep in Montana. Chief Mountain is a landmark on the southern horizon, 130 km away. Table Mountain, Avion Ridge and Carbondale Hill are just below the horizon due south and slightly west of the summit. Crowsnest Mountain and the Seven Sisters loom in the southwest. To the west, the open horizon is layered—valley foothills, small mountains, then the mighty mountains of the Continental Divide joining the sky. It is a grand amphitheatre summit.

The view is beyond spectacular, but you have to work for it because the way is rough and steep.

From the summit the entire Front Range is in view as far as Chief Mountain.

23 Southfork Lakes

Mode: foot
Rating: difficult
Time: 5 - 8 hours
Distance: 8 km
Maximum elevation: 2330 m
Elevation gain: 735 m
Map: 82 G/8 Beaver Mines

Southfork Lakes is quite unlike the other alpine places discussed in this book. Mount Galwey, Table Mountain and Thunder Mountain all offer viewpoints overlooking almost the entire western part of southernmost Alberta. The Southfork Lakes route ends in a cirque, surrounded by high curved walls of limestone and dolomite. The only horizon is presented through a narrow window ground out of the bedrock by a glacier on its way to join mightier glaciers in the valley below.

For a bigger horizon, the truly adventurous must ascend the wall to the cirque rim. From the summit of Southfork Mountain at 2330 m elevation, the view is as grand as any in the province.

The trail starts in a meadow of fescue grasses and flowers fringed with aspen and lodgepole pine. A narrow trail plunges east into a grove of trees near the river's edge and heads across the West Castle River's cold and swift waters. In late summer, the water should be down to knee or lower thigh depth. The river is less than 15 m across, but it is a powerful mountain river in any season.

On the other side, put your boots back on and head along the shore to the rotting foundations of an old wooden bridge. The trail follows a cutline that

The three Southfork Lakes fill the cirque and drain over the valley toward the Castle River.

Getting there

There is only one way to get to the trailhead below the western flank of Southfork Mountain. Follow Highway 774, the West Castle River Road, for 6 km from the bridge crossing the Castle River, and the intersection heading north for Castle Falls Campground and Carbondale Hill.

Watch for a narrow gravel road on the east side of Highway 774. Turn onto the gravel road and follow it to the end in a grassy meadow beside the West Castle River. The trailhead begins in a cutline on the east side of the meadow.

Camping

The closest campground is Castle Falls Campground, already described in Chapter 7 of this book. Much of the area is available for random camping, so if you have everything you need for comfort, you can probably find a good campsite closer to the trailhead.

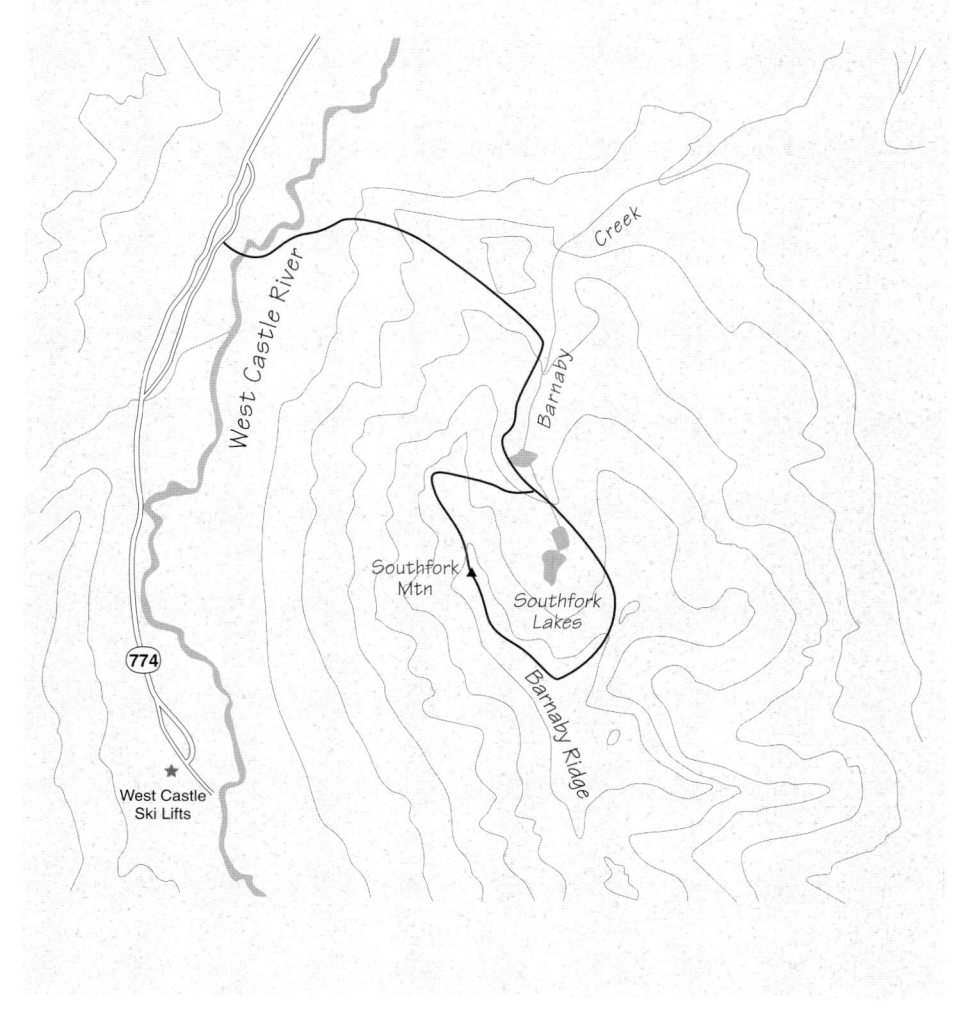

Cirques

Cirques, like summits and ridges, offer the best of mountain walking in southernmost Alberta, especially if there is a lake or tarn to camp beside. The high elevation, gracefully sculpted shapes, seclusion and a mighty challenge ahead strengthen a basic sense and appreciation of natural splendour and adventure.

Even with plenty of subtle variations, cirques are usually easy to recognize. Cirques are created by principles of nature in action on a spectacular scale, and the results are fairly uniform. Once you have seen and experienced the cirque below Southfork Mountain, you will know what to expect when you walk in other cirques.

Glacier physics

Perhaps 40,000 years ago, the last glacier began to form on the gently sloping northeast flank of Barnaby Ridge. In time, the glacier became large and heavy enough to begin moving downhill. Under enough pressure, ice becomes plastic and behaves like other plastic materials.

Gravity compresses the mass of snow and ice directly downward. The ice and snow are resting on an angled surface of rock, so the glacier moves both vertically and horizontally down the mountain and along the valley. The result is a shearing force acting along the downhill angle of the ice sheet. Drag and friction and simple slippage put out enough force to break the surface of the valley.

The same shearing force acts on a glacier through the thickness of the ice. There is just as much ice backed up above the top layers of a glacier as above the bottom layers. The whole sheet moves in unison downhill.

There are other principles at work. Drag and friction act along the sides and bottom of a glacier, where it makes grinding contact with the bedrock. The edges are slowed, so the centre of the ice mass moves faster than the edges. The centre of the glacier draws in fresh ice and debris from the sides and carries it downward.

The plastic ice of growing glaciers is loaded with debris shorn from their valleys, and the whole mass acts as a powerful grinder to sculpt its graceful walls. When the glaciers stopped growing and melted away, the ground debris was deposited in the centre of the valley, giving walkers a fine travelling surface.

The steep, shattered cliffs continue to rain debris into the cirque bowl.

The glacier destroyed Southfork Mountain to carve a steep valley joining the main glacier below.

The Southfork Lakes glacier

There were at least six glaciers on Barnaby Ridge alone, perhaps joined in an icefield at the highest elevations. The glacier that carved the Southfork Lakes cirque was one of the biggest on the mountain, at least several hundred metres thick.

The climate would only have been a little more severe than it is today for these glaciers to grow. During the Ice Age, winters were like winters in the subarctic north today, but summers were cooler and wetter. The ice would have been cold, no doubt, but not at all like the cold glaciers in the High Arctic or Antarctic.

The northwest face of Barnaby Ridge was shaped and formed long before the Ice Age, perhaps by earlier episodes of glaciation. The Castle River probably flowed under the northern brow of Barnaby Ridge back then just as it does today. The forming glacier clung to a moderately steep slope—neither so steep that snow avalanched off before making ice, and not so gentle there was no shear force to drive it downhill.

Finally, the underlying material. Barnaby Ridge is composed of base layers of Precambrian limestones with a cap of Cretaceous shales and sandstones. The glacier had soft, young material to work on at first, and eventually it was big and heavy enough to gouge into the harder, older limestones.

The glacier that filled the cirque containing Southfork Lakes was a relatively small glacier, but nimble. The glacier found the easiest way downhill—toward the north—and took it, slowly grinding the channel now filled by Barnaby Creek. Barnaby Creek curves off toward the northeast to join the ancient path of glaciers flowing in the same direction from valleys of the Castle and West Castle rivers. The debris from the tributary and main valley glaciers now fills the valley bottoms below the mountain's lofty summit.

West Castle River glides across a thick layer of glacial debris and through a spruce forest.

comes to the river beside the old bridge. This lower section of the trail near the river passes through a fine stand of white spruce choked with patches of green alder. In less than half a kilometre the base of Barnaby Ridge is met and the real work begins.

Straight up

From the base of the ridge, the upward trail is in clear view for the first 100 m of very steep ascent. The trail passes straight up the high-angled slope wandering a little to left and right in a parody of efficient switchbacks.

The slope is dressed with a few lodgepole pine and patches of grass, but the south- and west-facing hillside is exposed to the dry, pounding prevailing wind. Thin soils lie exposed and eroded, and plant growth is sparse. Most of the trail and surrounding hillside are covered with a layer of broken and crushed debris brought down from the heights.

Only the first 100 m of steep ascent is visible from the base of the ridge, but there are still 300 more metres of only slightly less steep ascent just beyond the sightline. The first 400 m of gain are achieved in only 1300 m of horizontal travel.

Higher slopes

At about 1800 m of elevation, the steep slope moderates and then levels off on the northwest-facing hump of the ridge. As soon as the surface is level enough to allow soil buildup, the sparse trees grow closer together in clumps until they once again form a forest.

At these higher elevations, the forest includes Engelmann spruce, Douglas fir and an occasional limber pine, reflecting the closeness of the Montane Ecoregion below and to the east. The grassy areas around the groves of trees are also distinctly montane in character, but the soils are very thin and exposed. The fescue grass is short, flowering species are sparse, and much of the surface is covered with creeping juniper, bearberry and lichen-encrusted boulders.

Subalpine trees

Many of the spruce trees were once as tall as 5 m, a good size for trees facing the teeth of prevailing weather from the west and northwest. But many of these larger trees were killed back from their tops. Now, the living plant is only 1 m high, with a rack of dead wood looming above.

These trees are very old to have achieved 5 m of growth, perhaps several hundred years old. At some point in their history the trees experienced a catastrophic setback. In any event, it happened long ago, so the evidence of what might have happened is blurred by time and weathering.

A fire may have "crowned" or leapt along the tops of the trees without burning and killing the lower trunk and branches. There is other evidence of fire on the hillside, mostly a few ancient charred bits of spruce wood.

Insects may have attacked the succulent, new, upper growth of the trees, killing back the tops. Again, there is some evidence in the form of insect-gnawed tracks in the standing and fallen trunks. Especially severe weather can kill trees. A combination of a dry summer and water stress in the trees, followed by a cold dry winter would be enough to kill the tops, the most exposed and tender part of a tree. Or it could be something else.

Upper Barnaby Creek

Once above the first, long steep section there is a chance to take a breather and look around. The trail curves around to the east and crosses a low col on the ridge crest. It then drops a few metres into the lee of the ridge. The forest closes in a little, with somewhat bigger and less distorted trees in the protection of the ridge.

Windswept pine and top-killed spruce near the tree line.

Southfork Lakes

Barnaby Creek trickles out of the cirque and through a bed of mossy cobbles.

The trail leads through the forest to Barnaby Creek, the stream draining the tarns 210 m higher up. The trail follows the stream into the cirque. From the stream bank to the tarns, the landscape quickly takes on the features of the Subalpine Ecoregion, leaving the last vestige of montane country behind.

Barnaby Creek is a delightful mountain stream. A sparkling trickle of water tumbles over shelves of rock softened with a dense pelt of vibrant green moss. Willow and birch shrubs crowd the edge of the water, with tiny but old spruce trees a metre or two away from the running water.

The first lake

There is 210 m of gain and 2 km of trail left to reach the upper lake, at a much easier grade through a fascinating forest of stunted Engelmann spruce and Douglas fir. Wherever there is space, sunlight, soil and moisture flowers sparkle in the undergrowth.

Quite suddenly, the trail comes over the lip of the cirque and there is the first lake, a milky blue jewel held in the lower, gentler part of the cirque. The first lake is surrounded on all sides by subalpine forest, part of the forest growing along upper Barnaby Creek. The trail stays on the west side of the creek and rounds the lake on a long traverse of a scree slope covered with sparse subalpine trees.

On the south end of the first lake, the trail heads up a 90 m-high slope toward the second lake. The climb is needed to get over a shelf of harder material in the bedrock that thwarted the power of the glacier. The entire shelf is covered with a thick layer of glacial debris, left behind when the glacier melted away.

The lower part of this slope is forested, but the forests begin to thin out on the approaching margin between subalpine and alpine landscapes. A few metres up the curving wall of the cirque is the krummholz zone and the beginning of rockland. Again, the trail passes over a brow of hard rock and there is the second lake.

The second lake

The second lake is almost perfectly round. It has a thin garland of trees on most sides, but rarely more than a few trees deep. The forest is thicker on the north-facing wall, where there is less exposure to sun dessication. With their backs to the winds, these slopes are on the lee side of the cirque, ready to capture wind-driven snow. The trees take advantage of abundant water and shelter.

The second lake is separated from the third lake by a low dam of glacial debris, the terminal moraine of a dying glacier. If, some day, torrential rains fill the third lake, the stream will carve through the dam quickly enough. The dam supports a weird forest of half-killed and full-killed spruce, juniper and bearberry.

The third lake

The third lake is where trees give out completely and the landscape is purely alpine. There is still a thick forest on the north-facing slope, but there are no trees on the east, west and south-facing slopes.

The view up the walls of the cirque takes in sweeping heights of scree and gently tilted beds of limestones, sandstones and shales.

To the north lies the channel the glacier carved out of the cirque. The view out this window is framed in towering rock and looks out over Carbondale Hill, Table Mountain, Crowsnest Mountain and the southern end of the Livingstone Range. It is an entirely spectacular place to camp for a night.

The hard ridge held back the glacier long enough to carve a lakebed overlooking Crowsnest Mountain.

Southfork Lakes

Glacial rubble reaches from the upper lake to the summit.

Southfork Mountain summit

Very strong hikers and scramblers could make the route in a day trip—the entire 9 km and 955 m of gain to the top of Southfork Mountain. My friends and I made it a two night and three day expedition. We spent the entire second day climbing the cirque wall and travelling all the way around it.

We chose to go up the steep and broken northeastern wall of the cirque. This involved an early morning climb up 245 m of loose, very steep scree until we reached a band of equally steep and loose shale rockwalls. Above the scree slopes and rockwalls, and we were on the rim of the cirque. We followed the cirque clockwise with the sun to the summit of Southfork Mountain, and revelled in the view.

The great landmarks of southernmost Alberta were visible on a horizon cleared by the dry force of a fullblown chinook—Avion Ridge to the south, the High Rock Range to the west, the Livingstone Range to the north, the southern Porcupine Hills to the northeast and the Clark Range to the east. From this great elevation, the transitions from grassland to parkland, parkland to foothills, foothills to subalpine, and subalpine to alpine landscapes are as clear as the mountain air.

The summit of Southfork Mountain.

Special Places for a Quick Visit

Bertha Lake

Waterton Lakes National Park is the place to find good, well-maintained trails leading to alpine country. There are several trails built to national parks standards and accessible to anyone wanting an interesting but not too demanding mountain experience. The Bertha Lake trail is a favourite amongst the park's visitors.

The trailhead is in the townsite with ample parking in view of a bakery and coffee shop. The distance to the lake at the end of the trail is 6.9 km and 470 m elevation gain, and usually takes five hours to complete.

A little less than midway along the trail there is an alternative destination—Bertha Falls, including a stout bridge across Bertha Creek, dabbling pools amongst the riverbed rocks, picnic tables, toilets and resident gray jays. Lots of travellers turn back here, about an hour or more from the trailhead and the bakery.

The first part of the trail along the west shore of Upper Waterton Lake is broad and well equipped with natural history signs and benches. The finest viewpoints offer sweeping views down the length of a classic glacial U-shaped valley all the way into Montana.

Reaching Bertha Creek, the trail veers west, following the course of the creek through a thick forest of mountain trees. Each species is marked with a plaque. The trees thin where the trail drops to the level of Bertha Creek and into a fringe of alder and willow, exposed bedrock, and a thin flow of water over the lip of a hanging valley.

Above Bertha Falls the trail narrows and gains elevation across a series of switchbacks through a forest shaded from the summer sun. At the end, the last steep pitch lands at the origin of Bertha Creek, a blue gem lake resting in a cirque surrounded by landmark mountains. If you have the time, there is a good trail going all the way around the lake.

The Bertha Lake trail is about the best opportunity to see classic glacial alpine landscapes without grinding your way up a mountain.

Bertha Lake.

Special Places

The road to Plateau Mountain.

Plateau Mountain

Reaching the summit of Plateau Mountain can be either a lot of work or not so much work, depending on the route and toys taken. "Work" remains the operative word in any case. The reward is a landscape that is quite unlike any other in the Alpine Ecoregion.

Plateau Mountain stands at about 2524 m elevation, or about 344 m above the trailhead off Highway 940. The entire trail follows well-maintained gravel roads used to service gas wells on the plateau. The access roads are famous amongst mountain bikers, and on this route bikers have the advantage over hikers when it comes to covering territory.

During the last glacial age of the Pleistocene, the summit of Plateau Mountain escaped innundation by ice. It was a nunatak standing lonely and tall like an island above a sea of ice. Plateau Mountain was not hacked and hewn into cirques, cliffs, ridges and jagged peaks like the Rockies farther west. Instead, it is a mesa with a top 14 sq. km in size, almost 9 km long from north to south, and up to 3 km wide in places. Once at the top, the narrow roads crossing and crisscrossing the broad plateau are first-rate for leisurely foot and especially cycle travel. The view is spectacular in every direction and easy to enjoy.

There are many rare and unusual plants living on the summit of Plateau Mountain. During the Ice Age, the summit was a refugium or sanctuary from glacial devastation where plants and animals survived and helped repopulate the land when the glaciers disappeared.

Plateau Mountain is one of the largest expanses of tundra landscape in southern Alberta. Geological features include "patterned ground" found in the high Arctic, formed when frost and cold sort and churn surface debris into round or honeycomb patterns neatly marked out by connecting rows of blocky stones. The centres in the pattern are filled with much finer materials grown over with tough grasses, sedges and flowers. There are few other places in Alberta with a similar heritage.

264

Recommended readings

Landscape perspective

Alberta Environmental Protection 1994 *Natural Regions and Subregions of Alberta: Summary.* Edmonton: Alberta Environmental Protection. Staple bound, 18 pages, 7 maps. Off market. No ISBN number.

Alberta Environmental Protection 1996 *The Status of Alberta Wildlife.* Edmonton: Alberta Environmental Protection. Coilbound, 42 pages, map, appendices. Free. ISBN 0-7732-5051-4.

Alberta Wilderness Association 1986 *Eastern Slopes Wildlands: Our Living Heritage.* Calgary: The Alberta Wilderness Association. Softcover, 119 pages, 11 maps, 20+ plates, 20+ illustrations, appendices. $11.00. ISBN 0-920074-05-7.

Archibald, J. H., G. D. Klappstein and I. G. W. Corns 1996 *Field Guide to Ecosites of Southwestern Alberta.* Ottawa: Natural Resources Canada. Softcover, 300 pages, map in pocket, 20 plates, 200+ illustrations, index, bibliography, glossary, appendices. $25.00. ISBN 0-660-16439-6.

Barry, P. S. 1991 *Mystical Themes in Milk River Rock Art.* Edmonton: University of Alberta Press.

Beaty, Chester B. 1975 *The Landscapes of Southern Alberta: A Regional Geomorphology.* Lethbridge: University of Lethbridge. Softcover, 95 pages, bibliography, 115 figures. $6.75 ISBN 0-919555-61-6.

Dickinson, Dawn and Dennis Baresco 1996 *Prairie River: A Canoe and Wildlife Viewing Guide to the South Saskatchewan River.* Medicine Hat: Grasslands Naturalists. Softcover, 150 pages, bibliography, 12 maps, 50+ illustrations. $15.00. No ISBN number.

Gadd, Ben 1995 *Handbook of the Canadian Rockies.* Second edition. Jasper: Corax Press. Softcover, 831 pages, index, bibliography, 300+ illustrations, 30+ maps. $45.00. ISBN 0-9692631-1-2.

Gayton, Don 1996 *Landscapes of the Interior.* Gabriola Island (British Columbia): New Society Publishers. Softcover, 176 pages, bibliography. $17.95. ISBN 1-55092-285-8.

Hardy, W. G. (editor) 1967 *Alberta: A Natural History.* Edmonton: Hurtig. Hardcover, 343 pages, index, bibliography, 20+ maps, 150+ illustrations, 100+ plates. Out of print. No ISBN.

Hummel, Monte (editor) 1995 *Protecting Canada's Endangered Spaces: An Owner's Manual.* Toronto: Key Porter Books Limited. Softcover, 251 pages, index, bibliography, appendices, 11 maps, 32 plates, 30+ illustrations. $29.95. ISBN 1-55013-710-7.

Lethbridge Naturalists' Society 1988 *The Lethbridge River Valley Nature Field Guide.* Lethbridge: Lethbridge Naturalists' Society. Staple cover, 26 pages, map. No ISBN.

Recommended readings

Pringle, Heather 1986 *A Guide to Waterton Lakes National Park*. Vancouver: Douglas and McIntyre. Softcover, 128 pages, index, bibliography, 3 maps, 10+ plates, 15+ illustrations. $11.00. ISBN 0-88894-459-4.

Reid, Gordon 1992 *Head-Smashed-In Buffalo Jump*. Toronto: Stoddart Publishing. Softcover, 48 pages, bibliography, map, 25 plates. $10.95. ISBN 0-919783-39-2.

Royal Tyrrell Museum of Palaeontology 1994 *The Land Before Us: The Making of Ancient Alberta*. Red Deer: Discovery Books. Softcover, 96 pages, index, bibliography, 75+ plates, 25+ maps. $19.95. ISBN 0-88995-123-3.

Strong, W. L. Ecological Land Surveys Ltd. 1992 *Ecoregions and Ecodistricts of Alberta*. Edmonton: Alberta Forestry, Lands and Wildlife. Softcover, Volume 1: 77 pages, bibliography, 18 tables, 34 figures, 2 maps. $15.00. Volumes 2 and 3: 350 pages of technical climate tables. $20.00. ISBN 0-86499-839-2.

Wallis, Cliff 1980 *Montane, Foothills Parkland and Southwest Rivers Natural Landscapes Survey*. Edmonton: Alberta Recreation and Parks. Staple bound, 66 pages, bibliography, 10 maps. Out of print. No ISBN.

Whitney, Stephen 1985 *The Audubon Society Nature Guides: Western Forests*. New York: Alfred A. Knopf. Softcover, 670 pages, index, bibliography, 618 colour plates. $22.00 ISBN 0-394-73127-1.

Willock, Thomas 1990 *A Prairie Coulee*. Edmonton: Lone Pine Publishing. Softcover, 88 pages, index, bibliography, 43 plates, 12 figures. $8.95 ISBN 0-919-433-56-1.

Natural history guidebooks

Budd, Archibald C. and Keith F. Best 1964 *Wild Plants of the Canadian Prairies*. Ottawa: Queen's Printer. 519 pages, index, map, 171 figures. Out of print. No ISBN.

Droppo, Olga 1988 *A Field Guide to Alberta Berries*. Calgary: Calgary Field Naturalists' Society. Coilbound, 224 pages, 200+ illustrations, glossary, bibliography, index. $11.00. ISBN 0-921224-03-6.

Dzikowski, Peter and Richard T. Heywood 1990 *Agroclimatic Atlas of Alberta*. Edmonton: Alberta Agriculture. Staple bound, 31 pages, 17 maps, bibliography. Off market. No ISBN.

Farrar, John Laird 1995 *Trees in Canada*. Ottawa: Natural Resources Canada. 502 pages, index, glossary, bibliography, 100+ plates, 100+ illustrations. $45.00. ISBN 1-55041-199-3.

Johnson, Derek, Linda Kershaw, Andy MacKinnon and Jim Pojar 1995 *Plants of the Western Boreal Forest and Aspen Parkland*. Edmonton: Lone Pine Publishing. Softcover, 392 pages, index, bibliography, glossary, 3 maps, 400+ plates, 100+ illustrations. $24.95. ISBN 1-55105-058-7.

Kuijt, Job 1972 *Common Coulee Plants of Southern Alberta*. Lethbridge: University of Lethbridge. 130 pages, index, bibliography, 124 illustrations. $7.95 No ISBN.

Recommended readings

Looman, Jan 1982 *Prairie Grasses: Identified and Described by Vegetative Characters*. Ottawa: Agriculture Canada. 244 pages, index, 8 figures, 241 illustrations. $18.00. ISBN 0-660-11094-6.

Looman, Jan 1983 111 *Range and Forage Plants of the Canadian Prairies*. Ottawa: Agriculture Canada. Softcover, 255 pages, index, map, 240 illustrations. $11.00. ISBN 0-660-11387-2.

Nelson, Joseph and Martin J. Paetz 1992 *The Fishes of Alberta*. Edmonton: University of Alberta Press. Softcover, 437 pages, index, bibliography, glossary, 30 maps, 70 illustrations, 50 plates. $22.95. ISBN 0-88864-235-9.

Pordsil, A. E. 1979 *Rocky Mountain Wild Flowers*. Ottawa: National Museums of Canada. Softcover, 454 pages, index, glossary, 450+ illustrations. $11.95. ISBN 0-660-00073-3.

Robbins, Chandler S., Bertel Bruun and Herbert S. Zim 1966 *Birds of North America*. New York: Golden Press. Softcover, 340 pages, index, bibliography, 500+ maps, 500+ illustrations. $15.95. No ISBN.

Salt, W. Ray and Jim R. Salt 1976 *The Birds of Alberta*. Edmonton: Hurtig. Hardcover, 498 pages, index, 50+ maps, 100+ illustrations. Out of print. ISBN 0-88830-108-1.

Scotter, George W. and Hälle Flygare 1986 *Wildflowers of the Canadian Rockies*. Toronto: Hurtig Publishers Ltd. Softcover, 170 pages, index, bibliography, map, 200+ plates, 4 illustrations. $24.99. ISBN 0-88830-286-X.

Scotter, George W. and Tom J. Ulrich 1995 *Mammals of the Canadian Rockies*. Saskatoon: Fifth House. Softcover, 185 pages, index, bibliography, glossary, 3 maps, 150 plates, 10 illustrations. $20.00. ISBN 1-895618-55-X.

Scotter, George W., Tom J. Ulrich and Edgar T. Jones 1990 *Birds of the Canadian Rockies*. Saskatoon: Western Producer Prairie Books. Softcover, 170 pages, index, bibliography, glossary, 3 maps, 200+ plates. $19.00. ISBN 0-88833-305-6.

Semenchuk, Glen P. (editor) 1992 *The Atlas of Breeding Birds of Alberta*. Edmonton: Federation of Alberta Naturalists. Hardcover, 391 pages, index, bibliography, glossary, 300+ plates, 300+ maps. $45.00. ISBN 0-9696134-0-7.

Spellenberg, Richard 1979 *The Audubon Society Field Guide to North American Wildflowers: Western Region*. New York: Alfred A. Knopf. Softcover, 862 pages, 666 plates, 40 illustrations, glossary, index. $25.50. ISBN 0-394-50431-3.

Stelfox, J. Brad (editor) 1993 *Hoofed Mammals of Alberta*. Edmonton: Lone Pine Publishing. Softcover, 241 pages, index, bibliography, 20 maps, 100 illustrations. $19.95. ISBN 1-55105-037-4.

Tannas, Kathy 1997 *Common Plants of the Western Rangelands*. Lethbridge: Lethbridge Community College. Coil bound, 2 volumes, 622 pages, index, glossary, 200+ illustrations, 200+ plates. $59.95. No ISBN number.

Wilkinson, Kathleen 1990 *Trees and Shrubs of Alberta*. Edmonton: Lone Pine Publishing. Softcover, 191 pages, index, bibliography, glossary, 1 map, 150+ plates, 20 illustrations. $19.95. ISBN0-919433-39-1.

Recommended readings

Trail guides

Alberta Forestry, Lands and Wildlife 1990 *Alberta Wildlife Viewing Guide.* Edmonton: Lone Pine Publishing. Softcover, 96 pages, index, bibliography, 30 maps, 50+ plates. $7.95. ISBN 0-919433-78-2. (Cypress Hills Provincial Park, Police Outpost Provincial Park, Police Point Park, Red Rock Coulee and Writing-On-Stone Provincial Park)

Ambrosi, Joey 1984 *Hiking Alberta's Southwest.* Vancouver: Douglas and McIntyre. Softcover, 166 pages, index, bibliography, 20 maps, 20 illustrations. $9.00. ISBN 0-88894-426-8. (Cabin Ridge, Carbondale Hill, Ironstone Lookout, Salter Creek, Southfork Lakes, South Twin Creek, Table Mountain and Whaleback Ridge)

Blaxley, Bob 1997 *The Whaleback: A Walking Guide.* Calgary: Rocky Mountain Books. Softcover, 96 pages, bibliography, glossary, 70+ photographs, 6 maps. $12.95 ISBN 0-921102-56-9.

Buhrmann, Hans and David Young 1982 *Canoeing Chinook Country Rivers.* Buhrmann and Young. Softcover, 154 pages, glossary, bibliography, 20 maps, 30 illustrations. $9.95. No ISBN number. (Milk River, Oldman River, South Saskatchewan River and St. Mary River)

Daffern, Gillean 1997 *Kananaskis Country Trail Guide*, Volume 2, Third edition. Calgary: Rocky Mountain Books. Softcover, 320 pages, 16 maps, 150+ photos, index. $16.95. ISBN 0-921102-48-8. (Plateau Mountain, Salter Creek and Upper Oldman River)

Eastcott, Doug and Gerhardt Lepp 1993 *Backcountry Biking in the Canadian Rockies.* Calgary: Rocky Mountain Books. Softcover, 352 pages, index, 57 maps, 60 illustrations. $16.95. ISBN 0-921102-21-6. (Carbondale Hill, Dutch Creek, Plateau Mountain and Willoughby Ridge)

Finlay, Joy and Cam Finlay 1987 *Parks in Alberta.* Edmonton: Hurtig Publishers Ltd. Softcover, 243 pages, 3 maps, 27 plates. $17.95. ISBN 0-88830-312-2. (Cypress Hills Provincial Park, Lethbridge Coulee Trails, Police Outpost Lake Provincial Park, Police Point Park, Taber Provincial Park, Woolford Provincial Park, Writing-On-Stone Provincial Park)

Kane, Allen 1999 *Scrambles in the Canadian Rockies.* Calgary: Rocky Mountain Books. Softcover, 336 pages, index, glossary, 5 maps, 100+ illustrations. $21.95. ISBN 0-921102-67-4. (Mount Galwey)

Pole, Graeme 1994 *Classic Hikes in the Canadian Rockies.* Canmore, Alberta: Altitude Publishing Canada. Ring binder, 304 pages, index, bibliography, 25 maps, 200+ plates. $24.95. ISBN 1-55153-009-0. (Goat Lake and Bertha Lake)

Ross, Jane and William Tracy 1992 *Hiking the Historic Crowsnest Pass.* Calgary: Rocky Mountain Books. Softcover, 160 pages, index, glossary, bibliography, 20 maps, 30 illustrations. $14.95. ISBN 0-921102-01-1. (Ironstone Lookout, Willoughby Ridge)

Spring, Vicky 1994 *Glacier National Park and Waterton Lakes National Park: A Complete Recreation Guide.* Calgary: Rocky Mountain Books. Softcover, 224 pages, index, 30 maps, 100+ illustrations. $15.95. ISBN 0-921102-19-4. (Bertha Lake, Goat Lake, Wishbone Trail)

Index

aboriginal 31, 53, 61, 107, 130, 136, 171, 174, 183
Agoseris *Agoseris aurantiaca* 151
agriculture 15, 22, 24, 105, 109, 113, 120
alder *Alnus* 209, 225
Alexander Wilderness Park 87, 91, 96
alpine 205, 262
Alpine Ecoregion 16, 17, 25, 26, 29, 194, 200, 205, 226, 239, 265
alpine fir *Abies lasiocarpa* 214
alpine forget-me-not *Myosotis alpestris* 140, 214
alpine larch *Larix lyallii* 214
American kestrel 62
Andy Good Peak 153
anemone 161
antelope 24
apricot mallow *Sphaeralcea coccinea* 35, 92
aquifer 57
archaeology 43, 107, 156, 183
arnica 214, 219, 251
aspen *Populus tremuloides* 15, 113, 120, 124, 128-135, 137, 139-143, 150, 160, 169, 177, 182, 185, 189, 193, 199, 201, 207, 213, 216, 221, 231, 241
Aspen Parkland Ecoregion 15, 24, 85, 122, 123, 198, 238, 239
aster *Aster* spp. 129, 161, 165
avalanches 25
Avion Ridge 127, 153, 196, 197, 201, 202, 204, 243, 246, 253
awned wheat grass 163
badlands 6, 45, 79
Baird's sparrow *Ammodramus bairdii* 85
balsamroot *Balsamorhiza sagitta* 39, 112, 137, 140, 164
Banff National Park 197
Barnaby Creek 257, 259, 260
Barnaby Ridge 153, 243, 246, 256-258
Battle Creek 183
Bauerman Creek 197, 199, 201, 203, 204
bear 21
bearberry *Arctostaphylos* spp. 58, 129, 179, 189, 201, 207, 213, 214, 231, 233, 249, 251, 258, 261
beardtongue 151, 237
Bearpaw Sea 48
Bear's Hump 235
Beauvais Lake 241
beaver *Castor canadensis* 52, 77, 80, 94, 96, 106
Beaver Creek 109, 167, 172, 176, 177, 179, 184, 187, 190, 247
Beaver Mines Lake 239-241
Beaverdam Creek 160, 161, 163-165
Bebb willow *Salix bebbiana* 112, 121, 161, 163, 249
bedstraw *Galium* spp. 173, 219
Belly River 86, 145, 198, 227
Belly River Sandstones 146
belted kingfisher *Ceryle alcyon* 96
bergamot *Monarda fistulosa* 129, 173, 231
Bertha Creek 263
Bertha Falls 263
Bertha Lake 263
Big Coulee 166
Big Rock 100
bighorn sheep *Ovis canadensis* 30, 136, 163, 190, 202, 215, 237, 243, 252
biological sciences 9
biological soil 23, 25
birch *Betula* spp. 201, 260
bison *Bison bison* 13, 24, 30, 32, 90, 107, 136, 174
black bear *Ursus americanus* 94, 158, 213
black cottonwood *Populus balsamifera* 52, 113, 128, 131, 160, 164, 182, 233
black currant 179
blackbird 95, 240
Blakiston Creek 38, 131, 198, 230-232, 234-236
blue beardtongue *Penstemon nitidus* 47, 233
blue camas *Camas quamash* 143
blue flax 92
blue grama grass 76
blue heron *Ardea herodias* 95
blue jay *Cyanocitta cristata* 165
blue wild rye 163
bluebell *Campanula rotundifolia* 92, 129, 184
bluegrass *Poa* spp. 63, 92
bluestem 103
Bob Creek 157, 160-162
bog birch *Betula glandulosa* 212
Bosporus 131, 235
Boundary Creek 143
Bow River 72
Bow-Crow Forest 134
box elder 55, 173
brome *Bromus* spp. 128
brook trout 183
brown trout 150, 183
brown-eyed Susan *Gaillardia aristata* 92, 94, 115, 129, 173, 184
Brunisols 25, 85, 195, 219
buckbrush *Symphoricarpos occidentalis* 59, 68, 76, 79, 99, 112, 121, 125, 179, 221
buffalo berry *Shepherdia canadensis* 110, 150, 179, 213, 249
bull snake 182
bull trout *Salvelinus confluentus* 150
bullhead trout 247
bulrush *Scirpus* spp. 112, 179, 240
bunchberry 189
burrowing owl *Athene cunicularia* 43, 178
butte marigold *Hymenoxis acaulis* 47
buttercup *Ranunculus* sp. 161, 251
Cabin Ridge 205, 207, 211, 247
California golden trout 150
camel 30
Canada geese 58, 59, 77
Canada milk vetch *Astragalus canadensis* 173
canoeing 71
Carbondale Hill 109, 148, 151, 172, 175, 184, 241, 246, 253, 261
Carbondale River 145, 227
Carboniferous 208
caribou 136
Castle River 145, 148-153, 167, 203, 204, 227, 239, 243, 257
Castle River Falls 148-150
Cataract Creek 217, 225
cattail 179
cattle 70
Cenozoic era 87, 102, 234
Chain Lakes 134, 145, 216, 222
Chain Lakes Provincial Park 134, 217
Chernozems 24, 42, 47, 59, 66, 68, 84, 85, 111, 115, 125, 135, 150, 160, 173, 179, 231, 233
chickadee *Parus atricapillus* 219
chickweed 60
Chief Mountain 127, 132, 139, 145, 176, 198, 253
chinook wind 27, 32, 92, 96, 104, 108, 111, 141, 153, 170, 190, 196, 215, 222, 223, 234
chokecherry 185
cinnamon teal 143
cirque 201, 202, 205, 208, 213, 214, 228, 238, 243, 252, 254, 256, 260-263, 265
Clark Range 239, 262
Clark's nutcracker *Nucifraga columbiana* 165, 210
clearcut 215, 220
clematis *Clematis columbiana* 140, 161, 179
cliff swallow *Petrochelidon pyrrhonta* 77, 102
climate 6, 8, 9, 14, 18, 19, 22, 24, 26, 28, 29, 32
coal 105, 121
Colorado rubber plant *Hymenoxis richardsonii* 47, 92
Columbian ground squirrel *Spermophilus columbianus* 143, 202, 214
common juniper *Juniperus communis* 249
concretion 48, 51, 59, 62, 67, 179
cone flower 103
Continental Divide 6, 7, 8, 27, 28, 48, 153, 170, 193, 194, 202, 204, 205, 208, 210, 213, 214, 222, 238, 243, 246, 248, 253
continental drift 21
Coppermine Creek 231-233
cottontail rabbit *Sylvilagus nuttallii* 95
cottonwood *Populus* spp. 18, 42, 85, 93 112, 117
cougar *Felis concolor* 158, 183
coulee 19, 20, 45, 50-52, 58, 62, 63, 65, 68-70, 75, 77, 88-92, 96, 140, 179, 185
cow parsnip *Heracleum lanatum* 128, 138, 165, 173, 199, 201
coyote *Canis latrans* 77, 78, 80, 94-96, 176, 219, 221, 222
creeping juniper *Juniperus horizontalis* 47, 152, 249, 258
crested wheat grass *Agropyron cristatum* 60, 92, 115, 151
Cretaceous 21, 48, 49, 51, 56, 66, 68, 75, 87, 100, 101, 105, 107, 108, 119, 121, 138, 143, 146, 147, 151, 152, 157, 172, 180, 191, 208, 218, 234, 250, 257
crocus 60
crow *Corvus brachyrhyncos* 29, 43, 94, 165, 219
Crowsnest Highway 145, 191

269

Index

Crowsnest Mountain 253, 261
Crowsnest Pass 8, 16, 139, 152, 198, 240
Crowsnest River 191, 227
Crowsnest Trail 6, 7, 16, 88, 149, 198
Crowsnest Volcanics 151
cushion cactus *Coyphantha vivipara* 92, 94
cushion vetch *Astragalus gilviflorus* 47, 189
cut-leaved anemone *Anemone multifida* 249
cutthroat trout *Oncorhynchus clarki* 150, 183, 247
Cypress Hills 8, 91, 100, 104, 145, 147, 177, 179
Cypress Hills Formation 180, 184
Dardenelles 129, 131
Davis Coulee 53, 60, 62
Dawson, George 225
death camas *Zigadenus venenosus* 161
deer *Cervicae* 24, 219
deer mouse *Peromyscus maniculatus* 167
Devonian 208
dinosaur 48
Dinosaur Provincial Park 48
dipper 212, 225
Douglas fir *Pseudotsuga menziesii* 140, 148, 152, 156, 164, 165, 169, 182, 193, 210, 251, 258, 260
downy woodpecker *Picoides pubescens* 96
draba *Draba* spp. 233, 251
Dry Mixed Grass Ecoregion 15, 17, 22, 24, 26, 27, 29, 30, 41, 76, 83-85, 111, 145, 181
Dryas *Dryas octopetala* 39, 251
Dutch Creek 193, 248
dwarf birch *Betula glandulosa* 251
dwarf clubmoss 47
earth sciences 9
eastern brook trout 150
Eastern Slopes 198
ecodistrict 8, 9, 11, 13, 17-19, 28, 145
ecoregion 8-11, 13, 14, 17-19, 28, 29, 113, 145
ecosite 8, 9, 11, 13, 18, 19
elevation 19
elk *Cervus elaphus* 24, 30, 136, 153, 162, 174, 176, 183, 190, 204, 215, 221, 222
Elkwater Lake 179, 184
Engelmann spruce *Picea engelmannii* 135, 140, 148, 152, 154, 155, 195, 201, 210, 214, 216, 217, 222, 241, 251, 258, 260
erratic 97, 100, 104, 121, 146
European timothy *Phleum* spp. 151, 173
false Solomon's seal *Smilacina stellata* 179, 249
farmer 44, 57, 155
farming 63, 85
fescue *Festuce* spp. 36, 92
Fescue Grass Ecoregion 15, 26, 109, 125, 167, 168, 170, 213
fire 134, 151, 174, 214, 259
fire lookout 151, 154, 166
fire suppression 175, 185
fireweed *Epilobium angustifolium* 128, 199, 249
First Nations 32, 86, 155
flax 62
fleabane *Erigeron* spp. 112, 161, 173, 199, 231, 249
flicker 77
flood 25, 91, 115, 129, 150, 225, 230, 241, 245
floodplain 18, 25, 42, 43, 52, 57, 59, 76, 81, 86, 88, 89, 96, 99, 103, 105, 108, 111-115, 121, 132, 138, 150, 152, 212, 231
foothills 6, 20, 24, 28, 101, 111, 116, 123-125, 136, 141, 148, 155, 168, 170, 173, 175, 194, 198, 205, 223, 235, 262
forestry industry 155, 158, 162, 220
Fort Walsh National Historic Park 189
Fort Whoop-Up 89
Forty Mile Coulee 70, 91
fox *Vulpes vulpes* 94-96
fringed brome grass *Bromus ciliatus* 160, 163
Front Ranges 193, 218, 253
garter snake *Thamnophis* spp. 85
gas well 265
geologic history 68, 226
geology 6, 8, 9, 11, 14, 17, 19, 20, 22, 28, 79, 80, 99, 265
geranium *Geranium* spp. 219
glacial ages 21
glacial recession 236
glaciation 21, 145, 223, 227, 228
glacier lily *Erythronium grandiflorum* 182, 201, 214
glacier 21, 43, 58, 63, 66, 90, 91, 100, 102, 140, 147, 154, 178, 180-182, 193, 201, 208, 210, 213, 214, 218, 226, 228, 235, 239, 250, 256, 257, 260
Glacier National Park 116
Gleysols 25, 42, 115
goat 24
Goat Creek 201

Goat Lake 127, 197, 199, 201, 202, 204
golden aster *Chrysopsis villosa* 62, 249
golden bean *Thermopsis rhombifolia* 60, 69, 85, 92, 94, 99, 112, 140, 161, 184, 207
golden currant *Ribes aureum* 55, 81, 112, 121
golden eagle *Aquila chrysaetos* 77, 104, 106, 202, 210
goldenrod *Solidago* spp. 173, 231
gooseberry 185, 221, 237
grama grass *Bouelous gracilis* 42, 43, 45, 62, 63, 81, 84, 158, 189
Grand Forks 72, 73
grass-of-parnassus *Parnassia fimbriata* 214
grassland 6-8, 15, 17, 18, 30, 31, 41, 45, 53, 62, 63, 65, 66, 79, 81, 83, 89, 92, 94, 97, 100, 107, 110, 111, 116, 120, 123, 124, 128, 129, 132, 135, 138, 139, 141, 143, 144, 151, 161, 164, 166, 168-170, 181, 184, 189, 194, 198, 223, 230, 235, 253, 262
grassland coulee 42
gray jay *Perisoreus canadensis* 165, 202, 210, 237
gray partridge 183
gray wolf *Canis lupus* 30
grazing reserve 52
greasewood 178
great blue heron 129, 143
great horned owl *Bubo virginianus* 96, 185
grebe 143
Grinnell Formation 200
grizzly bear *Ursus arctos* 30, 183, 202, 213
ground cedar 179
ground squirrel 77, 94, 207
groundsel *Senecio* spp. 214, 233
grouse 221
grouseberry *Vaccinium scoparium* 251
Hailstone Butte 218, 222
hair grass *Agrostis scabra* 103, 129, 163
hairy woodpecker *Picoides villosus* 96
hanging valley 201, 228
hare *Lepus townsendii* 219, 222
hawk 94
hawkweed *Hieracium* spp. 213
Head-Smashed-In Buffalo Jump 107, 168
heart-leaf arnica *Arnica cordifolia* 179, 213
Helen Schuler Coulee Centre 89
High Rock Range 205, 210, 262
Hind, Henry Youle 66
Honey Coulee 137
hoodoo 49, 51, 53, 55, 56, 58-60, 62, 65, 77, 79
horned lark *Eremophila alpestris* 43, 47, 99
horse *Equus* spp. 30, 70, 126, 156, 158, 169, 171-174, 206
Horseshoe Canyon 177, 184, 187-190
horsetail rush *Equisetum pratense* 212
house wren 185
human history 8, 9, 22, 53
human sciences 9
hummingbird 94
Humphrey Coulee 62
hybridize 115, 155
Ice Age 22, 42, 43, 63, 66, 67, 75, 76, 80, 90, 104, 109, 118, 121, 131, 140, 146, 178, 180, 181, 186, 208, 218, 257, 265
Ice Age glacier 31, 140
Indian 156, 165
Indian paintbrush *Castilleja minitia* 151, 164, 184, 251
interglacials 21
Interior Plains 14, 20, 22, 24, 27, 32, 45, 48, 49, 56, 71, 75, 87, 90, 101, 102, 109, 110, 121, 146, 152, 170, 180, 222, 244, 250, 253
Ironstone Lookout 153
irrigation 73, 86, 105
irrigation agriculture 121
jackpine *Pinus banksiana* 186
Jacob's ladder 140
Jasper National Park 197
June grass *Koeleria gracilis* 42, 81, 84, 92, 99, 111, 115, 125, 160
juniper *Juniperus* spp. 110, 189, 207, 213, 223, 233, 251, 261
Jurassic 21, 147, 208
Kananaskis Country 217, 253
killdeer *Charadrius vociferus* 94
Kimball Park 101, 113, 218
kittentail 188
krummholz 202, 214, 246, 260
lake 15, 66, 67, 91, 110, 143, 204, 216, 218, 223, 234, 260, 261, 263
landform 8, 11, 14, 17, 19
landscape 8, 9, 11, 13, 14, 19, 117
landslide 25
larkspur *Delphinium* spp. 173

270

Index

lease land 144, 162
least chipmunk *Tamias minimus* 167
Lewis Range 246
Lewis Thrust 230, 234
limber pine *Pinus flexilis* 135, 148, 152, 156, 165, 182, 193, 210, 222, 223, 258
Livingstone Falls 217
Livingstone Fire Lookout 166
Livingstone Gap 38, 139, 156, 160, 166, 193, 206, 247-249
Livingstone Range 135, 145, 166, 168, 176, 210, 218, 246-248, 250, 251, 253, 261, 262
Livingstone River 193, 218, 227, 250, 253
Livingstone Thrust 234
locoweed 140
lodgepole pine *Pinus contorta* 110, 148, 150, 151, 156, 161, 164, 174, 177, 179, 182, 186, 187, 189, 193, 195, 207, 213, 216, 220, 222, 232, 241, 246, 254, 258
loess 90, 179, 181
logger 183
logging 138, 175, 215
long-billed curlew *Numenius americanus* 85
long-toed salamander 28
Lower Waterton Lake 129, 238
Lundbreck Falls 145, 191, 192
lupine *Lupinus* spp. 151, 161, 207, 231
Luvisols 24, 150, 164
lynx 221, 222
magpie *Pica pica* 94, 95, 165
mallard duck *Anus platyrhynchos* 240
mammoth 30, 104
Manitoba maple 55
marten 221
Maskinonge Lake 128, 236
mastodon 30
meadowlark *Sturnella neglecta* 43, 47, 99
Medicine Lodge Coulee 189
Memory Lake 211, 214
Mid Boreal Mixed Wood Ecoregion 14
Middle Waterton Lake 129, 131, 238
Milk River 15, 29, 42, 44-46, 49, 51-53, 57, 59, 61, 62, 86, 97, 98, 102, 114
Milk River Ridge 97, 101, 102, 104
milk vetch *Astragalus* spp. 69
Mill Creek 243
mineral soils 209
mining 158
mink 143
Missouri 29
Missouri River 91, 178, 180-182
Mixed Grass Ecoregion 15, 17, 18, 82-85, 87, 97, 109, 111, 167, 168, 181
Montane Ecoregion 14, 16, 17, 24, 26, 109, 125, 144, 145, 155, 156, 166, 168, 170, 182, 191, 193, 205, 213, 239, 258
moose *Alces alces* 24, 94, 136, 143, 153, 162, 163, 176, 179, 183, 190, 215, 221, 222
moraine 178, 204, 213, 229, 261
moss campion *Silene acaulis* 212, 251
moss phlox *Phlox hoodii* 26, 47, 60, 76, 188, 189
Mount Burke 225, 253
Mount Coulthard 153
Mount Crandell 235
Mount Galwey 109, 197, 198, 227, 230, 231, 233, 236, 237, 254
Mount Gass 213
mountain bluebird 185
mountain building 21, 56, 75, 101, 145, 151, 172, 186, 191, 208, 218, 223, 234, 250
mountain goat *Oreamnos americanus* 28, 136, 202, 215, 252
mountain heather *Cassiope mertensiana* 214, 246
mourning dove *Zenaidura macroura* 70, 185
mouse-ear chickweed *Cerastium arvense* 69, 213, 249
mule deer *Odocoileus hemionus* 43, 50, 52, 60, 69, 70, 77, 84, 85, 94, 96, 97, 103, 106, 136, 167, 179, 190, 202, 215, 225
musineon *Musineon divaricatum* 47
muskrat *Ondatra zibethica* 143
narrow-leaf cottonwood *Populus angustifolia* 113, 115, 116, 120, 121
natural gas 49, 57, 61, 215
needle-and-thread grass *Stipa comata* 42, 45, 59, 60, 62, 63, 76, 81, 84, 92, 99, 125, 189
Newman Peak 153, 202-204
nighthawk *Chordeiles minor* 43, 70, 223
nodding onion *Allium cernum* 131, 161
North Milk River 98, 104
North Twin Creek 217, 219
North-West Mounted Police 16, 60, 61, 120, 142

northern bedstraw *Galium boreale* 92, 125, 199, 213
northern hedysarum *Hedysarum boreale* 69, 92
northern pocket gopher 207
northern wheat grass *Agropyron dasystachyum* 92, 161
nunatak 100, 265
oat grass *Danthonia* spp. 163
oil and gas 72, 90, 158
Oldman River 6, 7, 15-18, 37, 72, 84, 86-89, 91, 92, 96, 105, 106, 108, 109, 116, 132, 133, 139, 152, 156, 157, 166, 167, 176, 193, 205-208, 211, 212, 214, 227, 247, 248, 250, 251, 253
Oregon grape *Berberis repens* 151
Outpost Wetlands Natural Area 143
Oyster Creek 213
pale Agoseris 173
pale big-eared bat *Myoms evoms evoms* 43
Paleocene 146
Paleozoic 247
Palliser, Captain John 13, 31, 60, 177, 183
Palliser Triangle 31, 70
parkland 8, 83, 120, 123, 125, 126, 128, 143, 144, 223, 262
Parry oat grass *Danthonia parryi* 111, 161, 231
partridge *Perdix perdix* 94
pasture sage *Artemisia frigida* 47, 99, 112
patterned ground 265
Pavan Park 83, 89, 95, 106
pearly everlasting *Antennaria microphylla* 112, 199
pelican *Pelecanus erythrorhynchos* 94, 106
petroleum 162
pigeon 59
pika *Ochotona princeps* 214
pike 236
pileated woodpecker 143
pincherry 185
Pinhorn Grazing Reserve 33, 45, 52, 99, 101
plains cottonwoods 76
plains grizzly bear 186
plains wolf 183
Plateau Mountain 139, 218, 225, 265
Pleistocene 90, 91, 100, 102, 152, 172, 180-182, 184, 227, 265
Pleistocene erratic 60
Pleistocene glacier 56
Pleistocene Ice Age 147, 154, 250
pocket gopher *Thomomys talpoides* 210
Police Coulee 53, 61
Police Outpost Lake 16, 142
Police Point 81
Popson Park 89
porcupine *Erethizon dorsatum* 81, 94, 96
Porcupine Hills 7, 36, 49, 100, 132, 134, 135, 139, 140, 145, 147, 151, 166-169, 172, 173, 176, 210, 218, 222, 246, 253, 262
Porcupine Hills Sandstone 138, 146
prairie anemone 207
prairie crocus *Anemone patens* 43, 99, 161, 164
prairie dog *Cynomys ludovicianus* 30
prairie falcon *Falco mexicanus* 43
prairie groundsel *Senecio canus* 62, 207
prairie onion *Allium textile* 161, 189
prairie rattlesnake 74
prairie rose *Rosa arkansana* 62, 69
prairie Townsendia *Townsendia hookeri* 35, 47, 60
Precambrian 146
precipitation 26, 31, 84, 110, 196
prickly pear cactus *Opuntia polyacantha* 35, 60, 62, 69, 92, 94
prickly rose 125, 231
pronghorn antelope *Antilocapra americana* 43, 50, 52, 77, 79, 97, 99, 136, 174, 182, 190
pronuba moth *P. yuccasella (Tegiticula y.)* 29
Proterozoic 20, 200, 234
Przewalski's horse 134
Purcell Supergroup 200
pussy willow 121
pussytoes *Antennaria microphylla* 99, 189, 249
raccoon *Procyon lotor* 18, 94
Racehorse Creek 248
rainbow trout 143, 150, 183
ranch 116, 157, 158
rancher 32, 44, 57, 60, 61, 104, 109, 155, 165, 183
ranunculus *Ranunculus* spp. 213
raspberry *Rubus strigosus* 151, 249
rattlesnake *Crotalus viridis* 18, 43, 72, 77, 78, 94, 178
raven *Corvus corax* 165
Red Rock Canyon 197, 200, 204
Red Rock Canyon Parkway 198, 232, 233
Red Rock Coulee 33, 63, 87, 146
Red Rock Creek 197, 200

271

Index

red squirrel 183, 221
red-osier dogwood *Cornus stolonifera* 249
red-sided garter snake 182
red-winged blackbird 179
Reesor Lake 183
refugium 265
Regosols 25, 42, 59, 85, 111, 115, 195, 231
Richardson's geranium *Geranium richardsonii* 161, 172, 173
Richardson's ground squirrel *Spermophilus richardsonii* 43, 104
ring-necked pheasant 183
river 42, 48, 67, 76, 85, 86, 91, 95, 102, 117, 118, 121, 195
rock art 53
rock dove 59, 62
rockland 8, 25, 194, 230
Rocky Mountain whitefish 150
Rocky Mountains 16, 21, 29, 71, 87, 90, 100, 102, 103, 110, 121, 144, 147, 151, 155, 168, 172, 180, 182, 191, 197, 200, 205, 226, 247, 250
rose *Rosa* spp. 76, 99, 121, 139, 150, 151, 163, 165, 179, 221, 249
round-leaf orchid 188
ruffed grouse 183
sage *Artemisia* ssp. 59, 76
sage grouse 182
Salter Creek 225
sandbar willow *Salix exigua* 42, 112, 115, 119, 131, 212, 249
sandhill crane 143
Sandy Point Park 79
saskatoon *Amelanchier alnifolia* 42, 81, 94, 99, 112, 121, 125, 128, 131, 139, 150, 163, 185, 249
savannah sparrow *Passerculus sandwichensis* 85, 143
saxifrage *Saxifraga* spp. 233, 246, 251
scientist 11
scorpion 178, 182
sedge *Carex* spp. 240
Selkirk Range 56
settler 14, 30, 60, 63, 70, 86, 109, 130, 134, 142, 183
Seven Sisters 253
sharp-tailed grouse *Pediocetes phasianellus* 47, 99
sheep 24
shooting star *Dodecatheon pauciflorum* 164, 184, 213
showy aster 179
shrubby cinquefoil *Potentilla fruticosa* 129, 161, 184, 207, 212, 213, 231, 249
silverberry *Elaeagnus commutata* 99, 110, 125
silvery lupine *Lupinus* spp. 112
skunk 81
small-flowered rocket *Erysimum inconspicuum* 69
smooth brome *Bromus glauca* 60, 92, 151
smooth gooseberry *Ribes oxyacanthoides* 112, 201, 249
smooth willow *Salix glauca* 212
snow 70, 95, 104, 176, 195, 233, 261
snowberry *Symphoricarpos albus* 125
snowfall 26
Snowshoe Cabin 204
soapweed *Yucca glauca* 29
Sofa Creek 129, 236
Sofa Mountain 121
soils 6, 8, 9, 11, 14, 17-20, 22, 28, 84, 109, 110, 194, 196, 208, 227, 251, 258
soils classification 23
Solonetzic 24
South Saskatchewan River 7, 15, 71, 79, 81, 86, 91, 106, 181
South Twin Creek 135, 216, 217, 219, 221
Southfork Lakes 254, 257
Southfork Mountain 246, 254, 256, 262
Spring Glen Campground 121
squirrel *Tamiasciurus hudsonicus* 187, 219
St. Mary River 15, 57, 86, 101, 113, 114, 116, 118, 120, 121, 145, 227
St. Mary River Formation 118
St. Mary River Sandstones 118, 146
Steller's jay *Cyanocitta stelleri* 165
sticky aster *Aster* spp. 173
sticky geranium *Geranium viscosissimum* 112, 125, 129, 161, 173
stonecrop *Sedum lanceolatum* 212, 213
strawberry *Fragaria glauca* 199, 213, 249
striped coral-root orchid 188
stunted thread-leaf sedge 47
subalpine 8, 24, 152, 154, 155, 175, 205, 213, 223, 225, 251, 262
Subalpine Ecoregion 16, 43, 127, 194, 195, 239, 260
subalpine fir *Abies lasiocarpa* 195, 201
subalpine hills 210
swan *Cygnus buccinator* 85

sweetgrass *Hierochloe odorata* 30
Sweetgrass Arch 101, 102
Sweetgrass Hills 46, 56, 57, 62, 253
swift fox *Vulpes velox* 30, 183
Table Mountain 40, 109, 153, 239, 243, 245, 247, 253, 254, 261
tafoni 56, 59
tarn 214, 229, 256
temperature 27
Tertiary 48, 180, 208
thimbleberry *Rubus parviflorus* 151
three-flowered avens *Geum triflorum* 69, 125, 161, 207, 213, 249
Thunder Mountain 109, 139, 166, 193, 210, 228, 247, 249, 252, 254
timothy *Phleum* spp. 128
tipi ring 43
topographic relief 17
topography 19
Triassic 21
Trout Creek 132
Trumpeter swan 183
tundra 99, 182
Twin River Grazing Reserve 34, 52, 97, 99
twinflower *Linnaea borealis* 189
U-shaped valley 208, 218, 228, 263
umbrella plant 62
Upper Waterton Lake 234, 263
vetch *Vicia* spp. 76, 151, 161, 207, 249
Vimy Ridge 131, 235
volcanic rock 151, 152
vole *Microtus* spp. 43
Ward Creek 133, 134
water 19
water birch *Betula occidentalis* 55
water gap 247, 250
Waterton Lakes 116, 230, 234
Waterton Lakes National Park 19, 20, 23, 26, 29, 30, 109, 114, 119, 124, 126, 127, 139, 190, 197-199, 204, 232, 233, 245, 263
Waterton River 15, 86, 129, 131, 176, 227
weasel 221
weather 9, 19, 28, 171
wellhead 46
West Castle River 150, 243, 254, 257, 258
western Canada violet 125
western cottonwood 55, 76, 79, 81, 89, 120, 121, 143
western painted turtle 182
western sparrow 85
wetland 15, 109, 138, 142, 161, 181, 188, 199, 220
Whaleback 172, 193, 253
Whaleback Ridge 37, 109, 135, 139, 145, 151, 156, 168, 184, 210, 215, 246-248
wheat grass *Agropyron* spp. 42, 43, 63, 99, 189
white beardtongue *Penstemon albidus* 92
white camas *Zygadenus elegans* 184
white mariposa 39
white pelican 77, 85, 95
white spruce *Picea glauca* 30, 110, 133, 141, 143, 148, 150, 151, 154, 155, 169, 177, 179, 182, 185, 187, 193, 195, 207, 213, 214, 216, 217, 220, 231, 241, 251, 258
white-tailed deer *Odocoileus virginianus* 32, 85, 94, 103, 136, 143, 190
whitebark pine *Pinus albicaulis* 152, 182, 210, 214, 237
wild blue flax *Linum perenne* 69
wild licorice 112
wild rose 42, 43, 59, 85, 94, 112, 129
wild strawberry 251
wild turkey 181, 183, 190
Willoughby Ridge 153
willow *Salix* spp. 52, 58, 110, 136, 140, 150, 201, 260
Willow Creek 132
Willow Creek Sandstones 146
willow herb *Epilobium glandulosum* 161
wind 25, 27, 41, 47, 58, 60, 73, 95, 110, 115, 161, 169, 203, 209, 238, 252, 261
Wishbone Trail 109, 126, 198, 238
wolf 30, 96, 153, 219
wolf willow *Elaeagnus commutata* 51, 121, 125, 129, 161, 163, 179, 249
Woolford Provincial Park 120
Writing-On-Stone Provincial Park 34, 44, 46, 53
yarrow *Achillea millefolium* 76, 85, 92, 94, 99, 112, 129, 161, 165, 173, 184, 199, 207, 213
yellow bell *Fritillaria pudica* 35, 43, 47, 60
yellow salsify *Tragopogon dubius* 173
yellow umbrella plant 189
yellow warbler 185
yellow-bellied marmot *Marmota flaviventris* 29
yellow-headed blackbird 179